MAKING AFFIRMATIVE ACTION WORK IN HIGHER EDUCATION

An Analysis of Institutional and Federal Policies with Recommendations

A REPORT OF THE CARNEGIE COUNCIL
ON POLICY STUDIES IN HIGHER EDUCATION

*A report of the
Carnegie Council
on Policy Studies
in Higher Education*

MAKING AFFIRMATIVE ACTION WORK IN HIGHER EDUCATION

*An Analysis of Institutional and
Federal Policies with Recommendations*

 Jossey-Bass Publishers

San Francisco · Washington · London · 1975

MAKING AFFIRMATIVE ACTION WORK IN HIGHER EDUCATION
An Analysis of Institutional and Federal Policies with Recommendations
The Carnegie Council on Policy Studies in Higher Education

*This report is issued by the Carnegie Council on Policy Studies
in Higher Education with headquarters at 2150 Shattuck Avenue,
Berkeley, California 94704.*

*Copies are available from Jossey-Bass, San Francisco,
for the United States, Canada, and Possessions.
Copies for the rest of the world are available from
Jossey-Bass, London.*

Library of Congress Catalogue Card Number LC 75-27205

International Standard Book Number ISBN 0-87589-270-1

Manufactured in the United States of America

DESIGN BY WILLI BAUM

FIRST EDITION

Code 7518

The Carnegie Council Series

Contents

Preface

Affirmative action is today one of the most important issues before the higher education community. It affects the life chances of many individuals and the degree of independence of higher education from increasing governmental controls. It involves the highest principles of academic and political life, the goals and tactics of important interest groups, and the quality of public administration in an important area of action.

We fully realize the explosiveness of this issue, and are acquainted with the passions, ideologies, strong opinions, and established interests surrounding consideration of every aspect of it. We do not expect full agreement with our report. Indeed we have had intense internal debates within the Council—nevertheless a degree of consensus has developed, although individual members reserve their separate views on specific points and on forms of expression.

We have sought to take a fresh look at the current situation and to this end have brought in new information about institutional plans and practices obtained in a special survey of 132 colleges and universities.

We are concerned with further progress in achieving nondiscrimination and we set forth a series of proposals for action which we believe in each case will be helpful and are subject to early realization.

Fortunately, both higher education and the federal government are arriving at a fuller understanding of reality through experience. The time for basic reevaluation and new constructive action has arrived. After a shake-down cruise, better preparations are now being made for the long voyage ahead.

We recommend a course of action along what seem to us to be currently the best available routes, recognizing that some of them would not be the best routes if we were in the best of all possible worlds.

We run the risk of some inconsistencies in temporary methods in the course of seeking to overcome the enormous inconsistency between our stated national principle of nondiscrimination and the legacies of the past that continue, in reduced form, into the present. Righting the balance may take the leverage of means that would not be appropriate if a balance already existed. The difficult part is how to use this leverage temporarily to get a more properly balanced situation without causing imbalance in the other direction by overdoing it and without letting the temporary means become permanent encumbrances; how to overcome discrimination without moving to reverse discrimination; how to get equality of individual opportunity without entering into a policy of equality of group results; how to use mechanisms, like federal rules and bureaucracies, when needed without making them into eternal burdens.

The Golden Mean is elusive. Reasonable and well-informed persons who agree on the principles to be served may disagree on the means to serve them. We offer our best conclusions about means in the hope that they may be useful in moving higher education into a more tenable position in keeping with its own principles and those of the nation.

We treat here specifically only academic personnel, leaving aside nonacademic personnel, because they have no special characteristics that make them different from such personnel in many other situations. We also do not discuss policies for students, since these policies are a very important and substantial issue in their own right.

We have benefited from the advice of many persons, some with views contrary to those of this report but who nevertheless gave us the advantage of their most careful and helpful reviews as we prepared it, including: Elizabeth Abramowitz of the Institute for the Study of Educational Policy, Howard University;

Frederick E. Balderston, professor of business administration and director of the Center for Research in Management Science, University of California, Berkeley; Carolyn Shaw Bell, Katharine Coman Professor of Economics, Wellesley College; Mary Bunting, assistant to the president of Princeton University; Sharon Bush, staff member of the National Board on Graduate Education; Mariam K. Chamberlain, program officer of the Ford Foundation; Gloria L. Copeland, assistant vice-president of the University of California; Richard Dickerson, chief of the Educational Programs Division, Office of Voluntary Programs, Equal Employment Opportunity Commission; Miles Mark Fisher IV, executive secretary of the National Association for Equal Opportunity in Higher Education; John Fleming of the Institute for the Study of Educational Policy, Howard University; Robben Fleming, president of the University of Michigan; Martin Gerry, deputy director of the Office for Civil Rights, U.S. Department of Health, Education, and Welfare; Ruth Bader Ginsburg, professor of law, Columbia University; Peter Holmes, director of the Office for Civil Rights, U.S. Department of Health, Education, and Welfare; Ralph K. Huitt, executive director of the National Association of State Universities and Land-Grant Colleges; William J. Kilberg, solicitor of the U.S. Department of Labor; Eugene C. Lee, director of the Institute of Governmental Studies, and professor of political science, University of California, Berkeley; Mary M. Lepper, special assistant to the director of the Office for Civil Rights, U.S. Department of Health, Education, and Welfare; Richard A. Lester, professor of economics, Princeton University; Edward P. Levy, Civil Rights Division, U.S. Department of Health, Education, and Welfare; Thomas R. McConnell, professor emeritus of education, University of California, Berkeley; Roy McKinney, director of the Higher Education Division of the Office for Civil Rights, U.S. Department of Health, Education, and Welfare; Joseph B. Platt, president of Harvey Mudd College; John Rhinelander, general counsel, U.S. Department of Health, Education, and Welfare; Geraldine Rickman, president of Geraldine Rickman Associates, Inc.; David Riesman, Henry Ford II Professor of Social Sciences, Harvard University; Bernice Sandler, executive associate, and director of the Project on the Status and Education of Women, Association of American Colleges; Paul Seabury, professor of political science, University of California, Berkeley; Virginia B. Smith, director of the Fund for the Improvement of Postsecondary Education; Emily Taylor, director of the Office for Women, American Council on Education; Kenneth Tollett, chairman of the Institute for the Study of Educational Policy, Howard University; Martin A. Trow, professor of sociology, University of California, Berkeley; and Jan Vetter, professor of law, University of California, Berkeley.

Above all, we express appreciation to the members of the Council staff who assisted in the development of this report and particularly to Margaret S. Gordon, who had the help of Ruth Goto and Jane McClosky.

William G. Bowen
President
Princeton University

Ernest L. Boyer
Chancellor
State University of New York

Nolen Ellison
President
Cuyahoga Community College

E. K. Fretwell, Jr.
President
State University of New York College at Buffalo

Rosemary Park
Professor of Education
University of California, Los Angeles

James A. Perkins
Chairman of the Board
International Council for Educational Development

Alan Pifer, *ex officio*
President
The Carnegie Foundation for the Advancement of Teaching

Lois Rice
Vice-President
College Entrance Examination Board

Pauline Tompkins
President
Cedar Crest College

Clifton R. Wharton, Jr.
President
Michigan State University

William Van Alstyne
Professor of Law
Duke University

Clark Kerr
Chairman
Carnegie Council on Policy Studies in Higher Education

1

Problems and Viewpoints

Nondiscrimination in employment, promotion, and pay is a high national priority in higher education, as in other segments of American society. The priority given to this policy is fully in keeping with the American commitment to equality of opportunity.

The historical record of many institutions of higher education in employing, promoting, and paying women and members of minority groups has been grossly inadequate in meeting the test of equality of opportunity.[1]

Substantial progress has recently been made, however, and further progress is now being made by many institutions.

Affirmative action, nevertheless, is needed to overcome the residue of a past record of discrimination which was partially purposive and partially inadvertent. It will be needed until a better record of nondiscrimination has been established, a situation where there is nondiscrimination on the basis of sex, race, and ethnic origin, and discrimination only on the basis of ability and contribution to institutional needs. Affirmative action does

---

[1]Two able observers wrote in 1958: "Women scholars are not taken seriously and cannot look forward to a normal academic career . . . . Discrimination on the basis of race appears to be nearly absolute" (Caplow and McGee, 1965).

not mean entitlements to proportional representation. It means actions to eliminate discrimination: creation of more adequate pools of talent, active searches for talent wherever it exists, revision of policies and practices that permitted or abetted discrimination, development of expectations for a staff whose composition does not reflect the impacts of discrimination, provision of judicial processes to hear complaints, and the making of decisions without improper regard for sex, race, or ethnic origin. We join with the AAUP ("The Sixtieth Annual Meeting," 1974) in urging "all institutions involved in higher education to pursue affirmative action in good faith."

We now stand in a transition period between actual past deficiencies of major proportions and potential future achievement of true equality of opportunity. This report is concerned with policies and procedures for this transition period.

We should not, in the course of handling the problems of transition, build a permanent bureaucratic structure of detailed federal controls. We need, instead, transitional policies and procedures for a transitional period. As the problem of achieving equality of opportunity changes in its contours (and it is changing) and in its gravity, the governmental superstructure of policies and procedures should reflect these changes. One grave danger is that rigid and heavy-handed controls may survive any reasonable need for their continued imposition.

The way out of the transition period should be contemplated even while we are still on the way into it. Past inequities should be eliminated as soon as possible, but so also should current controls when they are no longer needed. The federal government now intrudes further into the internal academic life of colleges and universities than almost any state government has ever gone, even temporarily. To whatever extent this may be necessary now, it should not become a condition ad infinitum. The necessary ends can be accomplished better and with less cost than such permanent intrusion would entail. Today's temporary necessity should not become tomorrow's curse.

We favor a basic review in 1980 of the situation at that time and of what amount and kind of federal involvement is still necessary; and reviews each five years thereafter, if and as needed.[2]

There are at least two tragedies involved in this transition period:

- One, that it should be necessary at all. Higher education long ago, in keeping with its own principles of finding merit wherever it could be found and rewarding it, should have been searching more actively for merit among women and minorities. It has failed its own principles and impoverished its own performance by the neglect of large pools of potential academic competence. It has looked for merit mostly within 40 percent of the population and largely neglected the other 60 percent. The accumulated loss of talent is staggering to contemplate. It has been a very major source of inefficiency in the academic world in the utilization of potentially available resources.
- Two, that it should take place in the 1970s and beyond. The 1960s saw a doubling of faculty members. The 1980s may even see a slight decline. The effort at redress of past errors comes 10 years too late to be easily effective. Now there are too few new appointments and too many candidates even from among the majority male group alone. The transition will take longer and will involve more individual disappointments than if it it had taken place earlier. We do not expect, however, that the very ablest, including white males, will fail to find some opportunities within higher education—although, often, they will not be appointed at institutions of their first choice, their talents will not be lost to use.[3]

[2] Specific actions might be taken, for example, exempting those community colleges that have a good record from controls on employment of women. Other actions of decontrol should be considered periodically. The HEW *Guidelines* of 1972 anticipated "that deficiencies in the utilization of minorities and women" would mostly be overcome within a five-year period, presumably then reducing the need for federal controls. This implied that the program was to be a temporary one. The 1977 date for basic completion, however, was quite unrealistic.

[3] New faculty hires ran at the rate of about 30,000 a year in the peak hir-

Nevertheless, the transition must take place, and higher education will be better and stronger and more effective as a result of it, but there also will be costs. Transition periods are seldom easy, and this one is no exception. They also are inherently complex, without the clarity of principle and the certainty of procedure that ideally might be wished.

Theme number one: Colleges and universities are increasingly assuming and should continue to assume the initiative in securing equality of opportunity in higher education. They can now carry the initiative far better than the federal government and, in doing so, can reduce the burden of federal controls before they become too overwhelming and too permanent. Colleges and universities, themselves, not the federal government, should now be on the first line of attack on the problem. The federal presence, however, should be maintained both in case institutional efforts should later lag where adequate efforts are now being made, and in reserve for action against institutions which make no adequate efforts at all. The relationship between institutions and the federal government, in any event, should become more cooperative and less combative.

This is not to suggest that the federal initiatives of the 1960s and early 1970s were unwise. On the contrary, they were absolutely essential. They were among the initiatives that started colleges and universities on the road to developing their own policies and plans and to creating their own internal machinery. They raised the consciousness of the academic community about the existing gross inequities and triggered a collective sense of concern and even guilt about past inadequate performance. They encouraged women and minorities to organize and to speak out more strongly on their own behalfs. They created the possibility of financial retribution against institutions if progress was not made.

A great individual moral and organized institutional effort has been mobilized under federal prodding. New forces have

---

ing years of the 1960s and are likely to average about 6,000 a year in the 1980s, entirely or almost entirely for replacements, not for expansion (see Cartter, forthcoming).

been set in motion. New directions have been identified. Attitudes have been changed, behavior modified, new habits introduced. These may turn out to have been the great federal contributions. The immense, lethargic, hesitant corpus of higher education has been roused, and its internal concern and energy have been released. The federal government has generated motion that higher education had not developed on its own.

The next stage calls more for action by higher education itself and less by government, and higher education now seems both more willing and more able to take that action. More and more good plans are being developed. Higher education has, by and large, committed itself to progress. And progress is being made. There is now no overall "demand gap,"[4] as far as we can tell; but this is not the same as saying that there is no discrimination still remaining:

Group	Pool of "qualified persons" (holders of Ph.D.) as percent of total	Percentage of "ladder" faculty in four-year colleges and universities
Majority women	16 to 17 percent	18 percent
Minorities	4 to 5 percent	4 to 5 percent

There is substantial evidence of good faith efforts.

Caveat: The distribution of women and minorities among institutions, among fields of specialization and among ranks, and for minorities among subgroups, is still quite uneven.

The record of recent progress is likely to be continued: the commitment is there; the policies and plans are being developed or are already in place; the internal bureaucracy has usually already been established; the internal constituencies of women

[4]The historical dimensions of the "demand gap" are difficult to determine. For a definition of the demand gap and the supply gap, see Section 2, pp. 37 to 41. An adjustment has been made to exclude noncitizens from the data.

and minorities on faculties, with many student supporters—some of them quite insistent—now usually exist and have been highly energized.

The federal government has supported many new developments in many areas of action that were then largely taken over by other institutions—collective bargaining by industry and unions, research and development by industry and universities, the land-grant movement by the states, vocational education by local school districts, among many others. One can hope that this devolution of responsibility is taking place in affirmative action also. This does not mean that a federal presence should not be maintained for some time to come. It should be. Rather, it means that the greatest of the federal contributions may already have been made and that the further role of the federal government should be increasingly more supplemental and less primary.

Caveat: This assumes (1) that institutions now making progress will continue to do so and (2) that the number of institutions that do not follow a progressive course will be relatively small.

Institutions, as they increasingly assume the primary responsibility, should, in particular, be sure that they:

- Have a carefully developed affirmative action plan and the administrative and advisory mechanisms to make it a working document. We cannot emphasize too strongly the importance of the nature and the quality of the individual plan.
- Make annual public reports on status and progress in relation to this plan.
- Actively recruit women and minorities into the pool of names for consideration for openings.
- "Select the most qualified candidate" as federal policy now requires regardless of race, sex, or ethnic origin.[5]

[5] The Carnegie Commission on Higher Education (1973d) suggested that the most qualified candidate be chosen with some reference, where appropriate to the position to be filled, to the potential contributions of women and minorities as inspiring "models" and as helpful "mentors." A commis-

· Provide fair procedures for processing complaints.

In this instance, at least, one price of liberty is internal progress.

As our survey of progress by individual institutions demonstrates, a number of institutions, on their own, are now going quite beyond the narrow limits of the Berkeley plan—the only plan fully approved by the federal government and advanced by HEW as a model for other institutions. It is, by comparison, a retrogressive plan. The federal government, in some of its efforts, is now acting more as a brake than as an accelerator.

Theme number two: The supply aspects of the equality of opportunity effort are now generally more important than the demand aspects. Demand for new hires, of course, encourages supply of new Ph.D.'s and other qualified persons. Increased demand is one of the best ways of increasing supply, and demand has been increased. But there are other ways of increasing supply, such as better financial support for low-income students in college and for graduate studies, and they also should be pursued. The federal government should put more of its money where its policies are. Demand, overall, cannot be much more intensified without causing unfortunate results, given the current supply situation:

Group	Pool of "qualified persons" (holders of Ph.D.) as percent of total	Percentage of total labor force composed of members of group
Majority women	16 to 17 percent	38 percent
Minorities	4 to 5 percent	14 to 15 percent

---

sion of the AAUP ("Affirmative Action in Higher Education," 1973) has spoken of the academic value of "a balance of qualities within a department," of "consideration of different kinds of skills and interests in different persons," of "consideration of diversity of characteristics among the faculty," of efforts to broaden a department "from its unisex or unirace sameness," of projecting an "example of mutually able men and women, and mutually able blacks and whites," of "richness which a variety of intellectual perspectives and life experiences can bring to the educational program" as warranting, for such reasons, "the affirmative consideration of race or sex" (see Appendix B for the full text of the report).

The greater effort should now be made on the supply side by the federal government and by institutions. We suggest, among other things, that each affirmative action plan include a "supply plan" wherever the institution contributes to the supply of potential faculty members. Affirmative action officers should be given responsibilities on the supply, as well as the demand, side.

The supply problem breaks into two parts: women and minorities. The supply gap is smaller for women, and it is easier to fill because the problems of origins in low-income families and of other sources of deprivations are less universal.

Overall, in obtaining a higher proportion of women and minorities in faculties, nothing is so persuasive as a good supply of highly able and well-trained people.

Theme number three: A better distribution of women and minorities among institutions and among fields of specialization and ranks is badly needed, even though there appears to be no overall demand gap. This requires strong efforts on the supply side as well as continuing influence on the demand side. Related to this is the desirability of providing more opportunities for women and minorities in administrative positions, and of more equitable treatment of lecturers and instructors and part-time persons in all ranks—many of those in each of these classifications are women.

Theme number four: Efforts at "fine-tuning" by the federal government can lead to ludicrous results and be quite counterproductive. The smaller the unit controlled (for example, the department of classics) and the smaller the disadvantaged group (for example, Native Americans), the less likelihood an institution's plan will call for any change:

- If the unit has three members and the pool is as large as 20 percent of all recent Ph.D. recipients in that field, no effort is officially called for to fulfill the required plan.
- If the pool is 0.5 percent, even a unit of 100 will require no action to meet the required terms.

Also, small units can lead to discriminatory results as between women and members of minority groups, since women usually form the larger pool:

- If women are 20 percent of the pool, they may warrant a place in a department of 5 or 10 members in order to reach "parity."
- If blacks are 2 percent of the pool, they may not warrant a place in a department of 5 or 10 members to reach parity—only in a department of 50, which is quite an unusually large size for a department.

The Berkeley plan, which HEW has been seeking to make the model for all universities in the nation, is a case in point. By looking at departments as the unit and by looking at five subdivisions of minorities as the pool (blacks, Asians, Chicanos, Native Americans, and "other minorities"), only two departments "need" Asians and only one any blacks; none "need" Chicanos or Native Americans or members of "other minorities" for the foreseeable future—which extends to as long as 30 years—to reach "parity."[6] However, 31 departments (of a total of 75) "need" women, who are not divided into subpools, in order to reach "parity." For example, the dramatic arts department requires 0.05 Native Americans to reach "parity," and 1.62 women. Were women divided into subpools—which they quite easily could be because there are substantial variations among them in terms of quantifiable characteristics—their situation would more closely parallel that of minorities.

Statistical games potentially can be played. The smaller the unit, the less the likelihood of a "need," and units can be made smaller in size. The smaller the minority group, the less the likelihood of a sufficient pool of qualified persons to require action, and minorities can be divided almost endlessly. We are

---

[6]The goals are to be revised each year, but the fact that they are determined on a narrow departmental basis and that minorities are divided into subgroups makes it less likely that additional departments will be found to "need" minorities.

against approaches that, in the future, could reward the shrewd gamesman and enthrone the computer. Statistics are no substitute for action, and it should be realized that they serve better in defense (one major plan required 60 to 70 thousand statistical calculations) than on offense—the defense can drown the offense in data. A barrier of paper work can keep the pilgrim from ever reaching "The Castle," almost without the pilgrim knowing why. Affirmative action should not be allowed to degenerate into a "numbers racket," into a monstrous piece of fakery.

The search for perfect justice can even lead to no justice at all. Asians may be overrepresented from an aggregated point of view, but what about Hong Kong-born Chinese, Filipinos, Samoans (there are more of them in mainland United States than in American Samoa)? (The Berkeley plan states that it intends later to present "subcategories" of Asians.) Blacks may be underrepresented, but those of ghetto or rural-South origin may not be represented at all; and what about them? Persons of Hispanic descent divide, among other distinct categories, into Puerto Ricans, Cubans, and Chicanos—each with different educational experiences; and should they each be recognized? Women from high-income families or from certain religious backgrounds (such as Quakers and Mormons), or both, may be quite advantaged as against those from low-income families and from other religious backgrounds; and what about justice within the overall classification of women? There are more differences within the Asian group, within the black group, within the Hispanic group, and within the totality of women than between each of these categories in their entirety and the overall category of majority males. Yet, as we have seen, dividing and then subdividing can lead to no results at all.

The general rule may be stated: the finer the tuning, the grosser the results. Yet we recognize the strong desires of those who wish to eliminate every potential pocket of discrimination on campus, however small, and to give a chance to every disadvantaged group, however miniscule its contribution to a pool of qualified persons. Unfortunately, the smaller the pocket and the smaller the pool, the smaller the chance of drawing someone from the pool to place in the pocket in the name of "parity."

This is a real dilemma that must be confronted—the claims of perfection against the hope for accomplishments. Choices must be made. All good things are not compatible. We favor the designation of broader units and broader pools, with the proviso that any excessive concentrations in any discipline, except as related to special subject matter (black studies, Latin-American studies, as examples), may justify special inquiry.

The federal government, in a pluralistic democracy, should not, and even cannot, assure equal results in each potentially smaller and smaller unit for each potentially almost endlessly divided subgroup. The limits of governmental power must be recognized and the demands of common sense acknowledged, even if perfect justice in statistical results is not attained—to overreach power or to ignore common sense is to fail. The government cannot control all individual actions; it cannot sit at every committee table; it cannot coerce acceptance by colleagues; it cannot force the respect of students. To get equality of statistical results, the government would need an enormous amount of power and would have to impose a network of detailed controls—both of which would strain the bonds that hold a democracy together. And common sense suggests that extreme positions can defeat themselves.

The wiser course of action for the federal government is to look at goals and pools broadly; to allow institutions of higher education to exercise their best judgments in individual cases; to concentrate more on fair processes rather than on statistical projections; to recognize that merit in the academic enterprise draws more support than preference solely on grounds of sex or race or ethnic origin; to pursue equality of actual opportunities rather than equality of forced results in the academic endeavor; to concentrate on problems that not only need to be solved but that can be solved.

Theme number five: Goals, broadly defined as to academic units included and groups covered, and timetables should be continued during the current transition period as part of the federal affirmative action program. We say this while rejecting fine-tuning efforts by the federal government.

We define *goal* as: the object to which effort or ambition is directed. Goals are not quotas. *Quota* means: the part of share of a total which belongs, is given, or is due, to one. The verb that goes with goal is strive; with quota, the word is impose. The failure to meet a goal calls for an inquiry into the reasons for failure; to fail to meet a quota calls for a penalty. The goal may be viewed as normal expectations of what would happen if there were no discrimination.

We define *timetable* as a statistical forecast of the expected date by which a goal might prospectively be met, of when a nondiscriminatory result might be obtained. Meeting such forecasts should be viewed not as a certainty but as a probability within fairly wide margins of error. Two reasons argue for this "probability approach": (1) the data on which the forecasts are made are often inadequate and always out of date; and (2) the competition among institutions for scarce personnel resources may make the supply situation quite an erratic one—forecasts are made institution by institution and do not take account of the forecasts and the actions of all the other institutions operating in the same market. What one institution can do in accordance with its plan is affected by what all others are doing in connection with their plans, and there will be some inconsistencies.

Goals should not be fine-tuned for the reasons given above. They apply more equitably to broader units and broader groups of people than to narrower units and narrower groups. The broader units also give the institution more leeway for the exercise of academic judgment. Thus we favor the unit of the entire faculty in a small college; the school in a larger college or university; and the division (humanities, social sciences, natural sciences) of a very large school in the largest universities. Timetables also should not be fine-tuned. They can be no better than the data that lie behind them and the data are less than totally precise.

With these comments in mind, we favor goals and timetables at this stage of transition:

• They give an assurance to women and members of minority groups that real concern is being evidenced about their access

to equality of opportunity. The statement of goals and time-tables carries an implied promise of progress.
· They require careful analysis of existing staffing patterns and of the potential supply of qualified persons. Thus facts, though often imprecise, are substituted for sometimes prejudiced fancy. In the absence of any facts, excessive asserted expectations too often confront excessive covert opposition —both ill informed.
· They help introduce debates over realistic possibilities as an alternative to ideological battles with inflamed rhetoric.
· They provide one possible basis for compliance through due process, as an alternative to what might otherwise be institutional guerilla warfare.
· They thus, in total, serve as a basis for turning a highly emotional revolution over the life chances of many individuals into a process of fact finding, discussion focused on realistic alternatives, and adjudication.
· They are one reasonable way, if properly employed, of monitoring the integrity of the academic enterprise, which cannot claim, on its earlier record, an exemption from some surveillance.

To the outsiders, goals and timetables hold out hope of steady improvement; to the insiders, the expectation of rational solutions arrived at in an orderly manner. These are the processes by which many earlier social conflicts have been brought within the influence of peaceful conduct.

We see the process as operating much like that of the courts in reviewing the composition of juries. The courts have not reviewed the composition of an individual jury by itself but have been concerned, rather, with any "continuing and significant disparity" in jury selections as compared with jury-eligible persons ("Affirmative Action in Higher Education," 1973). If such disparity is found to exist, then the burden of proof is on those involved in the selection process.

Theme number six: The federal affirmative action program is confused, even chaotic, and should be brought quickly into closer conformance with good governmental practices. Some confusion may be inevitable in the early stages of a major new endeavor, but it is inexcusable as a long-term condition once experience has illuminated the difficulties. These include:

• Too many regulations and guidelines, in some cases inconsistent with each other, and these regulations and guidelines too little informed by a knowledge of the special characteristics of higher education.
• Too many agencies duplicating, even feuding, with each other, and demanding the same data.
• Too few staff persons, and they, in turn, often too little qualified for their responsibilities. Some of them are more dedicated to their personal crusades than to impartial enforcement of federal laws and regulations.
• Too long delays in processing plans and complaints, with too little certainty of the resulting actions (as among the regions of HEW).
• Too many remedies through too many channels. The remedies now exhaust the parties.
• Too little contact, on a consultative basis, with the world of higher education.
• Too antielitist an approach, singling out the most prestigious research universities, out of about 1,000 institutions subject to affirmative action requirements, for action that is, on occasion, quite precipitate.
• Too hypocritical a posture by the agencies involved in not having applied their own rules to the recruitment and employment of their own staffs—for example, failure to take an early approach to "parity" in their own staffs.

Few federal programs are now so near self-destruction. Seldom has such a good cause spawned such a badly developed series of federal mechanisms.

We favor improvement, believing that a federal influence remains essential during the current transition period. There are those who favor maintenance of the status quo in terms of federal positions and actions, however unfortunate—in fact, the more unfortunate the better—on the grounds that its growing ineffectiveness will make it in due course essentially inoperative —a result that they favor. We do not.

Generally, the federal government should cultivate and work with the many elements of goodwill and decency in higher education. Currently, however, it is creating a backlash of resentment against federal conduct. This backlash is different from the backlash against affirmative action as a policy, although the two backlashes may reinforce each other. Some of the second is inevitable, but the former is not, and should be avoided. The current government program is now on a trajectory toward an unnecessary confrontation with higher education and, also, toward impotence. This course can be and should be quickly reversed.

We make a number of suggestions for improvements, including clarified assignment of responsibilities: policy and policy review to the Department of Labor; evaluation and approval of plans to the Department of Health, Education, and Welfare; and processing of individual cases to the Equal Employment Opportunity Commission.

Theme number seven: Compliance should rest on persuasion in the vast majority of cases, and on punishment that fits the crime for the small minority.

We favor maximum use of internal grievance procedures to settle individual cases. This will avoid overburdening the courts and federal agencies. We recognize, however, that such procedures fit the cases of insiders better than they do those of outsiders trying to get in; the latter may not be eligible under, and are unlikely to be confident about, internal procedures. Outsiders, in particular, must have direct access to governmental agencies and to the courts. In cases involving insiders, however, we would hope that the agencies and the courts would respect internal procedures and seek to give their support to them, provided the procedures are fair and the decisions do not violate the law.

We favor overall compliance actions against institutions through due process and on the basis of their overall performance including:

- The quality of their plans, policies and procedures
- Their recent progress on the demand side
- Their contributions on the supply side
- Their general adherence to broadly stated goals and time-tables, provided this adherence is consistent with the elimination and avoidance of discrimination whether direct or reverse

We favor a series of penalties to fit the nature and the degree of noncompliance, and not just the currently available, but never used, atomic bomb of total withdrawal of contracts—the power not to spend is the power to destroy some institutions. This penalty potentially falls much more disastrously on some institutions—the research universities—than on others and even does no damage at all to some. It also falls more disastrously on some departments—particularly science, though the difficulty may be in other departments, for example, the humanities. Just declaring an institution out of compliance and nothing more, for example, would set at work powerful internal and external forces to bring corrections. It might be a useful first step. The atomic bomb is not necessarily always the best first step, but it should be reserved for serious cases of noncompliance.

The *Washington Post* ("The Rebellion of the Chancellors," 1975) has editorialized on the "Frankenstein regulations," the "torrent of statistics," the "blizzards of paper." It noted that "the government now has an opportunity to rethink and reform the reflexive, oppressive and unproductive way it has been dealing with the objectives in this area" and warned that "if it fails to do so it will ultimately so thoroughly discredit the original intention of those who sought to bring more fairness to American institutional life that it will (if it hasn't done so already) do that cause more harm than good." Such a basic review, happily, is now underway.

Observations. We make these general and specific observations:

- Expectations for the near future should be realistic. More women than members of minorities will be employed. Among women, more will come from high-income families than low, from religious traditions that place a high premium on educational attainments than from those that do not. More will come from blacks than from Hispanic sources because the former have more of a heritage of professional attainment for women than do the latter.

Among minorities, more will be Asians than members of other minorities and, among Asians, proportionately more will be U.S.-born Chinese and Japanese; more will be drawn from among urban middle-class blacks than from the rural working class; and more persons of Hispanic culture will be of Cuban than of Puerto Rican background. In each case, this is true because of the current composition of the pools of qualified persons and the relative ease of expanding these pools. The major early beneficiaries are going to be those relatively better off already.

· Foreign-born blacks, Asians, and Latin-Americans who have become citizens or permanent residents should not be rejected in the pools. They also can serve as "models" and "mentors." Further, higher education benefits from its cosmopolitan components and should reject parochial tendencies.

· Collective bargaining should be watched for its impacts on affirmative action. Unions, of necessity, represent their member "ins" more than the nonmember "outs." Unionization may, in some cases, already be a protective reaction to affirmative action. Seniority and tenure protect those already on the job, and, among those on the job, those with the longer service.

· Charges of "reverse discrimination" by majority males will grow in volume and intensity as the number of faculty openings declines between now and the early 1980s, and they will meet with widespread public support.

· White males will continue to be the dominant group in faculties at least until the year 2000. Their acceptance of new approaches is crucial to effective implementation. If they were to become "good soldier Schweiks," then sabotage could be quite effective.

- Patterns of action change. After World War II, women were more concerned with the home today, more with careers as well.
- Many women, even after affirmative action has become fully effective in opening positions to them, will still find themselves in a disadvantaged competitive situation vis-à-vis males, particularly with males who have wives to help them with their academic work, or to manage their family and social lives, or both. Some may thus seek more fundamental changes in higher education and society.[7]
- Some leaders in the women's movement favor concentration of academic women in selected departments or schools so that they may have power bases from which to operate. They, thus, are doubtful about the value, from a power point of view, of scattering women broadly across all areas.[8]
- Colleges and universities are vulnerable institutions. They have little power. They depend heavily on marginal money granted to them by others. Under undue pressure of power or money, they may make unwise long-run concessions affecting their quality. And civic courage in fighting for quality is often in scarce supply.
- Affirmative action will take more time to be effective than the five years suggested earlier (1972) by the federal government. Once reasonably effective, however, it will have brought in additional sources of talent for higher education while serving to enhance equality of opportunity in society.

We are concerned here with an aspect of the "American dilemma"—the contrast between high principle and actual practice. The important principle of nondiscrimination in academic employment is involved. It deserves the best efforts of institutions and governments—which are not yet being given—to assist

[7] For a most perceptive and challenging presentation of this point of view, see Hochschild (1975). See also Johnson and Stafford (1974) on how women, on the average, fail to accumulate as much "human capital" in the course of their careers.

[8] See Howe (1975).

its supremacy over past contrary practices. In asserting this supremacy, we count more on the awakened morality and capacity for reform of the academic community than on the ministrations of an expanding bureaucracy.

We believe, also, that more progress will be made by changing emphases, when warranted, as from the federal government to institutions of higher education and from demand to supply, than by standing rigidly on the same spot arguing old controversies.

Above all, we believe in equality of opportunity for individuals and protection of merit in a truly interracial society where people can make their own choices and are not born as members of "blocks" and placed irretrievably in lifelong categories. In the academic community, in particular, each individual should be viewed on the basis of her or his own abilities and contributions, free from discrimination, pro or con, on the basis of extraneous characteristics. We should not in the course of solving the current problem of past and present discrimination create a new problem for the future by building a block-versus-block mentality, a block-versus-block society. How we handle the transition period of today can substantially affect, for better or worse, the posttransition period of tomorrow.

2

Women and Minorities
on Faculties–
Recent Changes

During the 1960s, with their unprecedentedly rapid enrollment growth, women lost relative ground on faculties of four-year colleges and universities, except at the instructor level (Table 1).

Table 1. Women as a percentage of faculty members in four-year colleges and universities, by rank, 1959-60 to 1974-75

Faculty rank	NEA data[a]			NCES data[a]	
	1959-60	1965-66	1971-72	1972-73	1974-75
All ranks	19.1	18.4	19.0	20.6	22.0
Professor	9.9	8.7	8.6	9.4	9.4
Associate professor	17.5	15.1	14.6	15.8	16.2
Assistant professor	21.7	19.4	20.7	23.1	26.3
Instructor and other	29.3	32.5	39.4	43.5	47.6

[a]National Education Association data and National Center for Educational Statistics data.

Sources: National Education Association (1972, p. 13); Jacobson (1973, p. 1); and "Faculty Salaries Shown Rising" (1975, p. 6).

This reflects, in part, the heavy emphasis on childbearing and childrearing in the years after World War II. Fewer women prepared for entry into the academic labor market. Under the impact of affirmative action, the women's movement, and other forces that have led or encouraged more women to seek Ph.D.'s, this trend has been reversed in the early 1970s. Increases in the proportion of women among faculty members have continued to occur at the instructor level, but they have also occurred at a significant rate at the assistant professor level, where, by 1974-75, the percentage who were women was well above the level of the early 1960s. The trend has been reversed, also, at the associate and full professor levels, but the proportions of women at these levels had not yet reached those of 1959-60 by the 1974-75 academic year.

The familiar pattern of relatively small percentages of women in universities, intermediate proportions in other four-year institutions, and largest proportions in two-year colleges has not been altered by the gains of recent years (Table 2).

Table 2. Women as a percentage of full-time faculty members, by rank and type of institution, 1972-73 and 1974-75

Type of institution and rank	1972-73	1974-75
All institutions	22.3%	24.1%
Professors	9.8	10.3
Associate professors	16.3	16.9
Assistant professors	23.8	27.1
Instructors and other	38.0	39.4
Universities	16.4	18.5
Professors	6.3	6.3
Associate professors	12.5	13.3
Assistant professors	19.8	23.9
Instructors and other	44.4	46.4
Other four-year institutions	23.4	25.0
Professors	12.5	12.9
Associate professors	18.1	18.7

(continued on next page)

Table 2 *(continued)*

Type of institution and rank	1972-73	1974-75
Other four-year institutions *(continued)*		
Assistant professors	25.1	28.1
Instructors and other	43.1	45.5
Two-year institutions	32.9	33.3
Professors	22.1	24.8
Associate professors	25.0	24.9
Assistant professors	31.9	34.4
Instructors and other	35.9	34.9

Sources: Jacobson (1973, p. 1); "Faculty Salaries Shown Rising" (1975, p. 6); and U.S. National Center for Educational Statistics (1975, p. 89).

Moreover, except in two-year colleges, recent gains have been largely confined to the instructor and assistant professor level. This is to be expected, because most hiring is done at those levels, and it takes time for changes in sex ratios to be reflected at higher levels. Data for future years should be more revealing in this respect.

National Data

A recent study by Cartter and Ruhter (1975) shows that female Ph.D.'s gained ground relative to male Ph.D.'s in hiring for the faculties of prestigious universities between 1967 and 1973. Women accounted for 28 percent of the new Ph.D.'s hired by the top 10 universities in 1973, compared with only 4.4 percent in 1967. Among the next 20 universities, women represented 25 percent of new hires in 1973, against 13 percent in 1967. These gains for women, moreover, were achieved in a market that, overall, was deteriorating for both men and women. The proportion of male Ph.D.'s hired by universities among all institutions of higher education declined from 62 percent in 1967 to 42 percent in 1973, while the proportion hired by four-year colleges rose sharply, and relatively more of these male Ph.D.'s accepted positions in two-year colleges and in elementary and secondary schools. Among women, the relative proportions hired by these groups of institutions changed much less, although there was an increase in the percentage hired by two-year colleges (Tables 6 and 7, Appendix A).

Consistent with the Cartter-Ruhter findings are the results of a large-scale 1973 survey of men and women who received their doctor's degrees in 1950, 1960, and 1968. Among those who received their doctor's degrees in 1968, a larger proportion (40 percent) of the women than of the men (35 percent) who were employed full time were in universities. Among the 1950 and 1960 doctoral recipients, however, the percentages of men employed in universities were appreciably higher than those of women (Centra, 1974, p. 53).

The situation differs by field of study. A University of Michigan survey (1974, p. 24) of its 1971 and 1972 recipients of doctorates showed that, among those employed in teaching institutions, 50 percent of the men, but only 16 percent of the women, in the biological and medical sciences were at schools comparable or almost comparable in stature to the University of Michigan. In the social sciences and humanities, that difference did not emerge, while in the physical sciences the numbers of women involved were too small to provide reliable results. The study also showed, however, that the percentages of women who were "unsatisfactorily placed" were considerably larger than the corresponding percentages of men in nearly all fields, among the 1971 graduates, and rose much more sharply for the 1972, as compared with the 1971 graduates, for women than for men. (Those classified by their departments as unsatisfactorily placed were unemployed, underemployed, employed outside their own field, or in an uncertain employment status.) The study also showed that single women were about as likely as men to have firm contracts or commitments at the time of receiving the degree, but that the percentage of married women with firm contracts or commitments was considerably smaller (ibid., pp. 23-24).[1]

[1] Consistent with the University of Michigan results are data from a 1973 survey of doctoral scientists and engineers in the United States, which showed that 3.9 percent of the women, compared with 0.9 percent of the men, were unemployed. Furthermore, unemployment rates for women,

Special studies that have been conducted in particular disciplines indicate that national statistics may conceal some of the difficulties that women continue to encounter in competing with men, particularly in traditionally male fields and in prestigious universities.[2] A survey of faculty members in economics departments in 1974-75, for example, indicated that, both for full-time and for part-time faculty positions, new hires of women were more likely to be at the instructor and "other" (probably chiefly lecturer) levels than in the case of men. The survey also showed that there had been little change from the preceding year in the substantial proportions of economics departments with all-male faculties (Reagan, 1975). Even more striking are the results of a survey of doctoral-granting chemistry departments, which showed that in 1973 two-thirds of the 184 departments had no women in their professorial ranks (assistant, associate, or full professor). Among the departments in Research Universities I, 80 percent had no women. Only 2 percent of the faculty members in professorial ranks in the 184 departments were women, whereas women had received 9.9 percent of the Ph.D.'s granted by these departments in 1971-72 (Green, 1974).

Thus, although national statistics indicate that women Ph.D.'s are being hired—primarily at instructor and assistant professor levels—in rising proportions, there continue to be problems in many of the traditional male fields. We are not suggesting that in all fields and in all departments, there should be an exact match between proportions of women among recent national Ph.D. recipients and recently hired faculty members, but extremely wide disparities may be indicative of a failure to seek out qualified women in traditionally male departments.

---

but not for men, were considerably above the overall rates in the 30 to 34 and 35 to 39 age groups. As in national labor force statistics, an individual was classified as unemployed only if actively seeking work (National Academy of Sciences, 1974, p. 25).

[2]The Cartter-Ruhter study did not shed much light on variations by field, providing data on percentages of women among those hired only for biology, economics, and English. In addition, no information was provided on the ranks or types of faculty positions for which men and women were hired, nor on new hires other than holders of doctor's degrees.

The higher proportions of women among faculty members in four-year and two-year colleges than in universities could disappear in a less favorable job market for Ph.D.'s, as men accept positions in colleges that they would have considered unsuitable in the past.

Minority groups have been much more sparsely represented on faculties than have women, and data relating to them are considerably less adequate. Comparison of the results of faculty surveys conducted by the American Council on Education in 1968-69 and 1972-73 showed slight increases in the relative representation of minority groups between the two years, especially in the "other" category, which includes Native American, Mexican-American, Puerto Rican, and some unspecified groups (Bayer, 1970, p. 12; and 1973, p. 31). However, the data for the two years are not precisely comparable and are not presented here. The 1972-73 data indicated that minorities comprised about 5 percent of all faculty members. Proportions of black faculty members, and especially of black women, were appreciably higher in "other four-year institutions" than in universities. This undoubtedly reflects the fact that most of the black colleges—the colleges historically founded for Negroes—are among the other four-year institutions.

At this point, we need to identify the minority groups with which we shall be especially concerned. They are the groups that include many educationally disadvantaged persons, because of low income, inferior education in ghetto schools, and other economic and social handicaps. We have in mind primarily blacks, persons of Latin American origin (chiefly Chicanos and Puerto Ricans), Native Americans (or American Indians), and certain minority groups of Asian ancestry, such as Filipinos. Chinese-Americans and Japanese-Americans are not generally educationally disadvantaged. They are well represented among students, faculty members, and nonfaculty researchers in higher education, especially in the physical sciences and in the health professions. However, recent immigrants of Chinese and Japanese origin may be educationally disadvantaged (especially the many Chinese coming recently from Hong Kong).

Although the U.S. National Center for Educational Statistics has conducted two recent surveys that have provided data on the sexual composition of faculties, as shown in Table 2, there is a serious deficiency of data relating to the racial composition of faculty members. This deficiency will be partially overcome (so far as current data are concerned) when returns from colleges and universities to a newly developed federal questionnaire, "EEO-6," due November 30, 1975, are received. Completion of this questionnaire is required jointly by the Equal Employment Opportunity Commission (EEOC), the Office for Civil Rights (OCR—in the Department of Health, Education, and Welfare) and the Office of Federal Contract Compliance (OFCC—in the Department of Labor).

Carnegie Council Survey Data

In the spring of 1975, the Carnegie Council undertook a survey of affirmative action policies of colleges and universities to develop data for the present report. The sample of institutions was planned to include a representative group of campuses in the various categories of the Carnegie Commission classification of institutions of higher education, which is described in Appendix B. Included in the sample were the largest public and the largest private campus in each of four categories of the classification in each of the two largest states in each of the nine geographical regions as defined by the U.S. Bureau of the Census —the four categories were Research Universities I, Research Universities II, Doctoral Universities (I and II combined), and Comprehensive Universities and Colleges (I and II combined). In the case of Liberal Arts Colleges I and II, we selected the two largest private colleges in each of the states, because there are relatively few public liberal arts colleges. Similarly, in the case of two-year colleges, we selected the two largest public campuses in each state, because public institutions account for 96 percent of total enrollment in two-year colleges. (In the case of multicampus institutions, the unit in the Carnegie classification is a campus.)

Thus, the sample was biased toward larger campuses, but this seemed appropriate for our purposes, because larger institutions are more likely to be covered by federal requirements for

affirmative action. In addition, the sample included a larger proportion of universities—and especially of Research Universities
I—than of other types of institutions, because there tend to be
far fewer universities in any given state than other four-year
institutions or public two-year colleges. This again was appropriate, because the universities have been far more involved with
federal government agencies than other groups of institutions.
Although the total sample included only 10 percent of the institutions in the relevant categories of the Carnegie classification,
it included 62 percent of Research Universities I (Table 8,
Appendix A).[3]

A letter requesting selected documents and a brief questionnaire (see Appendix B) were sent to the president or chief
campus officer of each institution in the sample about March
17-18, 1975. Responses were requested by April 15, and many
were received by that date, but some arrived later. By early
July, 132 institutions had responded, and the overall response
rate was 64 percent, with the response rates of the various
groups of universities exceeding those of other four-year institutions and two-year colleges. The higher response rate from universities was probably explained by two factors: (1) they are
more involved with federal government agencies on affirmative
action matters, and (2) they are more likely than smaller institutions to have well-organized affirmative action offices to which
to delegate responsibility for handling this type of inquiry. In
most instances, responsibility for assembling and forwarding the
various documents was delegated by the chief campus officer to
a vice-president, vice-chancellor, or affirmative action officer.

Many of the respondents provided data on recent changes

---

[3]The number of institutions included in the sample, for some types of
institutions, is smaller than would be expected on the basis of the number
of states included because of the absence of particular types of institutions
in some states. In addition, we included a few institutions that did not fall
strictly into the sample, because they were known to have had extensive
negotiations with federal government agencies, or because we had access to
their affirmative action plans from sources other than our survey. This
seemed legitimate for this particular survey, because its objectives were not
primarily statistical, but were rather to develop information on the characteristics of affirmative action policies.

in the sexual and racial composition of their faculties and of other groups of academic and nonacademic employees. As we expected, the data are not easily additive for groups of institutions, because they do not always relate to the same years and do not always provide comparable detail. In fact, the number of respondents providing usable data was too small to justify presenting the results in statistical form, but large enough to suggest certain comments on what the data show.

The data on sexual and racial composition of faculty members (usually for either 1973-74 or 1974-75) suggested the following generalizations:

1. Among the universities, women accounted for a somewhat smaller percentage of faculty members in Research Universities I than the 18.5 percent shown for all universities by the NCES data presented in Table 2. Proportions who were women at each rank were also smaller than indicated by the NCES national data.

2. Percentages who were women at each rank tended to be higher in Research Universities II than in Research Universities I and higher in Doctoral-Granting Universities than in Research Universities II. Among universities as a whole, the proportions who were women were very close to those shown by NCES data for 1974-75. These results are not inconsistent with those shown by Cartter and Ruhter, because the Cartter-Ruhter data were focused on new hires, rather than on total faculty. In view of the fact that there have traditionally been few women in Research Universities I, rising proportions of women among new hires would not necessarily bring the proportion of women in these prestigious institutions up to percentages in other groups of institutions in the span of a few years.

3. Proportions who were women in four-year and two-year colleges tended to be higher than in universities, as in the NCES data.

4. The overall percentage of minorities among faculty members was about the same as revealed by the ACE data for 1972-73 (5 percent), but the pattern of variations among types of

institutions differed from that for women. Percentages of minorities among faculty members were slightly higher in Research Universities I than in other groups of institutions, but the differences were not large enough to be statistically significant. Furthermore, among those institutions that provided data for specific minority groups, Asians tended to explain the larger percentages of minorities in prestigious universities, which are more likely to have medical schools and specialized science departments, where Asians are frequently found.[4]

5. The percentages of minority faculty members who were women did not differ appreciably from the percentages of nonminority faculty members who were women, but this meant, in the light of the small proportions of minority faculty members overall, that the number of minority women was extremely small in many institutions.

6. Reflecting the fact that most of the hiring of women in recent years has been at the assistant professor level, the percentages of women in this rank tend to be very much higher than at the associate and full professor levels. Thus substantial increases in the percentages who are women in the higher ranks are likely to take place in the coming years if the newly hired women are promoted in reasonable proportions. Progress at the higher ranks is likely to be slower for members of minority groups, because there are less substantial differences in their relative representation by rank, probably reflecting the much smaller pools of qualified persons among minorities than among women.

7. Among those institutions that provided relevant data, the percentages of women and minorities among new hires (usually for 1973-74) tended to be significantly higher than among total faculty members. However, it was chiefly Research Universities I that provided this information, and, even in that group, only 40 percent of our respondents included such data. It is entirely possible that the institutions provid-

---

[4]We did not receive data from enough two-year colleges to provide reliable information on the racial composition of their faculties.

ing this information tended to have higher percentages of women and minorities among their new hires than institutions that did not provide the data.

8. Only six of our respondents—all Research Universities I— provided data on promotions by race and sex in recent years. For these six institutions, women and minorities tended to comprise a larger proportion of persons recently promoted to associate and full professor positions than of overall incumbents in those ranks in the relevant institutions. However, as in the case of appointments to assistant professor positions, the institutions that provided the data may not be representative of all Research Universities I.

Lecturers and Nonfaculty Academic Personnel

Thus far, we have been concentrating our attention on faculty members in regular, or "ladder," faculty ranks. Usually only faculty members in these ranks are eligible for promotion. In fact, instructors are not always eligible for promotion because, in some cases, they are advanced graduate students who are not likely to be hired for permanent faculty positions. A good many institutions, indeed, have policies of not appointing their own doctoral recipients to assistant professor positions, lest departments become too ingrown, that is, unduly dominated by the views and approaches of leading senior faculty members. These policies have been attacked as discriminatory against married women, who are not free to accept faculty positions in areas distant from their homes, and in some cases they have been modified under the impact of affirmative action policies.

Women make up a sizable proportion of lecturers, and there have been accusations in many institutions that an important type of discrimination is the tendency to keep women in this nonladder and nontenured status. In some cases, married women have been held in this position because of antinepotism rules, in some cases because they lack the Ph.D., and in some cases because they wish to work only part time, and departmental or institutional policies discourage appointing part-time faculty members to regular, or ladder, positions. The availability of qualified married women has made it possible for colleges and universities to use their services as lecturers when and as needed, without having to make a long-term commitment (Bernard, 1964, p. 100). Some married women are content to provide their services in this manner, either because they do not want to go through the arduous program of completing the work for a Ph.D. or because they prefer to work part time. On the other hand, there are many women lecturers who have the doctorate and who resent retention in this second-class status, which, among other things, sometimes prevents their membership in the faculty governing body.

In 1974-75, there were only 2,450 lecturers among 255,500 full-time faculty members in institutions of higher education, and most of these were in universities.[5] The great majority of lecturers, however, are part time. In any case, our data indicate that the number of lecturers in some leading research universities is considerably larger, relatively, than these overall data would suggest. Some institutions have made commendable efforts, under the impact of affirmative action, to identify and reclassify lecturers who are qualified for faculty status, but affirmative action documents received from many of the campuses in our sample make no mention of such efforts.

There are other groups of nonfaculty academic personnel who also tend to occupy second-class status in relation to the faculty on university campuses. These include nonfaculty researchers and librarians particularly. The problems of these two groups are not identical, but they have been of special concern to women's groups because there are substantial proportions of women among nonfaculty researchers, and women tend to predominate among librarians. Nonfaculty researchers complain especially about their lack of job security and in some cases about their lack of promotional opportunities. They are often working on "soft money"—available to the institution only for one or a few years—and thus there are difficult financing problems involved for the institution in guaranteeing them any form of job security. Librarians complain of low pay in relation to

[5] These data have been compiled by the U.S. National Center for Educational Statistics, but were not shown separately in Table 2.

faculty members and frequently find themselves blocked in positions with poor promotional opportunities.

The problems of these groups have been a focus of controversy on campuses and, in some cases, reviews of the qualifications of nonfaculty researchers, as in the case of lecturers, have led to opportunities for faculty appointments for some of them. As we shall see in Section 7, moreover, they have been included under the new types of grievance procedures that have developed under the impetus of affirmative action, whereas regular faculty members have long been protected by the right to appeal to a committee of the academic senate.

Some lecturers (for example, lawyers and physicians) who are practitioners in their fields receive high salaries for their part-time services. On the other hand, there are many lecturers and other faculty members on part-time appointments who are paid a flat fee for teaching a course, often at a rate considerably below the corresponding part-time fraction of a regular faculty member's salary. In some cases, but not invariably, the lower pay of part-time faculty members reflects the fact that, unlike many faculty members, they spend no part of their time on research.

Academic Administration

If women have been thinly represented on faculties, especially in traditionally male fields, they have been even more rarely represented in top academic administrative positions. The Catholic women's colleges have been an exception, but many Catholic women's colleges have either become coeducational or gone out of existence in the last 15 years or so. Independent women's colleges tended to depart from their earlier tradition of having a woman as president during the 1950s and 1960s, but there has been something of a reverse movement back toward women presidents in recent years.

A study conducted about five years ago showed that women constituted a larger proportion of head librarians and of placement directors than of other academic administrators, but this reflected in large part the fact that they held a majority of these posts in small colleges and in women's colleges (Olman, 1970, p. 16). A more recent study of a large sample of men and women holding doctor's degrees indicated that 11 percent of the men, compared with less than 5 percent of the women, held administrative positions (other than department chairmen). More than two-thirds of these men, but less than one-half of the women, were deans or presidents (Centra, 1974, p. 58).

We know of no data relating to the relative representation of minorities in academic administration. This paucity of data will be overcome when EEO-6 returns are available.

Degree Recipients

Data on recipients of master's and doctor's degrees play an important role in federal guidelines for the determination of "availability pools" in affirmative action programs. Thus, it is of the greatest importance that they should be made available as promptly as possible by the federal agencies that gather them.

Even in relation to women, the data on recipients of doctoral degrees are not fully satisfactory, because of the lag in publication of statistics in a period of rapid increases in the proportion of women among doctoral degree recipients. Following a drop after 1930 and slow gains from 1950 to 1970, this proportion rose rapidly from 1970 to 1973 and, in the latter year, exceeded the historic highs of 1920 and 1930:

Women as a percentage of total recipients of doctoral degrees, selected years, 1900 to 1973[6]

Year	Percent
1900	5.8
1910	9.9
1920	15.1
1930	15.1
1940	13.0
1950	5.7
1960	10.5
1970	13.3
1973	18.0

[6]Data for the years 1900 to 1970 are from American Council on Education (1973, p. 1771). The figure for 1973 is from National Research Council/National Academy of Sciences (1974b, p. 8). It should be noted that the actual peak in the relative representation of women among recipients was during World War II, but this reflected the drop in male recipients during those years.

Despite some tendency for increasing numbers of women to receive doctor's degrees in traditionally male fields, such as the physical sciences, in recent years, a survey conducted by the University of Washington of doctorates granted in 1969 to 1972 and of estimated doctorates for the years 1972-75 shows that these changes have not appreciably altered traditional sexual differences in choice of fields. The survey was conducted among institutions belonging to the Association of American Universities, members of which award about 60 percent of all doctor's degrees (McCarthy and Wolfle, forthcoming).

This result may, however, be seen in a somewhat different perspective if we compare changes in the distribution of doctoral degree recipients by field for *both* men and women from 1967-68 to 1972-73 (Table 11, Appendix A). This was a period when job opportunities for persons with advanced degrees in the natural sciences and engineering were deteriorating, and the decline in percentages of women receiving doctorates in those fields occurred along with declines in the proportions of doctorates awarded to men in those fields. Engineering was an exception—the percentage of men receiving doctorates in engineering declined, while the proportion of women achieving engineering doctorates rose somewhat from its previously extremely low level. In this connection, the number of doctor's degrees awarded to women increased from 2,900 to 6,100, or about 110 percent, during this period, while the number of doctor's degrees awarded to men rose by about 40 percent. In the cases of both men and women, the *number* of doctor's degrees awarded in the natural sciences and engineering rose over the five-year period, even though the proportions of degrees awarded in these fields declined. For women, the percentage increases in numbers tended to be greater than for men in each of the science and engineering fields shown separately in Table 11.

Although we know that the proportion of minority-group members among doctoral recipients has been very small, it is only in very recent years that any data have been available on this question, and the deficiency of information is still very serious. Frequently cited is a survey sponsored by the Ford Foundation, which showed that in 1968 the proportion of all doctorates held by blacks was at most 1 percent.

In 1973, for the first time, the Commission on Human Resources of the National Research Council compiled data on the racial and ethnic characteristics of recipients of doctor's degrees in 1973 and also of a sample of persons included in the Comprehensive Roster of Doctoral Scientists and Engineers (National Research Council/National Academy of Sciences, 1974a). These data are presented in Tables 9 and 10, Appendix A. They show, among other things, that 61 percent of the doctor's degrees awarded in 1973 to members of minority groups were received by Asians and that 87 percent of these were noncitizens. There were also noncitizens among black and Latin recipients of doctor's degrees. If U.S. citizens alone are considered, the percentages of minority-group members among doctorate recipients were as follows:

Blacks	2.7%
Asians	1.1
Latin (or Spanish-speaking)	0.8
Native American	0.5
All other	0.0[a]
Total	5.1

[a]Less than 0.05 percent

A second important point is that, although blacks, persons of Latin origin, and Native Americans represented a very small proportion of Ph.D. recipients in 1973, the numbers receiving doctor's degrees have been rising very rapidly. For this reason, measures of availability pools should probably be based on a moving average of percentages of minority-group members among Ph.D. recipients for, say, the most recent five years. A similar measure seems appropriate in the case of women because of the rapid increase in their relative representation among doctorate recipients.

Another important problem is the high degree of concentration of black recipients of doctor's degrees in the field of education. In 1973, no less than 60 percent of the doctor's degrees awarded to black U.S. citizens were in this field (ibid., p. 13). This is a reflection of a historical situation in which most of the blacks attending black colleges, and also to some extent, predominantly white colleges, expected to enter the teaching profession and to teach in the segregated schools and colleges of the South. Freeman (1974) among others has shown that this situation is changing, but the lapse of years between an individual's choice of a college major and the final achievement of a doctor's degree, especially in the field of education, can be very long.

In the case of Spanish-speaking doctorate recipients, a comparatively large proportion in 1973 received their degrees in "humanities and arts," probably reflecting some tendency to concentrate in Spanish-language studies. On the other hand, among the Asians (including both citizens and noncitizens) there was a high degree of concentration in the natural sciences, engineering, and mathematics.

The National Research Council (NCR) 1973 data on minority doctoral recipients included no breakdowns by sex, but we have been able to obtain from the National Board on Graduate Education the results of its special analysis of unpublished NRC data showing percentages of women recipients among the various racial and ethnic groups (National Board on Graduate Education, forthcoming):

Women as a percentage of recipients of
doctor's degrees among U.S. citizens, 1973

Total recipients (U.S. citizens)	19%
White	19
Black	26
Asian	19
Latin (or Spanish-speaking)	
Puerto Rican	19
Other	17
Native American	22

Particularly interesting is the fact that the percentage of women among doctoral recipients was highest for the black women. It should be noted, also, that women represented a higher proportion of native-born recipients than the 18 percent of all 1973 doctoral recipients shown in the previous text table. This is because there were relatively few women among the noncitizen doctoral recipients (indicated in the National Board on Graduate Education data, but not shown here).

Federal guidelines relating to affirmative action plans suggest that data on recent doctor's degrees awarded, by field, sex, and racial or ethnic group are appropriate sources of information for the determination of "availability pools" of potential candidates for positions in four-year institutions of higher education. We prefer the term *pools of qualified persons* to *availability pools*.

How do pools of qualified women and minorities compare with their "utilization" on faculties? Majority women have probably received about 16 to 17 percent of all doctor's degrees awarded to majority U.S. citizens, on the average, during the most recent five-year period for which data are available (1968 to 1973). Because a doctor's degree is not usually required for members of two-year college faculties, and often is not required for instructors in four-year colleges and universities, this percentage should be compared with the proportion of majority women among assistant, associate, and full professors in four-year colleges and universities—about 18 percent in 1974-75. On an aggregative national basis, therefore, it might be said that majority women are not underutilized on faculties of four-year colleges and universities. Another way of putting this point is that there is no overall "demand gap," that is, women are being employed to a relatively greater extent than would be indicated by their representation among qualified persons.

This is not, however, equivalent to saying that there is no discrimination against women on the faculties of four-year colleges and universities. Earlier, we suggested that, when the data for particular disciplines are examined, there may be a substantial gap between the proportion of women among Ph.D.'s and their percentage of faculty members, especially in prestigious universities. The data cited for the field of chemistry are particularly dramatic in this respect. It hardly seems likely that there would be no women in professorial ranks in chemistry in 80 percent of Research Universities I, when women have recently been receiving about 10 percent of the doctor's degrees in chemistry, in the absence of discrimination or, at the very least, if there were no indifference toward the existence of qualified women in the departments concerned.

Even so, if majority women are ever to reach a proportion of professorial faculty members in four-year colleges and universities corresponding to their percentage of majority persons in the labor force—currently about 38 percent—there will have to be a very large increase in their representation among recipients of doctor's degrees. From an average of 16 to 17 percent in the five years from 1968 to 1973 and 19 percent in 1973, they would have to increase their numbers among majority degree recipients to 38 percent. We may characterize this as the overall "supply gap" in relation to the employment of women in professorial ranks in four-year institutions.

Once again, however, there is enormous variation from field to field, and the supply gap is far more serious in such fields as the physical sciences and engineering than the overall averages would suggest. Whether the proportion of women among faculty members in these fields ever approaches their proportion of the total labor force depends on changes throughout the educational system—from the early grades on up—that will induce more women to aspire to careers in these fields and to prepare themselves accordingly, particularly through achieving adequate mathematical training.[7]

When we consider the situation for minorities, it also seems clear that the most serious problems are on the supply side. Probably the most reliable data for measuring the pools of qualified persons are those relating to degrees granted in 1969-72 and expected to be granted in 1972-75 by universities belonging to the Association of American Universities (collected by the University of Washington and reported by McCarthy and Wolfle). Among degrees awarded to U.S. citizens (most universities responding to the survey excluded noncitizens from their

[7]For more extensive discussion of these problems, see Carnegie Commission (1973c).

data), minorities accounted for 3.2 percent in 1969-72 and an estimated 5.8 percent in 1972-75. From our respondents' data and also from ACE data, we may roughly estimate that minorities have accounted for some 4 to 5 percent of faculty members in professorial ranks in four-year colleges and universities in the last few years. This again suggests that there is no overall "demand gap," but clearly the situation varies greatly from field to field, and the overall data should not be interpreted as indicating that there is no discrimination in individual fields and departments. To the extent that our respondents provided data on minorities by department or by groups of departments, and only a relatively small proportion of institutions (chiefly Research Universities I) did, we may report with some confidence that there are many departments, and some clusters of departments or schools, that have no minority members. This statement is even more true when we consider specific minority groups.

If we attempt to compare pools of qualified persons with "utilization" for specific minorities, we find that the data are very inadequate. Neither the University of Washington survey nor our own survey yielded much detail for individual minority groups. The best we can do is to compare the ACE data for faculty members in 1972-73 with the NRC data on degree recipients in 1973 (keeping in mind the fact that the faculty data include noncitizens):[8]

	Minorities as a percentage of	
	Faculty members, 1972-73	*Doctoral recipients (U.S. citizens, 1973)*
Black	2.9%	2.7%
Asian	1.5	1.1
Other	2.8	1.3

[8] For data on faculty members, see Bayer (1973, p. 31). The data relate to all faculty members in institutions of higher education; it is impossible to determine the percentages in professorial ranks in four-year institutions from the published tables. The data on doctoral recipients are from National Research Council/National Academy of Sciences (1974a).

These overall percentages do not suggest underutilization of minorities on an aggregative basis, but they tell us nothing about the situation in individual institutions and fields. The fact that "other minorities" form a larger percentage of faculty members than of doctoral recipients who are U.S. citizens is probably explained by the employment on faculties of noncitizens, primarily Latin Americans. These other minorities chiefly include persons of Latin origin and Native Americans. The 4-5 percent figure used for minority faculty members on page 5 has been roughly adjusted to exclude noncitizens but to include permanent residents.

What about the representation of minorities in the labor force? The current proportion of minorities among persons in the labor force is about 14 percent[9] of whom about 40 percent are minority women. Thus the supply gap is somewhat greater in percentage terms—though not in percentage points—for minorities than for majority women. Moreover, for minorities from families in urban ghetto and some rural areas, the handicaps involved in achieving doctor's or professional degrees are more deepseated than they are for most majority women.

Women have constituted about 40 percent of recipients of master's degrees in recent years and account for about one-third of faculty members in two-year colleges. Thus, there is something of a "demand gap," but it may be at least partially explained by the fact that many of the women receiving master's degrees (more than half of whom have been in the field of education) have in the past gone into elementary and secondary school teaching, not necessarily because they preferred it to college teaching. Even now, with the demand for schoolteachers sharply cut back, many of the women who receive master's degrees are employed as teachers and have been studying for their degrees on a part-time basis.

There are no data on minority recipients of master's degrees, and no very good data on minorities on faculties of two-year colleges.

[9]Computed from data in U.S. President (1974, Table A-3) and U.S. Bureau of the Census (1973).

Although the rate of enrollment growth in higher education has been slowing down, and enrollment is likely to be stationary or to decline somewhat in the 1980s, enrollment in public two-year colleges has continued to grow relatively rapidly in recent years. Prospects for future growth are more favorable for the two-year colleges than for four-year institutions, because they enroll relatively large numbers of adults in undergraduate programs and will not be affected as seriously as the four-year institutions in the 1980s by the decline in the traditional college-age population of 18- to 21-year-olds. Thus, there are likely to be relatively more opportunities for women and minority groups, as well as for majority males, in two-year colleges. Overcoming the current demand gap in the case of women on the faculties of two-year colleges should not present serious problems, assuming nondiscriminatory and affirmative action programs in those institutions, and a flow of women into master's programs at approximately the present rate. In the case of two-year colleges, overcoming the demand gap would also have the result of overcoming the supply gap for women. We cannot make the same statement about minorities, because the data are entirely inadequate.

We believe that an important part of each affirmative action plan of a doctoral-granting university should be a "supply plan," that is, a plan for giving maximum encouragement to women and minorities in achieving graduate and professional degrees. Only a few of the affirmative action plans that we have received from our respondents have given emphasis to this need, although many of the plans include statistics showing the racial and sexual composition of graduate and professional students. Examples of statements in affirmative action plans relating to this problem are the following:

> *Private research university—Northeast.* It is clear that so long as the pool of minority group doctorates is small, both short- and long-term faculty recruitment efforts will be frustrated by the limited availability of qualified candidates. Consequently . . . the University has decided that a significant component of its

Affirmative Action Program will be directed towards enlarging the pool. _____ feels that such a program would be of benefit to the academic community at large and hopes that its efforts will be paralleled by the graduate schools from which it normally recruits faculty candidates. . . .

During the past several years, both students and faculty members from the Graduate School visited the predominantly Negro colleges in the South to encourage students to apply for admission. . . .

Discussion of the problem and of possible alternative approaches led to the decision to shift the focus to Black student populations in universities in the Northeast, in the area from Boston to Washington.

Public research university—Northeast. Although affirmative action is thought of primarily in terms of employees, it is the University's view that one of its most essential contributions to affirmative action is to increase the pools of available minorities and women through the educational process. . . . The University will continue to recruit and accept students among those who are qualified, regardless of race, color, sex, national origin, religion, or age. Nevertheless, the University has been concerned that disciplines and programs and schools in which talented women and minority students seem to be under represented or not represented at all . . . attempt to identify and enroll qualified women and minority persons and break patterns of "clustering." These special efforts . . . have resulted already in significant progress for women and minorities, as can be seen from the accompanying [tables].

Public research university—South. Two types of programs can be developed to increase the numbers of female and minority students in the graduate programs at the _____ . The first is a thorough utilization of sources currently available by a strong recruitment effort directed toward female and minority students already at colleges and universities throughout the nation. Particular emphasis shall be made at those schools with predominantly female or minority faculty.

The second type of support of action programs is a long-range effort to increase the number of women and minorities available to be considered for admission to graduate school. We shall continue to support those types of programs which will enlarge the potential pool of qualified females and members of minority groups. Examples . . . are Project Upward Bound . . . and the Women's Walk-In Counseling Service.

Public research university—South. One point that has come up time and again in our efforts to increase the representation of blacks and females in our faculty ranks is the fact that, in a number of disciplines, there continues to be only a limited number of females, and even fewer blacks, who possess terminal degrees. This factor has made it increasingly clear that, if we are to meet our objective of significantly increasing the numbers of blacks and females on our faculty, it will be necessary for this and other universities in the nation to educate more blacks and females to the level of terminal degrees. . . .

One of the obstacles to increasing our enrollment of black and female graduate students is the shortage of financial support for such students. At a time when the need for such support is increasing, Federal aid for graduate students appears to be on the decline.

Not only has the number of women among graduate students and recipients of advanced degrees been increasing rapidly in very recent years, but there is also some evidence that discrimination against women in graduate education is receding.[10] This trend is likely to continue under the impact of Title IX of the Education Amendments of 1972—to be discussed more fully in Section 5—which prohibited discrimination on the basis of sex in admissions to graduate and professional schools, as well as to public undergraduate programs (with certain exceptions). Women continue, however, to need encouragement at all stages of education to aspire to careers that have been traditionally stereotyped as for males. In particular, they need encouragement to pursue the mathematical studies that are increasingly essential in many fields.

On the whole, however, the handicaps that face women are not as serious as those that face many members of minority groups in aspiring to graduate and professional education. The handicaps of minority-group members sometimes include relatively poor preparation and almost invariably include difficulties in financing prolonged graduate and professional education. Furthermore, the favorable job market that has prevailed for minority-group recipients of bachelor's and master's degrees, under the impact of affirmative action, in recent years, increases what economists would call the "opportunity costs" of advanced graduate education because of the favorable salaries that can be obtained in corporate jobs, especially for those trained in certain fields.[11]

---

[10]For a more detailed discussion, see Carnegie Commission (1973c, Section 6).

[11]Black male college graduates as a whole continue to have appreciably lower median incomes than white male graduates, but the difference has been narrowing, especially for young college graduates entering the labor market. Somewhat surprisingly, the median income of black female college graduates, while lower than that of black male graduates, has tended to exceed that of white female graduates in recent years. The explanation appears to be, not that black women graduates are usually paid more than comparable white women in similar jobs, but rather that they are more likely to work full time and less likely to drop out of the labor force when they are rearing young children. (See the discussion in Carnegie Commission, 1973b, p. 52; and 1973c, p. 26. See also Freeman, 1974; and U.S. Bureau of the Census, 1973 and 1975.)

All of this indicates that increasing the supply of doctorate recipients among minority groups calls for a concentrated national effort and for a significant expenditure of both public and private funds. In our recent report, *The Federal Role in Postsecondary Education,* we recommended an increased and stable federal program of fellowships for graduate students. We also recommended a continued increase in funds for the special federal programs, such as Upward Bound, that are designed to improve access of minority groups to undergraduate education.

Beyond these policies, special efforts are needed. Under the auspices of the American Economic Association, for example, a special seminar was conducted in the summer of 1974 for black juniors majoring in economics—primarily but not exclusively in black southern colleges—to improve their preparation for graduate education in the field. The seminar is to be continued for the same students in 1975. Similar programs are needed in other fields, especially those which, like economics, require mathematical skills. Such programs merit support from private foundations and from the federal government.

Recommendation 1: *All institutions of higher education with doctoral and professional programs should include within their affirmative action plans a "supply plan," that is, a plan designed to provide maximum opportunities for women and minorities to participate on a basis of equal opportunity in graduate and professional education.*

The plan should ensure, not only that there is no discrimination on the basis of race, national origin, or sex in admission to graduate and professional schools, or in the administration of financial aid, but also that positive efforts are made to recruit women and minorities along with majority male students, and that special programs are developed to improve, when needed, the preparation of women, minorities, and other persons who have been underprivileged in their prior education for graduate and professional education.

Special emphasis should be placed by high schools and other appropriate community agencies on the development of improved career and financial guidance, especially for young people from low-income families, who are less likely to receive informed guidance from parents and friends than those from more affluent families. Young women capable of aspiring to traditionally male careers need encouragement and guidance at an early stage. [12]

The federal government has a special responsibility to maintain stable financial support of graduate education. The Council's recent recommendation for 20,000 graduate fellowships and 2,000 traineeships should be promptly implemented. [13]

Universities and colleges need the active assistance and cooperation of other agencies and groups in achieving the purposes of Recommendation 1. The federal government should ensure, not only that there is an adequate and stable program of graduate fellowships, but also that there is no discrimination on the basis of race, national origin, or sex in the awarding of federal graduate fellowships. We have also recommended that federal funds for research in institutions of higher education increase with the gross national product. These federal funds play an important role in providing for research assistantships, which should also be available to graduate students on a strictly nondiscriminatory basis.

Private foundations, professional associations, and appropriate federal and state agencies should also give high priority to special programs designed to help women, minorities, and others overcome deficiencies in their preparation for graduate and professional education.

Married women desiring to study for graduate and profes-

[12] For a detailed discussion of this need, see Carnegie Commission (1973c, Section 4).

[13] The Council recommended (1) merit fellowships available for a two-year period to 5,000 beginning graduate students who are planning to undertake a doctoral program each year (or 10,000 fellowships at any one time), (2) predoctoral fellowships available for a two-year period on the basis of demonstrated academic ability for 5,000 graduate students advanced to candidacy for the Ph.D. or other doctoral degrees (also 10,000 at any one time), and (3) traineeships for a total of about 2,000 graduate students at any one time (Carnegie Council, 1975, Section 5).

sional degrees frequently encounter special obstacles, particularly if they are rearing young children or have been away from higher education for some years. These obstacles may include rules forbidding or discouraging part-time study, strict limitations on the length of time permitted for completion of the requirements for a degree, policies prohibiting access to fellowships on a part-time basis, antinepotism rules, policies forbidding credit for undergraduate records achieved some years ago, and the like.[14] An important aspect of affirmative action is the modification of such policies, which sometimes adversely affect men, as well as women, with family responsibilities.

Recommendation 2: *Graduate and professional schools should review their policies, where this has not been done, in order to revise any rules that discriminate against students on the basis of sex, marital status, or family responsibilities. Policies should include (1) rules permitting part-time study to accommodate men or women whose family circumstances necessitate part-time study, (2) policies permitting a moderate extension of the time period for completion of requirements for advanced and professional degrees for such students, (3) eligibility for fellowships for such part-time students,[15] (4) no discrimination on the basis of race, sex, or marital status in appointing teaching or research assistants or in awarding fellowships, (5) no antinepotism rules in connection with these appointments or awards, (6) and opportunities for persons entering graduate school after some years away from higher education to overcome special deficiencies in preparation, as in mathematics.*

Inadequacy of Data

Until very recently, as we have seen, data on the sexual and racial or ethnic characteristics of degree recipients and faculty

[14]For a more extensive discussion of these problems, see Carnegie Commission (1973c, Section 6).

[15]In most cases, the amount of the fellowship should be expected to reflect the part-time status of the student. Part-time study is not as practical a possibility in medical schools as in other graduate and professional schools.

members were inadequate or nonexistent. Data on minority women scarcely exist at all. These deficiencies are gradually being overcome, but efforts to improve the data, both by institutions of higher education and by federal agencies, need to be continued.

It also seems highly desirable that the Office for Civil Rights (OCR), as the agency most directly involved in enforcement of affirmative action, take responsibility for making available the most recent and reliable data on pools of qualified women and minorities. Thus far, individual institutions have been forced to devote considerable effort to collection of the data, and a few have gone so far as to conduct their own surveys of recipients of doctor's degrees from leading doctoral-granting institutions. A number of institutions of higher education responding to our survey suggested that OCR should take responsibility for compiling these data.

Recommendation 3: *The Council recommends that federal agencies—in particular, the National Center for Educational Statistics, the National Research Council/National Academy of Sciences, and the Equal Employment Opportunity Commission —improve their programs for collecting and promptly publishing data on the sexual and racial or selected ethnic characteristics of degree recipients and academic employees. There is a special need for breakdowns by sex within particular racial and ethnic groups.*

In addition, the Office for Civil Rights should assume the responsibility of making these data available to colleges and universities as soon as possible.

Salary Differentials

All the available data have shown that women tend to be paid less than men on the faculties of institutions of higher education—rank by rank, regardless of the type of institution. That these salary differences may be partially or wholly attributable to objective factors, such as relative research accomplishment and greater concentration of male faculty members in fields with particularly high salaries, has long been recognized. However, residual salary differentials in favor of men have been found in several studies that have attempted to control for all or many of the "predictor" variables that might objectively explain the salary differences. (A residual salary differential is an average difference between salaries of men and women that remains after controlling for all the measurable factors that might account for differences.) Whether or not these residual salary differences indicate discrimination against women has become a matter of controversy.

On the whole, there is less evidence of racial salary differentials than of sexual differences. Basing her analysis on data collected by the Carnegie Commission and the American Council on Education in 1968-69, Elizabeth Scott found a sizable residual sex difference in salaries after controlling for many predictor variables, but no clear indication of a significant residual salary difference on the basis of race. Her findings on this point are of considerable interest:

> There was a slight tendency for black men to have negative mean residuals when their salaries were predicted on the basis of the equation for all men, while there was a slight tendency for black women to have positive mean residuals when their salaries were predicted on the basis of the equation for all women. Somewhat similar relationships prevailed for Asian-Americans, but more irregularly. However, these differences were not statistically significant. On the other hand, the difference associated with sex persisted and was strong. Not only were the mean residuals for white men substantial and positive, but this was also true for black men, Asian-American men, and men of "other" races, and the mean residuals tended to be similar in amount to those for all men. Conversely, the residuals for women, regardless of race, tended to be negative in every field and type of institution (Carnegie Commission, 1973c, p. 209).

There are no recent data on racial differences in compen-

sation in higher education, but comments are frequently made
by informed persons to the effect that the salaries of minorities
—probably primarily of male minorities—have been driven up
above those of majority men with similar qualifications by the
intense competition for the limited supply of minority talent
under the impact of affirmative action. These comments tend to
relate chiefly to the salaries of minority men in prestigious research universities, and we have earlier commented on the
slightly higher proportion of minorities among faculty members
of Research Universities I than in other groups of institutions
(though we noted that the difference was not statistically significant). Even though most of the evidence is anecdotal, there
seems to be little question that the competition among leading
universities, at least for highly qualified minority men, has been
intense.

On sex-based salary differentials, there *are* recent data. In
1974-75, the average salary of all male faculty on full-time contracts for the academic year in all institutions of higher education was $16,000. The corresponding figure for women was
$13,200, or 83 percent of that for men. As compared with the
results of the comparable survey by NCES two years earlier,
there had been little change in overall male-female differentials
or in the pattern of differences within types of institutions and
academic ranks (Table 3). Percentage increases in salaries of
men and women over the two-year period differed only slightly,
with the pattern varying somewhat among ranks and among the
three major types of colleges and universities. Increases were
considerably smaller in private than in public institutions (see
Table 12, Appendix A), probably reflecting the more severe
financial difficulties facing many private colleges and universities.

Salary increases in public two-year colleges tended to be
somewhat larger, percentage-wise, than in public four-year colleges and universities. This was particularly true at the instructor level, and probably reflected exceptionally strong demand
for faculty members with specialized knowledge or experience
in a variety of vocational fields. Occupational programs in
public two-year colleges have been expanding very rapidly in

Table 3. Average salaries of full-time faculty members on
9-10-month contracts, by type of institution, rank, and sex,
1974-75, and percentage increases since 1972-73

Type and rank	Average salary 1974-75		Differ- ence	Percentage increase since 1972-73	
	Men	Women		Men	Women
All institutions	$16,000	$13,200	$2,800	10.9	11.3
Professor	21,000	18,400	2,600	9.3	8.6
Associate professor	16,000	15,200	800	11.0	10.5
Assistant professor	13,300	12,600	700	8.5	10.4
Instructor	13,500	11,800	1,700	22.9	16.5
Universities	17,400	13,600	3,800	9.8	9.2
Professor	22,700	20,100	2,600	8.1	10.7
Associate professor	16,700	15,800	900	11.1	10.2
Assistant professor	13,800	13,000	800	9.3	9.1
Instructor	11,000	10,500	500	9.4	10.9
Other four-year institutions	14,900	12,700	2,200	10.2	9.4
Professor	19,000	17,800	1,200	10.7	6.8
Associate professor	15,400	14,500	900	10.2	9.3
Assistant professor	12,800	12,200	600	7.2	10.4
Instructor	10,600	10,200	400	10.6	9.5
Two-year institutions	15,200	13,700	1,500	18.3	15.6
Professor	18,600	17,400	1,200	12.7	15.2
Associate professor	16,600	16,400	200	14.9	14.7
Assistant professor	13,800	13,500	300	12.7	12.5
Instructor	15,400	13,500	1,900	24.6	19.7

Sources: Jacobson (1973, p. 1) and U.S. National Center for Educational Statistics
(1975, p. 89). Percentage increases have been computed from unrounded data.

the last few years, and reports on the job market for teachers
continue to comment on shortages of vocational education
teachers.

The traditional pattern of relatively large male-female salary differentials in universities, intermediate differences in other

four-year institutions, and relatively small differentials in two-year colleges continued to prevail in 1974-75. However, in all three groups of institutions the overall male-female differential tended to be larger than the difference in any individual rank, indicating, as we have noted earlier, that women tend to be more heavily concentrated in the lower ranks. (The one exception to this pattern is the relatively larger differential at the instructor level in two-year colleges.)[16] Moreover, the male-female differential tended to vary with rank and was considerably larger at the full professor level than in lower ranks (again with the exception of instructors in two-year colleges). The largest difference of all appeared among full professors in private universities.

The relatively large male-female differential at the full professor level is partially explained by the fact that full professors' salaries in the natural sciences and on medical faculties, where women are rarely found, tend to be especially high. The particularly large differential at the full professor level in private universities probably reflects, in addition, the fact that private universities tend to have less formal salary structures than public universities and are more likely to compete for top male talent at tenured ranks by hiring from other institutions and offering salaries that are not restricted by formal salary scales. However, the difference between public and private universities in this respect should not be overstated, because prestigious full professors in public universities command "above-scale" salaries. Moreover, Elizabeth Scott's study showed that residual salary differentials tended to be especially large in highly paid fields.

A study that revealed residual salary differences between men and women on the basis of a 1968-69 survey of faculty members conducted by the Carnegie Commission and the American Council on Education was carried out by Astin and Bayer (1972). They repeated their analysis on the basis of an ACE 1972-73 faculty survey and found some reduction in residual

[16]This unusually large difference does not appear in the 1974-75 salary survey of the American Association of University Professors. In other respects, the pattern of differences revealed by the AAUP survey and the NCES survey is similar (Magarrell, 1975).

male-female differentials as compared with their analysis of the 1968-69 data:

> In 1968-69 an average raise for women of more than $1000 across all ranks would have been required for equity in accordance with the predictors of men's salaries. The comparable figure in 1972-73 was $600. Both these figures are conservative, inasmuch as they are based on accepting all preceding differentials, including ranks, as being not related to sex. If we exclude rank as a predictor of salary . . . application of the men's regression equation to the women's data yields an average gross salary differential in 1972-73 in excess of $1000 between the actual and the predicted salaries of academic women (Bayer and Astin, 1975, p. 800).

Thus, the Bayer-Astin findings, as those of Elizabeth Scott's analysis of the 1968-69 data, indicate that part of the residual sex difference is explained by the fact that women tend to be promoted less rapidly than men. Women are more likely, also, to be retained in lecturer positions, where salaries are relatively low, although there are some institutions in which lecturers are highly paid. In virtually all public institutions and in many private institutions that have formal salary structures, the discrimination does not take the form of paying a woman a lower salary than a man when she is in the same step of the same rank, but it does take the form of not moving her up through the steps and ranks as rapidly. Scott's analysis showed that in the sciences in Research Universities I, salaries increased with years of academic employment twice as rapidly for men as for women.

In spite of the prevalence of formal salary structures in public institutions, some of the cases, involving back-pay awards, in which sex discrimination in compensation in academic institutions has been found by federal or state agencies, or the courts, have been public universities and colleges.

A significant aspect of the Bayer-Astin findings is that, by

1972-73, residual sex differences in pay had largely disappeared in the junior ranks (instructor/lecturer, assistant professor), but continued to be sizable in the higher ranks, particularly at the full professor level. The residual difference, when actual salaries of women full professors were compared with salaries predicted on the basis of the regression equation for men full professors, amounted to $1,700. This the authors characterized as the "amount of underpayment in 1972-73 to women in high rank with characteristics statistically identical to men's in educational attainment, specialization, productivity, and so forth" (ibid.).

Nevertheless, differences in ability and accomplishment are not fully susceptible of statistical measurement. Convincing evidence of discrimination is more likely to be found as a result of intensive investigation of individual cases, and, indeed, has been found in some cases involving institutional, administrative (state and federal), and judicial decisions.

3

Academic Policies
Under the Impact
of Affirmative Action

The story of extensive federal involvement in the enforcement
of affirmative action policies in higher education began in 1970.
But campaigns for more equitable treatment of women and
minorities had begun on a number of campuses, especially the
larger ones, several years before. From the mid-1960s on, as predominantly white universities and colleges began to open their
doors to increasing numbers of minority students, they began to
be faced with complaints about the absence of minority faculty
members and, in some cases, responded by hiring minority faculty members, especially for black or ethnic studies programs.
Around 1968-69, there was growing evidence of organized
groups of women conducting surveys of the status of women
and pressing for modification of policies that they perceived as
discriminating against women on a number of campuses. Con-
spicuous among their early demands was insistence on the modification of antinepotism rules (policies restricting the employment of near relatives, sometimes on a campuswide basis, but
more frequently within the same department). These policies
had had the effect in many cases of barring married women
from employment in regular faculty positions, especially when
their spouses were in the same academic field.

Virtually all campuses are now affected in one way or another by federal government laws and regulations requiring nondiscrimination in the admission of students and in the hiring and promotion of academic and nonacademic employees. Under the provisions of federal Executive Order 11246, as amended, campuses seeking federal contracts must not only sign agreements pledging nondiscrimination, but in many cases must develop written affirmative action plans, including numerical goals and timetables for the hiring of women and minority groups in job classifications in which there are deficiencies in their relative representation. The requirement for affirmative action plans applies to all institutions employing 50 or more persons and receiving $50,000 or more in federal-contract funds.

Thus, although nearly all institutions are affected by nondiscrimination provisions, federal affirmative action requirements apply primarily to larger institutions, and especially to major research universities.

There is little question that academic employment policies have been altered under the impact of nondiscrimination and affirmative action requirements. Before discussing the ways in which they have been altered, we need to consider the special characteristics of the academic job market.

The Academic Job Market

In certain respects, the academic job market is unique, especially when compared with job markets for most white-collar and blue-collar workers. It is not quite so unique when compared with markets for specialized professional and managerial workers in government and in private industry.

Probably the most important characteristic of the academic job market, as it relates to the hiring of faculty members, is that highly specialized training and experience are sought. With certain exceptions, a four-year college or a university will have a preference for an individual with a doctor's degree. More importantly, the individual must have a doctor's degree in the particular academic discipline in which there is a vacancy, and, within that discipline, the recruiting department will frequently have a preference for an individual with considerable training in a subspecialty. That is, a recruiting department is likely to have identified a subspecialty which is not well represented, or not at all represented, on its existing faculty. In economics, the subspecialty might be industrial organization, econometrics, labor economics, or any one of a dozen or so important specialties. In the field of history, the department might be seeking a specialist in nineteenth-century American history, Oriental history, medieval history, and so on. This preference for highly specialized training and experience is likely to be even more important in making an appointment to an associate or full professorship than in making an appointment to an assistant professorship, but openings for assistant professors are often confined to a subspecialty within a discipline.

Second, candidates for appointments are carefully evaluated on the basis of their relative qualifications. If the appointment is to an assistant professorship, as most entry-level appointments to regular faculty positions are, the individual's record in graduate school, the quality of his or her doctor's thesis and any other papers or publications, recommendations from professors particularly familiar with the candidate, and impressions gained from personal interviews tend to be the most important considerations in the selection process. The individual's potential ability for research and teaching graduate students are likely to be given a relatively large weight in appointments to universities—especially research universities—whereas ability for teaching undergraduates may be given relatively more weight in appointments to other types of institutions. Selective liberal arts colleges, however, also tend, especially if they have graduate programs, to give weight to research and graduate teaching ability.

A third highly important consideration is the relative quality of the graduate or professional school in which the individual was trained. A department initiating a search for a candidate for appointment as assistant professor in a prestigious research university would have been likely, traditionally, to confine its search to the 10 or 12 departments considered the most distinguished in the particular specialty being sought. Departments in less prestigious institutions might recruit somewhat more broadly, but, nevertheless, would seek to attract candidates from relatively reputable graduate or professional schools.

Because of the preferences for highly qualified candidates from especially distinguished graduate or professional departments, search procedures, especially at prestigious institutions, tended traditionally to be conducted on a confidential basis. Openings were not advertised or publicized. Typically, the department chairman or the chairman of the department's personnel or search committee visited the relatively few departments from which applicants were to be sought and interviewed advanced candidates for the Ph.D. Women charge that the candidates who were recommended tended to be the male graduate students whom faculty members wanted to see placed in prestigious institutions. Minority groups have also complained that this pattern of recruitment was not well designed to identify qualified minority candidates.

Much has been made, in debates over affirmative action policies, of the charge that these recruitment procedures were carried on within an "old-boy network." There is some basis for this charge, but, to the extent that it implies that appointments traditionally have been made on the basis of friendship, rather than ability, it is not typically justified. Friendship may be a factor in certain cases, but the major considerations in departments that are highly concerned about their quality and prestige have been the candidate's individual qualifications and the standing of his or her graduate department.

Less distinguished universities and other types of colleges have tended to recruit somewhat more broadly than the prestigious research universities. Nevertheless, the traditional pattern has been not to publicize openings. Interviews with prospective candidates have been conducted at the candidate's university, at the university doing the hiring (by invitation), and at professional association meetings. Even at the association meetings, however, it has frequently been very difficult for job-seekers to discover which departments had openings, because representatives of those departments preferred to limit their interviewing to candidates who had already been recommended to them by the departments from which they usually hired.

Another exceedingly important characteristic of the academic job market, and one which is often not fully understood by persons unfamiliar with academic employment, is that appointments are usually initiated by departments. Representatives of a department undertake the search for candidates, a departmental committee screens the candidates, and typically the department as a whole, or the tenured members of the department, vote on the final selection. This tends to be less true in public two-year colleges, where faculty members have less power and responsibility in academic personnel matters than in other institutions, but it is generally true in four-year colleges and universities.

Once a department has made its selection, the recommendation of the department is typically reviewed by a dean and is usually subject to approval by the chief campus officer.[1] However, in relation to affirmative action requirements, traditional procedures usually called for review of the qualifications of the *recommended* candidate only. Often no attempt was made to consider the relative qualifications of other candidates that might have been considered by the department. Thus, if a qualified woman or minority candidate was passed over, the campus administration would not have been aware of the fact.

Review procedures are more complicated and more stringent on appointments or promotions to tenured positions than on initial appointments to assistant professorships. (Typically, a faculty member acquires tenured status when he or she is appointed to an associate professorship. From that point on, the faculty member is protected against dismissal except on very serious grounds of individual conduct or, in some cases, financial stringency within the institution).[2] In cases of

[1]The chief campus officer in a single-campus institution is the president. In a multicampus institution, it may be the chancellor, the campus president, or an official with some other title.

[2]Provisions relating to criteria for dismissal of tenured faculty members, as well as for rights of appeal to a faculty committee, usually follow quite closely the recommendations of the American Association of University Professors (1973, p. 2). For a special policy statement relating to termination of a faculty member because of financial exigency, see "Termination of Faculty Appointments . . ." (1974).

appointments or promotions to tenured positions, the departmental recommendation may go to a special review committee that includes a majority of faculty members from other (usually closely related) departments, along with a few representatives of the initiating department. Letters evaluating the candidate from distinguished scholars in the discipline, or the recommendation of a special committee of scholars from other institutions, are sometimes required. A department will sometimes support its selection with outside letters or recommendations even if not required to do so. Appointments and promotions to tenured positions sometimes require approval of the board of trustees, as well as the president, and, in multicampus institutions, frequently require the approval of the chief multicampus officer and sometimes, also, of the board of trustees.

In some respects, policies of major universities relating to appointments to tenured positions have differed in ways that are significant in relation to affirmative action policies. Harvard, for example, has long had a policy of restricting the number of tenured positions and of rarely appointing one of its assistant professors to an associate professorship. The number of assistant professors in some departments is quite large, and a good many of them have combinations of part-time teaching and part-time research appointments, but for the most part they are expected to look elsewhere for their more permanent positions, and tenured appointments are frequently made from outside the university. Some institutions, especially public institutions, on the other hand, have policies of discouraging departments from filling vacancies in associate or full professor ranks from the outside. When a professor retires, the department is expected to fill the vacancy by appointment of an assistant professor unless special permission is obtained to fill the position at a higher rank. Typically, promotions to associate professorships are made from among those assistant professors who have reached one of the top steps of the assistant professorship rank.[3]

Public universities and colleges usually have formal salary

[3]This discussion is based on generally available information, and not on responses to our survey.

structures that are similar to civil service salary schedules. The salary for each step of each rank is determined by the formal salary schedule, and there is a steady upward progression of salaries through the various steps and ranks. There may be as many as four to six steps within a rank—sometimes fewer. An individual will typically stay within a given step for the number of years, usually two or three, stipulated in the schedule. However, progression from one step to another is not automatic, but is based on a recommendation for a "merit increase," which is initiated by the department and subject to approval of the administration. Frequently there is an "above-scale" schedule of salaries for professors who have progressed through all the ranks and are deemed to merit additional increases, or who are in a position to bargain for such increases because of job offers from other institutions.

Private universities and colleges are somewhat less likely to have formal salary structures than public institutions, but the situation varies. The University of Chicago has long been known for its apparently complete absence of a formal salary structure and for its tendency to bargain individually with each faculty member and each potential appointee. In a number of other private universities and colleges, salary increases tend to be based more on individual merit and less on a formal salary schedule than in public institutions. Thus, a charge of salary discrimination might be expected to arise more readily in a private institution, but there have been awards of back pay to women who have been successful in complaints or court cases charging unequal pay in public, as well as in private, institutions.

In practice, the forces of market competition tend to moderate the impact of differences in salary policies between public and private institutions. During the period of rapid enrollment growth and keen competition for faculty members in the 1960s, public universities and colleges frequently hired assistant professors at, let us say, the third rather than the first step in order to meet offers of their competitors. Less prestigious public universities and colleges sometimes hired beginning faculty members at the associate professor level (though often initially without tenure) in order to meet the competition of more renowned campuses. Professors who were considering offers from other institutions were sometimes jumped several steps or given accelerated promotions to induce them to reject the offer. Competition was particularly intense in the natural sciences, where alternative demands from government and industry helped to enhance shortages. Faculty members in these fields were often promoted rapidly, so that average salaries exceeded those in other fields. A scientist who had a substantial research grant or contract that he could bring with him from another institution was in an especially strong bargaining position.

Under conditions of slowing enrollment growth, the academic job market of the 1970s is quite different from that of the 1960s, and enrollment is likely to be virtually stationary overall in the 1980s, chiefly because of the leveling off in the size of the college-age population that will result from the declining numbers of births that began about 1964-65. There are now far fewer new appointments to be made, relative to the size of the existing faculty, than there were in the 1960s. Offers from other institutions are less likely to be made to existing faculty members, and thus resignation rates are declining. Because so many young faculty members were hired in the 1960s, the average age of faculty members is currently rather low, and therefore retirement rates are low. All of this means relatively few vacancies, and far greater difficulty in adding women and minorities than would have been the case had the affirmative action movement started in the early 1960s. Some of our respondent institutions are contemplating appreciable reductions in the size of their faculties, and more may be expected to face this exigency in the 1980s. Thus, questions of whether dismissals will be based on seniority—a principle that would adversely affect recently hired women and minorities—or will avoid the principle of seniority in order to retain some of those women and minorities are likely to become much more urgent than they have been thus far.

The Prevalence and Status of Affirmative Action Plans

The great majority of respondents to the Council's survey of affirmative action policies had adopted affirmative action plans or were engaged in their preparation (Table 4).[4] In fact, among the respondent universities and the comprehensive universities and colleges, all reported that they had affirmative action plans that had been approved by the chief campus officer or that were in preparation, and most of these had been approved. Among the two-year colleges, also, all of our respondents had affirmative action plans or were developing them, but only about one-half of these had been approved by the chief campus officer. In the two liberal arts groups, 75 and 72 percent, respectively, had plans that had been approved or were in preparation.

The responsibility for enforcement of affirmative action in education (as well as certain other social service sectors of the economy) has been delegated by the Department of Labor to the Department of Health, Education, and Welfare, within which the Office for Civil Rights (OCR) is the responsible agency. A university or college need not submit its affirmative action plan to OCR for approval unless it becomes subject to a compliance review, either under routine enforcement of the executive order or as the result of the filing of a complaint.

Thus, it is not surprising to find that the great majority of universities, among our respondents with plans that had been approved at the campus level, had submitted their plans to OCR (Table 5), because universities are more likely to have sizable federal-contract funds, and to have come under compliance review, than other groups of institutions. Proportions that had submitted their plans for approval tended to be smaller for most other groups of institutions.

Of those plans that had been submitted to OCR, only 16 percent had been approved. This is consistent with other data indicating that very few plans have received official approval. The fact that so few of the plans of our respondent institutions had been approved would not be surprising if they had been submitted very recently, but in many cases they had been submitted several years ago, as the responses to our questionnaire indicated.

---

[4]For an earlier survey of affirmative action plans, conducted in 1972, see Weitzman (1973).

Table 4. Campus status of affirmative action plans, by type and control of institution

| Type and control of institution | Number of respondents providing information | Plan approved by chief campus officer or in preparation | | Total | | No plan or non-discrimination statement only | No information |
		Approved	In preparation	Number	Percent of respondents		
Total	131	100	22	122	93	9	1
Public	65	52	13	65	100	0	1
Private	66	48	9	57	86	9	0
Research Universities I	26	25	1	26	100	0	0
Public	15	14	1	15	100	0	0
Private	11	11	0	11	100	0	0
Research Universities II	17	14	3	17	100	0	0
Public	11	9	2	11	100	0	0
Private	6	5	1	6	100	0	0
Doctoral-Granting Universities	17	17	0	17	100	0	0
Public	9	9	0	9	100	0	0
Private	8	8	0	8	100	0	0
Comprehensive Universities and Colleges	20	17	3	20	100	0	0
Public	13	11	2	13	100	0	0
Private	7	6	1	7	100	0	0
Liberal Arts Colleges I, private	16	10	2	12	75	4	0
Liberal Arts Colleges II, private	18	8	5	13	72	5	0
Two-Year Colleges, public	17	9	8	17	100	0	1

Source: Carnegie Council Survey of Affirmative Action Policies, 1975.

Table 5. Status of affirmative action plans in relation to Office for Civil Rights, by type and control of institution

Type and control of institution	Number with plans	Submitted to OCR			Percent of submitted plans approved	Not submitted	No information
		Total	Approved	Pending			
Total	100	71	11	60	16	26	3
Public	52	42	5	37	12	7	3
Private	48	29	6	23	21	19	0
Research Universities I	25	23	7	16	30	2	0
Public	14	13	2	11	15	1	0
Private	11	10	5	5	50	1	0
Research Universities II	14	11	1	10	9	3	0
Public	9	8	1	7	13	1	0
Private	5	3	0	3	0	2	0
Doctoral-Granting Universities	17	13	1	12	8	3	1
Public	9	6	0	6	0	2	1
Private	8	7	1	6	14	1	0
Comprehensive Universities and Colleges	17	10	0	10	0	6	1
Public	11	8	0	8	0	2	1
Private	6	2	0	2	0	4	0
Liberal Arts Colleges I, private	10	4	0	4	0	6	0
Liberal Arts Colleges II, private	8	3	0	3	0	5	0
Two-Year Colleges, public	9	7	2	5	29	1	1

Source: Carnegie Council Survey of Affirmative Action Policies, 1975.

An institution's statement that its plan has been approved by OCR needs to be interpreted with caution. In one or two cases, an affirmative response on this point meant merely that informal assurance of approval had been given by the regional office. Moreover, the statement of the institution to the effect that its plan had been approved by OCR did not necessarily mean that there had been official action by the Department of Labor not to "assume jurisdiction" over the plan.

General Characteristics of Plans

As might have been expected, the affirmative action plans of universities tended to be more detailed than those of other institutions. This probably reflects the greater involvement of universities with federal and state agencies, as well as evidence that groups representing women and minorities have been especially active on university campuses. In any case, in discussing the features of affirmative action plans, we shall devote particular, but not exclusive, attention to those of universities.

Among the affirmative action plans of universities, there was substantial similarity in the aspects of affirmative action covered, but considerable variation in the detail with which the plans were spelled out, especially in relation to the specification of goals and timetables. Some of the plans had not reached the stage of specifying goals and timetables, although nearly all of them indicated the general procedure that was to be followed by administrative units in developing them. In addition, and significantly, the plans of universities that have been involved in protracted negotiations with OCR tend to be much lengthier and more specific than those of most other institutions.

The Elements of a Good Plan

Before considering affirmative action plans in detail, we should like to outline the elements of a good plan, drawing on features of a few of the most carefully developed plans among those available to us. The plan should include the following provisions:

1. An introductory statement indicating that the institution

will follow strictly nondiscriminatory policies in all aspects of employment of academic and nonacademic personnel.

2. A statement that the president or chief campus officer has overall responsibility for affirmative action.

3. A clear delegation of responsibility by the president for development and implementation of affirmative action policies to a top campus official reporting directly to the president, together with a carefully developed list of that official's affirmative action responsibilities. (We give examples of these responsibilities below.)

4. Provision, on large campuses, for a full-time affirmative action officer, reporting directly to the "top campus official" designated under 3, with a staff appropriate to the size of the campus. On smaller campuses, the functions of an affirmative action officer may be delegated to an administrator or faculty member on a part-time basis. The functions of the affirmative action officer should be carefully developed and listed.

5. Provision for an affirmative action committee or committees, with membership structures developed in consultation with all affected and interested groups on campus. On larger campuses, there may be a need for separate committees for academic and nonacademic personnel, as well as for special committees for schools, colleges, or groups of departments. Consideration may be given to inclusion of students. The functions of the committee or committees should be carefully developed and listed. (We give examples below.)

6. Provisions for dissemination of the affirmative action plan to all persons associated with the institution, including students, and to appropriate media and organizations external to the campus.

7. Faculty employment
   a. Presentation of data on racial, selected ethnic, and sexual composition of the faculty by department and rank for the most recent three or four years.
   b. Presentation of data (usually Ph.D.'s awarded in the most recent five-year period for four-year colleges and universities—master's degrees for two-year colleges) relating to

pools of qualified persons by race, selected ethnic groups, and sex for each academic field in which instruction is offered. Analysis of relationships between utilization ratios and ratios of qualified persons for each department.

c. Determination of goals and timetables for appropriate campus units (usually groups of departments, schools or colleges, or, on smaller campuses, the entire campus) after careful consideration of the overall impact on the composition of the faculty.

d. A statement of appropriate recruitment procedures to ensure nondiscriminatory recruitment by each department, including provisions for maintaining records on these procedures.

e. A statement of requirements for nondiscriminatory selection, including a provision for maintaining full records on the selection process.

f. A provision for review of each appointment by appropriate administrators, including the top campus official to whom responsibility for affirmative action has been delegated. Departments should be required to provide data on screening procedures, as well as comparative data on candidates considered in the final selection process. (Depending on the total number of candidates, this might include, say, the six or seven candidates evaluated after initial screening of all candidates.)

g. A provision for strictly nondiscriminatory procedures in promotion decisions, for a search for outside candidates in appropriate cases (especially when there are few or no women or minorities in the rank from which promotion is to be made), and for careful administrative review of promotion decisions, including review by the top campus official responsible for affirmative action. As in selection procedures, comparative data should be provided on the candidates considered for the promotion.

h. Provision for salary analyses, to determine whether there are inequities on a sexual or racial basis, and whether there are equitable salary and fringe benefit provisions for such groups as lecturers.

    i. Provision for a review of the status of lecturers, particularly to determine whether there are individuals who should be reclassified to regular faculty positions.

    j. Revision of policies relating to part-time appointments and employment of near relatives to remove discrimination on the basis of marital status and/or family responsibilities.

8. Similar provisions for nonfaculty academic personnel.

9. Similar provisions for nonacademic personnel, except for methods of determining pools of qualified persons, which will typically be related to the characteristics of the labor force in the surrounding labor market area.

10. Provision for development, in consultation with all affected groups on campus, of adequate grievance procedures available to all employees—faculty, nonfaculty academic, and nonacademic personnel.

Institutional Responsibilities

Before discussing particular aspects of affirmative action plans, we should like to emphasize the importance we attach to a genuine and vigorous institutional effort to overcome past patterns of discrimination. Policies and procedures that are nondiscriminatory in practice, and not just on paper, should lie at the heart of the effort. All relevant officials, from the board of trustees on down to department chairmen, and heads of other campus units, should be fully involved in an effort that is genuinely designed to accomplish nondiscrimination and affirmative action, and is not simply designed to comply routinely with federal requirements or to respond politically to campus pressure groups.

Recommendation 4: *The primary and long-term responsibility for affirmative action in higher education should be assumed by colleges and universities themselves. They should take the initiative in developing effective affirmative action policies without waiting to be coerced in that direction by federal or state agencies. Federal and state policy should be supplemental to institutional efforts and for only such period of time as it is essential.*

    Among institutions, research universities need to take their affirmative action responsibilities especially seriously, because they have traditionally had few women or minorities on their faculties, and they are particularly subject to federal government interference if they do not comply with federal affirmative action requirements.

Effective pursuit of affirmative action policies requires, not just the adoption of an adequate plan, but also procedures that ensure the involvement of decision-makers at all levels of the institution in furtherance of the objectives—the board of trustees, the administration, the academic senate, faculty members in individual schools and departments, and all others involved in the selection and promotion of academic and non-academic employees.

An annual report providing data on changes in the sexual and racial composition of employment should be published.

The Administration of Affirmative Action

If the institution's commitment to affirmative action is to be fully carried out, the first requirement is that responsibility for implementation of affirmative action be clearly assigned. Probably the most important single factor in ensuring that there is a genuine institutional commitment is the determination of the president or chief campus officer to carry out an effective affirmative action program. Thus, an administrative arrangement under which the primary responsibility for implementing the affirmative action policy is delegated to an official who reports directly to the chief campus officer will generally be preferable. On larger campuses, this individual may be a special assistant to the president, a vice-president, or a vice-chancellor. Under the individual with primary responsibility, there will usually be an affirmative action officer with a staff that will vary with the size of the campus. On large campuses, assigning the responsibility to a special assistant to the president or chancellor may have advantages over assigning it to a vice-president or vice-chancellor whose responsibilities may cover a wide range. However, the best solution will vary from campus to campus, because of differences in administrative relationships and in the personalities involved.

The *Higher Education Guidelines* relating to the enforcement of Executive Order 11246 (see Appendix B) state that "an administrative procedure must be set up to organize and monitor the affirmative action program." They go on to quote from the relevant Department of Labor regulation that "an executive of the contractor should be appointed as director of EEO programs, and that he or she should be given 'the necessary top management support and staffing to execute the assignment' " (U.S. Department of Health, Education, and Welfare, 1972, p. 15).

Most of the universities responding to our inquiry have designated a top administrative official as the person with chief responsibility for enforcement of affirmative action. Subject to his supervision, there is likely to be an affirmative action officer who very often is, in practice, a member of a minority group (usually a black). Sometimes the affirmative action officer is a woman, and occasionally a minority woman.[5] In some cases, there are separate affirmative action officers for academic and nonacademic employees.

Generally consistent with our views relating to effective delegation of responsibility for affirmative action is the administrative arrangement at Princeton (Princeton University, 1975). The provost, who is the general deputy of the president, is designated as the affirmative action officer of the university. "He is responsible for overall development, implementation and monitoring of all programs relating to Equal Opportunity and Affirmative Action. . . . Difficulties in regard to demands upon the Provost's time are intended to be ameliorated by the existence of two Assistant positions, the major responsibility of one of them being Affirmative Action matters." This assistant is given the title of affirmative action coordinator, whose responsibilities are outlined as follows:

• Oversight of developing, implementing, monitoring, and

[5] Here we are relying on general impressions. The documents we received in our survey did not usually provide information on the characteristics of affirmative action officers.

reporting university equal opportunity and affirmative action programs
- Maintaining and updating universitywide basic data files
- Coordinating preparation of utilization, salary analysis, and personnel mobility systems
- Receiving periodically from the dean of the faculty and the director of personnel services, departmental and office reports on recruitment, hiring, mobility, attrition, and overall affirmative action progress, and assessing them
- Preparing and presenting reports to the equal opportunity council and committees (described below)
- Serving as liaison between the university administration and interest groups in the university
- Preparing equal opportunity and affirmative action annual reports
- Overseeing development of policy statements, and internal and external communication techniques
- Keeping relevant administrative offices of the university informed of developments in equal opportunity and affirmative action areas

An example of a particularly strong provision for penalizing a department that fails to adhere to affirmative action requirements appears in the affirmative action plan of the University of California, Berkeley:

> The [Affirmative Action] Coordinator will also be invested with the delicate but vital responsibility of negotiating with departments or other units which have apparently failed to adhere to the requirements of the Affirmative Action Program. While it is anticipated that such situations will normally be remedied by negotiation and mutual agreement, the following remedies may be applied by the Administration in the cases where all other approaches have failed:
>
> (1) In individual cases a department or unit may not be permitted to make an appointment until the procedures described above, governing search and canvass for that appointment, have been met.

(2) In the rare case where a department or unit repeatedly fails to follow the prescribed procedures in particular specialities, or willful evasion of the Affirmative Action policy is otherwise shown, that department or unit may be instructed to suspend all new entry-level appointments until such time as the unsatisfactory situation has been corrected or the unit has satisfactorily demonstrated that it has exhausted all reasonable efforts to rectify the situation (University of California, Berkeley, 1975).

In addition, the effectiveness of the top administrative official and of the affirmative action officer will depend on their ability to work with all the officials and groups on campus who are concerned with implementation of affirmative action policies. This includes deans and department chairmen, along with women's, minority, and student groups concerned with these policies, and affirmative action committees.

Recommendation 5: *The Council recommends that primary responsibility for implementation of affirmative action policies be clearly assigned to a top official who reports directly to the president or chief campus officer. Reporting to this top official there should usually be, especially on larger campuses, a full-time affirmative action officer, with a staff appropriate to the size of the campus.*

The Role of Affirmative Action Committees

In most of the institutions with affirmative action plans, a special committee plays a role in the affirmative action program and works closely with the affirmative action officer. On larger campuses, there may be several campuswide committees, as well as special committees for individual schools and colleges.

About seven-tenths of our respondents that had adopted affirmative action plans reported that a special committee or committees concerned with affirmative action issues had been established (Table 13, Appendix A). Research Universities I, Comprehensive Universities and Colleges, and Two-Year Colleges with affirmative action plans were more likely to have established committees than other groups of institutions.

The names of these committees vary, and in a few cases information on their membership was not provided. However, they often include representatives of the administration and of both academic and nonacademic employees, with a provision in most instances that some of the members must be women or minorities. In a few cases, there is a *requirement* that a majority of the members of the committee be women or minorities, and about one-eighth of the institutions with such committees provide for student representation. On larger campuses, there are frequently separate committees for academic and nonacademic employees, as well as special committees for individual schools and colleges.

The functions of committees vary but usually include one or more of the following: (1) review of affirmative action plans, including goals and timetables, (2) review of progress in achieving affirmative action goals, (3) review of departmental recruitment, selection, and promotion procedures, and (4) much less frequently, serving as an appeal body in grievance cases, sometimes at the stage immediately following departmental consideration of the grievance and sometimes following administrative review of the case (usually by a dean). In about 14 percent of the institutions with committees, there was a provision for referring grievances to the committee.

We believe that campus committees or commissions are likely to play a significant role in the implementation of affirmative action policies, although we recognize that there are sometimes difficult conflicts that have to be resolved over their membership (including conflicts over the representation of particular minority groups). The principle to be followed is that all relevant groups on campus should be consulted before determining the basis of representation of affirmative action committees or their actual membership.

Among the functions of the affirmative action coordinator at Princeton, the first is "oversight of developing, implementing, monitoring and reporting University Equal Opportunity and Affirmative Action programs." The function of monitoring is of critical importance, and there is little question that women and minorities are likely to have greater confidence that this function will be effectively carried out if a committee (or committees) on which they are included plays a significant role in the monitoring process.

When we refer to "review of progress in achieving affirmative action goals" and to "review of departmental recruitment, selection, and promotion procedures" in discussing the function of these committees, we are referring to the monitoring process. It should not be conceived as a process of policing each individual appointment or promotion but rather as a process of ensuring that the procedures followed by departments in initiating appointments and promotions and of administrative officials in reviewing them are scrutinized frequently enough to ensure that the requirements of the affirmative action plan relating to recruitment, selection, and promotion are carefully carried out. Review of progress in achieving affirmative action goals and timetables is also important, as is review of lack of progress. A particularly crucial aspect of the monitoring process is its involvement with departments that have serious problems of underutilization of women and minorities.

Discussion of the composition and functions of committees on several campuses, illustrative of differing but relatively strong committee arrangements, will help to provide a clearer picture of the organization and roles of affirmative action committees.

At Michigan State University, a relatively recent policy statement provides for a Committee Against Discrimination which is composed of an executive secretary with voice but no vote and nine voting members. The nine members are distributed as follows: three faculty, one administrative-professional, one clerical-technical, one laborer, one graduate student, and two undergraduate students. The Faculty Committee on Committees selects the three faculty members, at least one of whom is female, who serve for three-year staggered terms. The Associated Students select the undergraduate members, one of whom is nonwhite and one female, who serve for two-year staggered terms. The graduate student member is selected by the

Council of Graduate Students for a two-year term. Each of the three nonacademic employee members is selected by the relevant employee association.

The functions of this committee are as follows:

1. To conduct . . . periodic reviews of the operation of the several units of the University, to identify policies or practices which may reflect discrimination after appropriate notification of the President. Upon formal request by majority vote . . . any unit of the University shall provide access to any and all records necessary for carrying out such reviews. . . . To the maximum extent consistent with the purposes of this procedure the confidentiality of personal records and the principle of privileged communication shall be respected by the Committee and its staff. Any alleged abuse of the investigative powers of this Committee may be appealed at any time directly to the President of the University who shall have authority to take appropriate action.
2. The Committee shall identify policies, practices, or patterns of behavior which may reflect discrimination as defined in this document and report same to the responsible officials of the unit. The Committee shall also recommend to such responsible officials such corrective action as it deems appropriate.
3. Any person or persons having knowledge of prohibited discrimination, but without a personal grievance, shall have the right to file a complaint with the Committee Against Discrimination . . . (Michigan State University, 1974).

A second illustration of a committee with carefully identified functions is found at Princeton. The committee is charged with responsibilities for affirmative action in relation to faculty and administrative employees and parallels another committee with responsibilities in relation to nonacademic employees. Chaired by a dean, it includes representatives of the various groups of academic employees (faculty, research, etc.), who are chosen after consultation with all the relevant groups on campus. The committee membership is "intended to include an ethnic, sex, age, and longevity diversity that reflects the University's Affirmative Action commitment." Its functions are as follows:

1. To review, at least annually, the faculty and professional staff's affirmative action program and analyze its effectiveness and weaknesses
2. To bring to the attention of the dean problems of affirmative action or equal employment from the perspectives of the staffs represented by the membership
3. To assist the dean in monitoring the affirmative action program
4. To assist the dean in disseminating affirmative action information
5. To review and evaluate reports issuing from the dean's office on matters of affirmative action and equal employment
6. To receive and react to reports prepared by the university for external agencies, such as HEW
7. To meet with individuals or groups who have information or concerns within the area of the committee's responsibility
8. To receive and respond to periodic progress reports from the university's affirmative action coordinator (Princeton University, 1975)

The affirmative action plan of the University of California, Berkeley, notes that the "Academic Senate Committee on the Status of Women and Ethnic Minorities has been particularly active and influential. It has been informed as to which department have authorizations to recruit for academic personnel, and members of the committee have met with department chairpersons to discuss search procedures and potential applicant pools." In addition, the Chancellor's Advisory Committee on Affirmative Action was established in June 1974 to replace separate advisory committees on academic and staff women which had existed previously. The committee is composed of academic personnel (both academic senate members and academic nonsenate employees), as well as nonacademic personnel. Students have been offered full membership, but the official student organization has opted for the present for participation as "observers." In addition, a number of special affirmative action committees for particular schools and colleges have been established (University of California, Berkeley, 1975).

We believe that appropriate committees are a particularly important aspect of affirmative action programs and that they should be given meaningful and clear responsibilities relating to the monitoring of recruitment, selection, and promotion procedures, as well as to progress toward the achievement of affirmative action goals. On some campuses, as we have seen, they also serve as appeal boards in grievance cases.

While providing several examples of apparently effective committee arrangements, we believe that these arrangements have to be worked out on each campus in a manner appropriate to its size, administrative structure, and the sexual and racial characteristics of academic and nonacademic employees and students. In some geographical areas, for example, blacks tend to be the only important racial minority group, whereas in other areas Mexican-Americans, Puerto Ricans, persons of Asian ancestry, and/or Native Americans may form a significant proportion of the population. Consultation with all relevant groups on campus is essential in working out problems of representation on affirmative action committees.

Recruitment

As we have seen, recruitment for faculty positions has tended traditionally to be carried on in a confidential manner. A major purpose of affirmative action plans has been to break down these confidential, and often exclusive, patterns of recruitment. This has also been an important objective of women's groups and minority caucuses. Some of these groups and caucuses have devoted considerable energy to the development of rosters of qualified candidates in particular fields and to disseminating information on faculty job openings.

Among the features most commonly found in university affirmative action plans relating to recruitment are the following:

1. An indication that the institution maintains a list of potential female and minority-group candidates for faculty positions or a list of specific suggested sources for recruiting such candidates (about three-fourths of the university plans and more than one-half of other plans)
2. A requirement that departmental search committees include women and minority-group members whenever possible (about one-third of the university plans and one-fifth of the other plans)
3. A requirement that the administration be given an opportunity to review the recruitment plan or some of its aspects for each vacancy to be filled (about one-third of the university plans and one sixth of the other plans)
4. A requirement that vacancies be advertised in specified media and that announcements of vacancies be sent to female and minority professional committees or caucuses, etc. (about three-fourths of the university plans and two-thirds of the other plans)
5. A requirement that all announcements of openings state that the institution is an "equal opportunity" or "affirmative action" employer (the great majority of all plans)
6. A requirement that there be a specific waiting period between announcement of a vacancy and selection (about one-sixth of all plans)

The formal features of plans, except, perhaps, for the requirement that search committees include women and minority-group members whenever possible, are probably less important than the spirit in which they are carried out. Advertising vacancies is not likely to be very effective if the applicants who respond to the ads are ignored. Notifying women's or minority group caucuses of vacancies is a meaningless gesture if the notification is sent at a very late date when the department has already made its selection.[6] Complaints continue to circulate that these things

[6] For documentation of the prevalence of such practices, see, for example, Hornig (1975).

happen. It is for reasons such as these that we have emphasized the importance of involving all relevant persons from the board of trustees on down in the affirmative action effort.

Federal *Guidelines* for the enforcement of Executive Order 11246 are quite explicit about methods of broadening recruitment procedures (see Appendix B), and the affirmative action plans of colleges and universities have clearly been influenced by these provisions and by consultation with relevant federal officials.

We believe that all departments should be required to submit their recruitment plans for administrative review and also for scrutiny by the appropriate affirmative action committee, if any, annually, well before the recruitment process begins. Whenever feasible, departmental search committees should include women and minority members.

Selection

Traditionally, departments have been required to submit documents justifying the recommendation for appointment of a particular candidate for a faculty position, but typically have not been required to provide evidence that candidates were considered in a strictly nondiscriminatory manner, regardless of race or sex. In fact, information relating to rejected candidates has not usually been required by campus administrators.

In contrast, a major feature of selection provisions of affirmative action plans is to require departments to maintain records relating to all candidates considered in the selection process (88 percent of the university plans and most other plans have such provisions). However, the plans differ somewhat in the requirements relating to the processing of these records:

1. Slightly more than one-half of the university plans and 30 percent of the other plans require that the records of recruitment and selection be reviewed by an administrative official (normally by the affirmative action officer or a vice-president or vice-chancellor especially charged with affirmative action responsibilities) before the preferred candidate can be offered a faculty position.

2. About 35 percent of the university plans and 45 percent of the other plans simply require that records of recruitment and selection be available at administrative request or be available for review at regular intervals.
3. About 30 percent of the university plans and 13 percent of the other plans require justification if the preferred candidate is a white male.

In a relatively small minority of universities, the plans either explicitly state or imply that women and minority candidates who are otherwise equally qualified in relation to white male candidates be considered additionally qualified by virtue of their sex, race, or ethnic group. These provisions were nearly all found in the plans of doctoral-granting universities and only rarely in those of research universities or of four-year or two-year colleges.

We believe that departments should be required to submit evidence indicating that women and minority candidates have been seriously considered along with majority males. The reasons for selection of the preferred candidate should be carefully stated, along with documentation indicating the relative qualifications of the recommended and rejected candidates. Clearly, when a department receives a very large number of applications for a given opening, it would be impractical to submit detailed documentation on more than, perhaps, six or seven leading candidates, but information on the criteria for initial screening out of other applicants should be provided.

In addition to the normal administrative review procedure, all recommendations for appointment should be reviewed by the top administrative official with particular affirmative action responsibilities. This review should be in addition to, and should not replace, review by the faculty committees that have traditionally been involved in the review process, especially on larger campuses.

These suggested selection procedures should be followed in all cases. Special requirements that the department submit documents justifying the selection if the preferred candidate is a white male, or is not a woman or member of a minority, are inconsistent with principles of nondiscriminatory selection.

Promotion

Of particular interest and significance in relation to affirmative action policies is the question of their impact on policies on promotion. As we have seen, review procedures on promotion to tenure or appointment to a tenured rank tend to be more extensive and in many cases to require approval at a higher administrative level than appointments to instructorships or assistant professorships. Most of our respondent universities have provided statements—some of them very lengthy—on their review procedures. We are concerned here, however, primarily with the question of whether those review procedures appear to have been modified in any way under the impact of affirmative action or whether there are special measures or policies that have been introduced to assure special scrutiny of promotions in relation to nondiscriminatory or affirmative action objectives.

We have scrutinized the promotion policies of universities and other institutions for indications of the impact of affirmative action on these policies. Some respondents provided no documents that shed light on promotion policies, while for others information on these policies was found in a variety of sources, including affirmative action plans, academic personnel manuals, and special administrative policy or procedural documents. Not including those institutions that merely had a provision that non-discriminatory policies should be followed in promotions, affirmative action and nondiscriminatory policies were found to have an impact on promotion policies in a variety of ways (several different types of impacts were found in some institutions):

	Number of responses	
	Universities	*Other institutions*
Procedure for periodic review of promotional experience by affirmative action officer or committee, or evidence that a recent review of promotional experience has been conducted	22	16

	Number of responses	
		Other
	Universities	institutions
Requirement that departmental committees or review committees must include qualified women or women and minorities	3	1
Policy emphasizing search for outside candidates	3	1
Women and minorities must be considered	7	6
Desirability of placing more emphasis on community service in evaluating qualifications of women or minorities	1	0
Specific requirement that nontenured faculty members who become pregnant be granted leaves of absence and permitted an extension of the time before a tenure decision is made	8	2
Statement that women and minorities should be promoted in proportion to their representation at the rank from which promotion occurs	1	0
Total number of institutions reflected by these responses	37	20

Of particular interest are policies reflected in selected quotations from these documents:

> *Report of special committee, public research university—West.* The criteria need to be augmented to truly reflect the "community service" aspects of faculty activities. The Faculty Code allows for this emphasis, but the allowance appears to be seldom utilized. For

the woman or minority faculty member, the exclusion or minimization of this criterion is a handicap. In the absence of adequate numbers, the minority and woman faculty member is often called upon to perform "extra" services, i.e., services over and beyond those expected of other faculty. It is not uncommon, for example, to be asked to serve on departmental, collegiate, and university committees as a minority or woman representative. Nor is it uncommon to find more graduate and undergraduate students seeking to confer with minority and women faculty members than would generally be true.

Administration directive, private research university— Northeast. A search committee appointed for the purpose of considering candidates for tenure positions should, at the beginning of its work, undertake a wide solicitation of names of possible candidates, specifically including the names of women and minority-group members. The responses should be collected in writing, to be submitted as part of the documentation of the search. These guidelines apply equally to cases where there is an internal candidate whom the department may wish to consider for promotion to tenure.

Administration directive, private research university— West. The President's Committee on Academic Appointments and Promotions has traditionally been composed of the three academic vice-presidents and the Dean of the Graduate School. In an effort to expand the affirmative action program of the University, the President has recently announced a basic change in the composition of this key committee. The University has been divided into four academic divisions: humanities, health sciences, social sciences, and basic sciences. Each division now has at least four faculty representatives, including women and minorities, serving with the four academic administrators as members of the Committee on Academic Appointments and Promotions for that specific division.

Affirmative Action Plan, September 30, 1974, University of California, Berkeley. Each Provost will provide to the Affirmative Action Officer numerical summaries of data for the following personnel actions:

—the applicants in the pool for each opening in the ladder ranks by ethnicity and sex;
—advancements to tenure and other promotions by ethnicity and sex;
—merit salary increases in the ladder ranks by ethnicity and sex;
  non-reappointments of Assistant Professors by ethnicity and sex;
  resignations of members of the Academic Senate by ethnicity and sex.

(Amendments to Affirmative Action Plan, February 18, 1975, University of California, Berkeley). It is the University's objective that women and minorities will be promoted to the Associate Professor and Full Professor ranks in proportion to those eligible for promotion in the Assistant Professor and Associate Professor ranks respectively in each department.

Among the persons who are eligible for promotion, the basis for any promotion decision will, of course, be the individual qualifications of the candidate. Since it is recognized that not all persons advanced to the tenure rank of Associate Professor achieve the qualifications for further advancement to the Full Professor rank, other avenues of salary increase will be explored for those persons, male and female, non-minority and minority, who may wish to consider an alternate career goal.

Goals and timetables, which are discussed in Section 5,

have a very important relationship to nondiscriminatory and affirmative action policies on promotion. But, at this stage, the main point to be emphasized is that affirmative action policies and procedures should call for careful documentation of recommendations on promotions by departments, to indicate that strictly nondiscriminatory policies were followed. Where traditional policies call for consideration of outside candidates, and in those departments that have few or no women or minorities at the assistant or associate level, a search for outside candidates should be a standard part of the procedures. Recommendations for promotion should be reviewed by the top administrative official responsible for affirmative action, in addition to review requirements under traditional procedures. Experience in promotions should be periodically reviewed by appropriate affirmative action committees.

Salary Analyses

An essential part of an institution's affirmative action policies and procedures is a thoroughgoing review of salary differences to determine whether there is discrimination against women and/or minorities on an individual basis or on a broader "class" basis. Careful execution of this responsibility will tend to reduce the probability of complaints filed by employees with federal or state agencies or of cases brought in court. Many institutions have conducted salary reviews as part of their affirmative action efforts and granted equity pay increases (in most cases to women faculty members), but it is also true that academic women have been responsible for many complaints of unequal pay filed with the Wage and Hour Administration of the Department of Labor and with other federal agencies in the last few years.

In public institutions of higher education with formal salary structures, women in regular faculty ranks normally receive compensation appropriate to their step and rank. Thus, overt salary discrimination is not likely to arise in these situations, but a charge of failure to grant a merit increase or promotion because of sexual or racial discrimination may be accompanied by a charge of unequal pay, because the higher step or rank would involve higher pay. However, many public institutions that have had formal salary structures for regular faculty ranks have sometimes lacked formal and/or equitable salary structures for such groups as lecturers (especially part-time lecturers), non-faculty research personnel, and librarians. Thus, an important part of a review of salary differences may involve the development of equitable salary structures for these groups and the establishment of appropriate relationships between the salary structures for these groups and those of the faculty.

Private institutions with less formal salary structures face a more difficult task than do other institutions in eliminating salary discrimination, because a more thoroughgoing analysis of relationships between sexual or racial differences in compensation and qualifications of the individuals involved is likely to be required.

Despite these problems, salary review is in some respects easier than other aspects of affirmative action, because it involves compensation to existing employees and "does not require the concurrence of as many individuals as is usually the case in making faculty appointments" (Pondrom, 1975, p. 428). The more difficult problems are likely to be budgetary. Back-pay awards present particular difficulties in public institutions with annual state budgets and in the more financially pinched private colleges and universities that have extremely limited discretionary funds. The problems are not insuperable but may require "a one-time conversion of money from vacant positions into funds for equity increases as a supplement to available merit money" (ibid.).

Recommendation 6: *The affirmative action plans of institutions of higher education should include carefully framed provisions ensuring strict observance of nondiscriminatory procedures in recruitment, selection, and promotions, and providing for analyses of salary differentials.*

The mere inclusion of appropriate provisions will not ensure nondiscrimination unless there are adequate requirements for administrative review, including review by affirmative action officials, of recruitment plans, selection procedures, and promotion procedures.

Where affirmative action committees have been appointed,

*such committees should periodically review departmental proce-
dures and experience in recruitment, selection, and promotions.*

Part-Time Appointments

There frequently has been no provision for part-time faculty
appointments except in lecturer or other nonladder faculty
positions, or when faculty members were partly on research or
administrative appointments. These policies have seriously
impaired opportunities for women, and sometimes for men,
with family responsibilities to obtain regular faculty appointments and promotions. One change urged by women's groups is
the adoption of policies that would permit part-time appointments on the regular or ladder faculty.

The results of our affirmative action survey indicate that
such recommendations have not been widely adopted. About
three-tenths of our respondents provided no information that
would shed light on whether part-time regular faculty appointments were or were not permitted, while another tenth indicated that part-time policies were currently under revision. This
left about three-fifths of all institutions—including about two-
thirds of the universities and about 55 percent of other institutions—that provided information on the status of part-time
appointments to regular faculty positions.

Among the universities providing information (excluding
those in which part-time policies were under revision), 38 percent permitted part-time faculty appointments in regular or ladder ranks, while 22 percent permitted part-time appointees to
be eligible for promotion to tenure. A slightly smaller proportion (19 percent) permitted a person promoted to tenure to
continue to serve on a part-time basis. Among the other (nonuniversity) institutions for which information was available, the
proportion permitting part-time appointments in regular faculty
positions was somewhat lower than that for universities, but dis-
tinctly smaller percentages allowed an individual to be eligible
for promotion to tenure or to occupy a tenure position on a
part-time basis.

In most cases, part-time appointments in regular faculty
ranks could not be on less than 50 percent of a full-time basis.

On behalf of these part-time policies, some of the documents we received (usually reports of special committees) pointed out that, increasingly, married couples were interested in considering academic positions in which both husband and wife would be employed part time and would share household responsibilities.

We believe that regular faculty appointments should not be permitted for persons whose principal employment or main employment commitment is elsewhere. The policy statement on "senior appointments with reduced loads" adopted by the American Association of University Professors in 1971 recognizes this problem by stating that "these [part-time] appointments would not normally be encouraged if the individual is seeking reduction of the academic commitment in order to accept another position."

Recommendation 7: *Part-time appointments should be permitted in regular faculty ranks for persons whose sole employment commitment is to the college or university, and not elsewhere.[7] Under appropriate conditions, these appointments may lead to tenure on a part-time basis.*

Policies relating to promotions should allow for a moderate extension of the usual period for qualification for promotion for persons who have been granted leaves of absence or who have been employed part time because of family responsibilities.

Lecturers and Nonfaculty Academic Employees

Qualified women and minority-group members are sometimes permanently classified in lectureships and in nonfaculty research positions, with little prospect of appointment to regular faculty positions or of acquiring tenure. Frequently, antinepotism policies have prevented the appointment of married women holding such positions to the faculty.

A few of the universities responding to our survey provide

[7] For additional discussion, and more detailed recommendations, see Carnegie Commission (1973c, Section 8).

information—in their affirmative action plans or in other documents—indicating that they have conducted or intend to conduct a systematic review of persons in lectureships and nonfaculty academic positions to determine whether there are individuals who are qualified for reclassification to regular faculty positions among these groups. Some universities have reported significant progress in identifying and reclassifying such persons.

Oberlin College has gone so far as to abolish the position of lecturer, indicating that its action was the result of an "analysis of the connection between the status of lecturer and the discriminatory effects of the antinepotism rule on married women.[8]

In other cases, institutions have undertaken systematic reviews of the status of nonfaculty academic personnel with a view to modifying personnel policies that have tended to have a discriminatory impact on such employees—for example, lack of access to fringe benefits. Another example of inadequate personnel policies, especially in some large research universities, has been the absence of equitable salary structures for research personnel. Librarians, who are usually classified as academic personnel, also tend to complain about inequitable or inadequate salary structures.

Recommendation 8: *As part of their affirmative action policies, colleges and universities should systematically review the status of lecturers and nonfaculty academic employees on their campuses. The purposes of such reviews should be (1) to identify and reclassify individuals who are qualified for regular faculty positions and (2) to ensure that lecturers and nonfaculty academic employees are covered by fringe benefits (on a prorated basis if they are part time) and are compensated on the basis of equitable salary structures.[9]*

[8] See Carnegie Commission (1973c, p. 263).

[9] Fringe benefits may not be appropriate for employees on less than a half-time basis or for part-time employees whose principal employment is elsewhere.

Antinepotism Rules

Traditionally, universities and colleges have prohibited employment of near relatives within the same department and, less frequently, within the same campus or within the institution as a whole. Such policies have been the subject of many complaints, on the ground that they have had a particularly adverse effect on the employment of married women, many of whom held degrees in the same fields as their husbands. Under the influence of federal regulations and pressure from women's groups on campuses, in many cases these policies have been revised (usually to conform with the provisions of the *Higher Education Guidelines* of October 1972 –see Appendix B). Employment of near relatives within the same department is now frequently permitted in universities, with the proviso that a near relative may not be involved in a decision relating to his or her relative or may not be employed in supervisory subordinate relationships.

Most of the universities responding to our survey provided information on antinepotism policies, while other institutions provided such information much less frequently. We shall therefore confine our analysis to the respondent universities:

	Antinepotism policies of respondent universities
(1) No restrictions on employment of near relatives	5
(2) Employment of near relatives within the same department is permitted, but employment in a supervisory-subordinate relationship is:[a]	
Prohibited or discouraged	12
Permitted only with administrative approval	5
	17
(3) Employment of near relatives within the same department is per-	

(continued on next page)

*Antinepotism policies
of respondent universities*

mitted, but participation in a decision concerning a near relative is prohibited[a]   14

(4) Employment of near relatives within the university is permitted, but employment within the same department is:

    Prohibited or discouraged   2

    Permitted only with administrative approval   6

                                       8

(5) Employment of near relatives within the university is:

    Discouraged   1

    Permitted only with administrative approval   1

                                       2

(6) Policy unspecified or unclear   11

(7) Policy currently undergoing revision   2

    Total providing information   59

[a]Some policies involve combinations of 2 and 3. Moreover, whatever the nepotism rule, most rules implicitly or explicitly prohibit participation in a decision concerning a near relative.

It should be noted that the policy statement of the American Association of University Professors relating to "Faculty Appointment and Family Relationship" adopted in 1971, opposes antinepotism rules, with the proviso that "faculty members should neither initiate nor participate in institutional decisions involving a direct benefit (initial appointment, retention, promotion, salary, leave of absence, etc.) to members of their immediate families" (American Association of University Professors, 1973, p. 23).

Recommendation 9: *Employment of near relatives within the same department should be permitted, provided they are not in a supervisory-subordinate relationship and that neither is involved in an employment decision concerning the other.*[10]

Special Policies

The affirmative action policies discussed thus far have been strongly influenced by federal policies and cover aspects of employment policies that are specifically mentioned in federal regulations and guidelines.

Some institutions—especially Research Universities I—have gone beyond these policies by establishing special funds for the employment of women and minority groups and in other ways. Our discussion of affirmative action policies would be incomplete without mention of such policies.

Three of our respondent Research Universities I have established or sought to establish special funds for the employment of women and minorities. These are to be distinguished from budgetary allocations to meet the special costs of affirmative action programs, such as advertising costs. Here we are referring to special funds to pay all or part of the salaries of women or minorities hired for positions on the regular faculty.

> *Private research university—South.* We are seeking standby funds to permit hiring of Negro faculty whenever they become available. For example, we may hear of a qualified person graduating in mid-year, or perhaps of one leaving government service. Standby funds would make it possible to provide immediate employment, with the expectation that in subsequent years the employee's salary would be covered by school budgets. . . . _____'s location impedes its efforts to attract black faculty. We have thought, therefore, that headway may be made by

---

[10]Employment of two or more near relatives in a very small department would not be desirable.

increasing offers to teach in summer session. This may enable us to attract people who might initially be reluctant to accept a longer term appointment.

Public research university—South. Regardless of the growth of the university faculty during the next decade, it is particularly important that the university provide a special means for increasing the proportion of women and ethnic minority group members on the _____ faculty. It is recommended that the [board] establish a special faculty affirmative action fund beginning fiscal year 1974-75 in order to service that purpose exclusively. This special fund would be useful for the general purpose of hiring individuals who are outstanding scholars and teachers who may be expected to contribute significantly to the University's educational needs but who do not fit exactly the specifications for an existing faculty opening. . . .

Private research university—West. Because the _____ University faculty is not expected to grow appreciably during the next decade, it is particularly important to provide a special means for increasing the proportion of women and ethnic minority group members on the faculty. The Faculty Affirmative Action Fund serves that purpose exclusively. . . . The Fund may be used:
a) To supplement existing departmental or school budgets so that a highly desirable individual can be hired, when appropriate, at a higher rank than was anticipated when the position was defined.
b) To allow departments and schools to anticipate retirements in taking advantage of available talent. . . .
c) To allow departments and schools to create new positions when special opportunities arise.

Although there might be some question about the legality

of such special funds under federal nondiscrimination policies, they do serve to illustrate the determination of some universities to pursue effective affirmative action programs in the face of slow growth.

The other special policies that will be quoted are concerned with providing special training and development opportunities for potential or existing women and minority faculty members.

> *Private research university—Northeast.* Under a grant from the _____ Foundation, the University last summer provided additional training to eight minority teachers from developing colleges in the South.

> *Public research university—South.* The Institution intends to continue a significant effort to upgrade the knowledge and skills of the entire academic community by granting leaves of absence for study and professional development. _____ plans to financially encourage women and minority faculty in the completion of degrees, provide aid in publications, and sponsor symposia for industrial, professional, and governmental organizations.

Opportunities in Administration

An especially important aspect of affirmative action policies is the encouragement of opportunities for women and minorities to rise in the administrative hierarchy. In academic administration, deans and top administrators are typically selected from among persons who have served ably as department chairmen, or, in some cases, as directors of research institutes or other special units. Because department chairmen are often elected or appointed after a secret-ballot straw vote by department members has been conducted, the initiation of opportunities for women or minorities to serve as department chairmen must come within departments. However, through informal consultation and in other appropriate ways, the administration can provide leadership in ensuring that qualified female and minority members of departments are not overlooked in such selections.

On occasion, also, individuals who have not served as department chairmen are given opportunities to become familiar with administrative problems through serving as assistant deans, or in other assistant administrative positions. Administrations can bring women and minorities into the hierarchy in such ways, and should emphasize opportunities for such persons to participate in the numerous special seminars and conferences relating to the management of institutions of higher education that have developed in recent years.

Recommendation 10: *Institutions of higher education should emphasize policies and procedures that will provide opportunities for women and minorities to serve in administrative positions.*

We have omitted discussion of the impact of affirmative action policies and of federal requirements on maternity leave and other aspects of fringe benefits, because they are not central to academic policies and procedures and have not given rise to appreciable controversy. We have also omitted discussion of the need for child-care centers on campuses, because of our central focus on employment policies.[11]

It seems appropriate to conclude this discussion of affirmative action policies by pointing out that, in broadening their recruitment nets and more effectively documenting their selection and promotion decisions, colleges and universities are likely to raise the overall quality of their appointments, on the reasonable assumption that highly qualified persons have been overlooked under past exclusive and more confidential procedures.

[11]For recommendations on child-care centers, see Carnegie Commission (1973c, Section 9).

4

Background of
Federal Policies

The story of extensive federal involvement in the enforcement of affirmative action policies in higher education began with the filing of a complaint against the entire academic community by a small, relatively unknown, women's civil rights group, the Women's Equity Action League (WEAL) early in 1970. The WEAL complaint charged higher education with an "industry-wide" pattern of sex discrimination and included about 80 pages of documentation (Sandler, 1973). It has been followed by more than 500 class-action complaints filed by WEAL and other women's groups against individual institutions. Earlier there had been a certain amount of federal involvement in relation to employment opportunities for minority groups, but it had been on a relatively limited scale.

The WEAL action was brought under an executive order banning discrimination by employers having federal contracts. In January 1970, this order was largely unknown in the academic community, because it had been enforced only in other employment settings.

The Executive Order

Executive Order No. 11246,[1] issued by President Lyndon B. Johnson in September 1965, provides that all federal contracts

[1] The texts of many of the regulations and laws discussed in this section may be found in Committee on Education and Labor (1975, Part 2B). For

include clauses agreeing not to "discriminate against any employee or applicant for employment because of race, color, religion, or national origin." Nondiscrimination on the basis of sex was added to the requirements under Executive Order No. 11375, effective October 1968. The Department of Labor is responsible for issuing rules and regulations to carry out the purposes of the executive order and to enforce compliance, but it may delegate its compliance-enforcement powers to other federal agencies. In its application to colleges and universities, the order is enforced by the Office for Civil Rights (OCR) in the Department of Health, Education, and Welfare (HEW), but certain final decisions for colleges and universities must be made by the Secretary of Labor, on the recommendation of the Secretary of HEW.

Regulations on requirements for written affirmative action plans were first issued in May 1968, but these were superseded by Order No. 4, issued on February 5, 1970, in which the Department of Labor set forth requirements in greater detail. Revised Order No. 4, issued on December 4, 1971, applied to women as well as minorities. Each federal contractor was to develop a written affirmative action program, including numerical goals and timetables for the hiring of women and minority groups in job classifications in which they are represented in smaller proportions than their representation in the labor market.

Under these orders, educational institutions with federal contracts of over $10,000 are prohibited from discrimination in employment on the basis of sex, race, color, religion, and national origin. In addition, under Revised Order No. 4, all institutions employing 50 or more persons and receiving $50,000 or more in federal-contract funds must have affirmative action plans.[2] Institutions found in violation are subject to having any

---

a useful summary of federal regulations affecting women, see Education Commission of the States (1975a).

[2]This provision applied only to private institutions at first but was amended early in 1973 to apply, also, to public institutions. Thus, we find that a number of the private institutions in our sample developed affirmative action plans before public institutions began to do so.

pending government contracts delayed or denied and current contracts cancelled; they may also be declared ineligible for future contracts. About 900 institutions of higher education are subject to the requirements of the executive order (Holmes, 1975, p. 74).

Whenever a contractor is found to be in noncompliance, the compliance agency must issue a notice to the contractor giving him 30 days to "show cause" why sanction proceedings should not be instituted. If the contractor does not show good cause for its failure to develop a plan and does not actually develop and implement an acceptable plan within 30 days, the agency must immediately issue a notice of proposed cancellation or termination of the contract and provide an opportunity to the contractor for a hearing. The same procedure must be followed when the more severe sanction of debarment—declaring the contractor ineligible for future contracts—is proposed. In practice, the process of conciliation and negotiation with the contractor tends to go on over a protracted period, during which the awarding of new contracts has sometimes been delayed. Technically, however, even a delay in the awarding of a new contract should not be undertaken without a hearing.

Department of Labor regulations also provide that no contract of $1 million or more may be awarded unless a preaward clearance has been conducted by the compliance agency within 12 months prior to the award, and the contractor has been found to be in compliance or to be able to comply as the result of the submission of an acceptable affirmative action plan.

In addition, both individual and class complaints of discrimination in academic employment may be filed with OCR. Under Department of Labor regulations, complaints must be filed within 180 days of the discrimination alleged. However, under an agreement between the Equal Employment Opportunity Commission (EEOC) and the Office of Federal Contract Compliance in the Department of Labor, a practice has developed under which OCR refers individual complaints to the EEOC.

Thus far, the courts have held that there is no private cause of action in court under the executive orders, but decisions are somewhat conflicting on whether a private action can be brought after administrative remedies have been exhausted (Babcock et al., 1975, pp. 511-512).[3]

The Equal Pay Act of 1963

The first significant legislation relating to sex discrimination in employment was the Equal Pay Act of 1963,[4] which did not apply to administrative and professional employees until July 1972. All employees of educational institutions, public and private, are now covered by the act, which prohibits discrimination on the basis of sex in the payment of wages for equal work on jobs that require equal skill, effort, and responsibility, and that are performed in the same establishment under similar working conditions. The provisions apply to overtime pay and to employer contributions for most fringe benefits. Salary differences are permissible when based on (1) a seniority system, (2) a merit system, (3) a system that measures earnings by quantity or quality of production (an incentive system), and (4) a differential based on a factor other than sex.

The legislation is enforced by the Wage and Hour Administration of the Department of Labor. Complaints of discrimination in pay may be filed with that agency, but the agency can also conduct reviews without prior complaint. Department of Labor inspectors routinely check for equal pay violations, as well as investigating specific complaints. If a violation is found, the employer is asked to correct the inequity immediately, that is, raise the wages and provide back pay to the underpaid workers. Women who have suffered pay discrimination can recover

---

[3]In a 1964 case a circuit court ruled that administrative remedies must be exhausted before any private action may be brought, while a 1967 circuit court held that denial of administrative remedies was final and could not be reviewed by the courts. However, in an appeal of a 1970 district court case denying relief until administrative remedies had been exhausted, the court of appeals suggested that judicial review of administrative action might be available to the plaintiffs in the future. The cases involved are *Farmer v. Philadelphia Electric Company*, 329 F. 2d 3 (3d Cir. 1964); *Farkas v. Texas Instrument Inc.*, 275 F. 2d 629 (5th Cir. 1967); and *Hadnott v. Laird*, 317 F. Supp. 379 (D.D.C. 1970), *aff'd* F. 2d 304 (D.C. Cir. 1972).

[4]Public Law 88-38, June 10, 1963.

the difference between their wages and those paid to men for up to a two-year back period.[5]

The Department of Labor is authorized to go to court when the employer refuses to settle. In the vast majority of cases, the employer does settle, but the Department of Labor has filed about 700 lawsuits under the act. In the fall of 1974, it was reported that perhaps as many as a thousand institutions of higher education had been the subject of complaints filed under the Equal Pay Act (Sandler, 1975, p. 276). The evidence is that academic women have been far more active, in relation to their numbers, in bringing complaints under the act than women in any other sector of the economy.

Private actions may also be brought into a federal district court under this legislation. An employee "may sue for back pay and an additional sum, up to the amount of back pay, as liquidated damages, plus attorney's fees and court costs" (*Code of Federal Regulations*, Title 29, Section 800.166). However, the employee may not bring suit if relief has been granted under the administration of the Wage and Hour Administration, or if the Secretary of Labor has filed suit. But private suits, stimulated to some degree by the growth of public interest law groups, have been of growing importance.

Complaints of unequal pay can be filed with the EEOC and with OCR, because salary discrimination is illegal under Title VII of the Civil Rights Act of 1964, the executive order, and Title IX of the Education Amendments of 1972. Complaints of salary discrimination in these cases are usually combined with complaints of other types of employment discrimination, as they easily can be, for example, in the case of charges of discrimination in job classifications or promotions. Complaints filed under the Equal Pay Act, on the other hand, can involve only unequal pay, and, unlike those under Title VII or the executive order (but not unlike Title IX), they can be based only on sex, not on race or national origin. There are advantages to plaintiffs in suing under both

[5] Back pay may be awarded over a three-year period when a willful violation is found.

the Equal Pay Act and Title VII simultaneously (Babcock et al., 1975, p. 441).

In addition to the federal agencies involved, sex-based discrimination in pay is also banned under the many state equal pay acts, and discrimination in pay on grounds of either sex or race is frequently illegal under state fair employment practice acts. Regulations under the federal Equal Pay Act state that "no provisions of the Fair Labor Standards Act will excuse noncompliance with any State or other law establishing equal pay standards higher than the equal pay standards provided by section 6(d) of the Fair Labor Standards Act." They also provide that "compliance with other applicable legislation will not excuse noncompliance with the equal pay provisions of the Fair Labor Standards Act" (*Code of Federal Regulations,* Title 29, Section 800.160).

Title VI of the Civil Rights Act of 1964

Title VI of the Civil Rights Act of 1964[6] prohibits discrimination on the basis of race, color, or national origin under any program or activity receiving federal financial assistance. Federal funds may be withheld from any such program or activity if an institution is found in violation. The legislation specifically provides that it is not applicable to "any employment practice of any employer, employment agency, or labor organization except where a primary objective of the Federal financial assistance is to provide employment," but, under a long-accepted interpretation of Title VI, it has been considered applicable to discrimination in academic employment on the basis, for example, of race. Enforcement is coordinated under the Attorney General, who may delegate authority to other federal agencies granting funds. Authority for enforcement of the provisions in relation to education is delegated to OCR.

Title VII of the Civil Rights Act of 1964

Under Title VII of the Civil Rights Act of 1964,[7] discrimination in employment on the basis of sex, race, color, religion, and

[6] Public Law 88-352, July 2, 1964.

[7] Public Law 88-352, July 2, 1964; as amended by Public Law 92-261, March 24, 1972. Nonprofessional employees of private institutions of

national origin is prohibited. The provisions did not apply to academic employment until they were extended by the Equal Employment Opportunity Act of 1972, which brought educational institutions and employees of state and local governments under coverage. The legislation is administered by a five-member bipartisan Equal Employment Opportunity Commission (the EEOC) appointed by the President.

An interesting bit of legislative history relating to the enactment of Title VII is that sex was not originally included as a basis on which discrimination was prohibited. A sex amendment was introduced by Representative Howard W. Smith of Virginia, a foe of the proposed Civil Rights Act, in an attempt to surround the debate on the legislation with ridicule and laughter, and perhaps thus defeat it (Bird, with Briller, 1972, pp. 1-7). Nevertheless, the sex discrimination provision had previously been supported by the National Women's Party and other groups, and was strongly supported by many male and female members of Congress.

Unlike the executive order, Title VII does not require affirmative action, but only nondiscrimination, and the regulations that have been issued under the legislation do not include affirmative action requirements. However, a conciliation agreement or court order *may* require affirmative action, but only after a finding of discrimination.

Under the 1972 legislation, the EEOC was given authority to bring suit against private employers in an appropriate federal district court if conciliation efforts are not successful. The commission may bring charges both in individual cases and where it is alleged that a pattern of discrimination exists. In a case involving a public employer, the Attorney General is authorized to bring suit. Similarly, both individual and class complaints against public and private employers may be filed with the commission. Thus, its responsibilities overlap with those of OCR and of the Wage and Hour Administration. Several years ago, based on an underlying agreement between OFCC and EEOC, the Department of Health, Education, and Welfare (HEW) and

---

higher education, unlike other employees in higher education, were covered by the 1964 legislation.

the EEOC agreed that all individual cases, but not class complaints, filed with OCR under the executive order after March 24, 1972, would be forwarded to EEOC for investigation and action. This practice was abandoned for a time in April 1974, after OCR decided that it was sometimes difficult to distinguish between an individual and a class complaint (U.S. Commission on Civil Rights, 1975a, p. 308), but it was later resumed.

Title VII provides that the EEOC may cooperate with state and local agencies charged with the administration of state fair employment practice laws and may enter into written agreements with such agencies. In conformity with this provision, EEOC regulations call for deferral of charges to state and local agencies with which it has written agreements and for refraining from initiating its own proceedings on such charges until termination of state or local proceedings, or after 60 days, whichever comes first.

If a complainant wishes to bring a private action in a federal district court rather than await EEOC's efforts to investigate and conciliate, he or she must obtain an authorizing letter, known as a "right to sue" letter, from EEOC. This may be obtained, as a matter of right, after EEOC has had jurisdiction for 180 days. Having received a permission-to-sue letter, the complainant has only 90 days in which to commence litigation.[8] Title VII provides for injunctive and affirmative relief as well as back pay, and the granting of attorneys' fees to the prevailing party.

There is an advantage in bringing a case to court, because EEOC, which faces an enormous backlog of complaints, will rarely be able to complete action on a matter within slightly more than 180 days. On the other hand, the costs of going to court may be higher than the costs of processing a complaint through EEOC, partly because the complainant may have to bear the costs of developing data and evidence, which would be borne by the agency in the case of a complaint filed with EEOC.

According to Beaird (1972, p. 480), the courts have been

[8] For additional details, see Babcock et al. (1975, p. 371).

very liberal in protecting the rights of a complainant under Title VII to proceed directly to court once a right-to-sue letter has been obtained.

Title IX of the Education Amendments of 1972

Title IX of the Education Amendments of 1972[9] provides that "no person in the United States shall, on the basis of sex, be excluded from participation in, be denied the benefits of, or be subjected to discrimination under any educational program or activity receiving Federal financial assistance." Private undergraduate education is excepted, but only with respect to admissions, not with respect to equal treatment of the sexes after admission.[10]

Regulations for the enforcement of Title IX were first published by HEW in June 1974 and then were the subject of comments and criticisms by numerous interested groups and institutions. A year later, on May 27, 1975, President Ford signed the regulations, but only after there had been some modifications of the provisions as submitted by the Secretary of Health, Education, and Welfare (*Federal Register*, June 4, 1975).[11] Under the legislation, however, Congress had 45 days (until July 21, 1975) to pass a resolution disapproving them. In fact, Congress did not pass such a resolution, and the regulations were therefore finally approved.

The regulations are extensive, setting standards for meeting federal equal opportunity requirements relating to admissions, treatment of students, and employment. They have been the subject of controversy, particularly in relation to athletics. So

[9] Public Law 92-318, June 23, 1972.

[10] Also excepted from the admissions provisions are public institutions of undergraduate education that traditionally and continuously from their establishment admitted only members of one sex. None of Title IX's provisions apply to educational institutions that are controlled by religious organizations if the application of the legislation "would not be consistent with the religious tenets of such organization." Also exempt are institutions whose primary purpose is to provide training for the United States military services and the merchant marine.

[11] *Code of Federal Regulations*, Title 45, Part 86.

far as academic employment issues are concerned, they involve an additional set of regulations that further complicate the picture, although there are no essential differences between these and other regulations, except for certain differences relating to pension plans.[12] They require only nondiscriminatory practices in hiring and promotion and do not include affirmative action requirements comparable to those of the executive order. However, remedial measures can be required of an institution after a finding of discrimination.

Responsibility for enforcing the regulations rests with the Office for Civil Rights in HEW, but OCR may delegate responsibility to other federal agencies involved in providing federal funds to educational institutions. Pending final issuance by the department of a "consolidated procedural regulation applicable to Title IX and other civil rights authorities administered by the Department," the procedural requirements under Title VI of the Civil Rights Act are to apply.

The regulations require that "a recipient shall adopt and publish grievance procedures providing for prompt and equitable resolution of student and employee complaints alleging any action which would be prohibited by this part." No requirements are included, however, with respect to types of grievance procedures.

During congressional hearings on the regulations, questions were raised as to whether the legislation actually provided the authority to HEW to require grievance procedures. A question was also raised as to whether Title IX was intended to apply to employment at all. In fact, Title IX is unclear as to congres-

[12]The Title IX regulations, along with regulations under the executive order, allow employers either to provide equal contributions to pension plans or equal periodic pension benefits to employees of each sex. On the other hand, regulations for the enforcement of Title VII of the Civil Rights Act of 1964 provide that "it shall be an unlawful employment practice for an employer to have a pension or retirement plan . . . which differentiates in benefits on the basis of sex" (Paragraph 1604.9 of *Code of Federal Regulations*, Title 29, Chapter XIV). In announcing release of the regulations on May 27, 1975, the Secretary of HEW indicated that the President had directed that a report be prepared by October 15 recommending a single approach by federal agencies on this issue.

sional intent—the word "employment" is never specifically mentioned, but "each Federal department and agency which is empowered to extend Federal financial assistance to any education program or activity, by way of grant, loan, or contract . . . is authorized and directed to effectuate the provisions of section 901 [the central provision of the act] with respect to such program or activity. . . ."

When the White House released the regulations, proposed new procedural regulations were announced by HEW under which OCR would concentrate its civil rights-enforcement efforts on systematic reviews of school districts and institutions of higher education covered by Title VI of the Civil Rights Act, Title IX, and other civil rights statutes for which it is responsible, and would handle individual complaints primarily as they were incorporated in the compliance review process. OCR would respond to individuals and groups filing complaints by acknowledging their correspondence, notifying them of any related compliance investigations expected within the next 12 months, and informing them of applicable remedies at the federal, state, and local levels ("Ford Signs . . . ," 1975, p. 1).

The provisions concerning the handling of complaints were immediately criticized by supporters of vigorous nondiscrimination policies and will doubtless continue to be attacked. Whereas complaints of employment discrimination may be filed with other federal and state agencies, including the EEOC, the only other federal agency with authority to handle complaints relating to student issues is the Department of Justice.

However, private actions can be brought in federal courts under Title VI and probably, also, under Title IX.

State Legislation

State fair employment practice laws, some of which were enacted not long after World War II, generally antedate federal nondiscrimination legislation and tended originally to prohibit discrimination on the basis of race, religion, or national origin. Most of them, however, have more recently been amended to include discrimination on the basis of sex. In addition, many of the states have also enacted equal pay legislation, and some of them have antidiscrimination provisions in legislation relating to state contracts. According to a recent compilation prepared by the Education Commission of the States (1975b), there are 42 states with fair employment practice legislation and/or equal pay laws. The states without fair employment practice acts are generally in the deep South.

The majority of the state fair employment practice laws apply to public, as well as to private, employment. They do not, however, invariably apply to higher education. Their provisions follow quite closely those of Title VII of the federal Civil Rights Act, and they are usually administered by a state fair employment practice commission. Complaints of discrimination in employment can be filed with these state and some local agencies, and, as we have seen, EEOC regulations call for deferral of the processing of complaints that it has referred to state or local agencies. This deferral procedure, as well as the huge backlog of cases that has developed under EEOC, have induced increased resort to state and local agencies.

Internal Revenue Service

Under Section 501 (C)(3) of the Internal Revenue Code, covering qualifications for tax exempt status, institutions must provide evidence that they do not discriminate on the basis of race. On February 18, 1975, the IRS issued lengthy regulations relating to enforcement of these provisions in the case of private, nonprofit institutions. Aimed primarily at private schools that have sprung up to evade the impact of integration of public schools, the provisions apply also to private nonprofit colleges and universities. The regulations include, among other things, requirements regarding school facilities and programs, scholarship and loan programs, and applications for tax exempt status.

The new regulations have been strongly protested by several presidents of private universities, on the ground that they overlap and duplicate the requirements of other federal agencies, especially with respect to record-keeping and reporting. The IRS, it is maintained, can obtain the relevant data from the other federal agencies that impose similar requirements.

On the other hand, the regulations were also protested by civil rights advocates as not dealing adequately with the problem of all-white academies ("New IRS Private School Guidelines . . . ," 1975).

Civil Rights Legislation Dating from
the Reconstruction Period

Several provisions of the United States *Code* (Title 42), dating from the period immediately following the Civil War, have increasingly become the basis for court cases involving complaints of racial or sexual discrimination. The provisions involved are sections 1981, 1982, 1983, 1985(3), 1986, and 1988 (see Appendix B). Relief may be sought through private actions in federal district courts for race-based (but not sex-based) claims against private employers under paragraphs 1981 and 1982. Similar relief may be sought against public colleges on grounds of race or sex under the other sections listed above.[13]

There have been some conflicting court decisions on whether a plaintiff may bypass the time limitations of Title VII and proceed directly to court under section 1981. Several circuit courts have held that a section 1981 cause of action is not subject to the time limitations of Title VII, but the Seventh Circuit, while not disagreeing with that principle, has held that the charging parties must plead a reasonable excuse for bypassing the provisions of Title VII (Babcock et al., 1975, p. 373).[14]

Another significant aspect of court decisions relating to section 1981 is that the courts have held that the specific remedies provided by Congress in Title VII were not intended to preempt the "general remedial language of section 1981" (Beaird, 1972, p. 477).[15] In their decisions on this point, the courts have held "that a legislative intent to preserve previously

---

[13]For an informative discussion of cases brought under paragraph 1981, see Larson (1972).

[14]See, for example, *Hackett v. McGuire Bros. Inc.*, 445 F. 2d 442 (1971); *Sanders v. Dobbs Houses, Inc.*, 431 F. 2d 1097 (5th Cir. 1970, *cert. denied*, 401 U.S. 948) (1971); *Boudreaux v. Baton Rouge Contracting Co.*, 437 F. 2d 1011 (5th Cir. 1971); and *Waters v. Wisconsin Steel Works*, 427 F. 2d 476 (7th Cir. 1970), *cert. denied sub nom. United Order of American Bricklayers and Stone Masons, Local 21 v. Waters*, 400 U.S. 911 (1970).

[15]See the Sanders and Waters cases cited in the preceding footnote. See, also, Larson (1972).

existing causes of action was demonstrated in the congressional rejection, by more than a two-to-one margin, of an amendment by Senator Tower which would have excluded agencies other than the EEOC from dealing with practices covered by Title VII" (ibid.).

Constitutional Amendments

In addition to the numerous bases for private actions in court discussed thus far, there is a large and significant body of court decisions in which sexual or racial discrimination has been found (or not found) unconstitutional under equal protection and due process clauses of the Fifth and/or Fourteenth Amendments to the Constitution of the United States. One of the best known of these cases is *Brown v. Board of Education* (34 U.S. 483, 74 S. Ct. 686, 1954), in which the Supreme Court held that racial segregation in the public schools deprived minority-group children of equal educational opportunities. The cases brought under these constitutional amendments cover a very wide range of social and economic laws and conditions, including employment conditions. Any attempt to review them would be beyond the scope of this report, but the possibility of private actions in court under these constitutional amendments should not be ignored.[16]

It is also important to bear in mind the possibility that final ratification of the Equal Rights Amendment, adopted by Congress in 1972, would create another basis for action in sex-based cases of discrimination. In fact, ratification of the Equal Rights Amendment would require extensive legislative activity by Congress and state legislatures to eliminate conflicts between the amendment and existing legislation. This activity would probably relate less to conditions of employment—already extensively covered by federal and state legislation—than to such matters as marital relations, primarily a concern of state law.

[16]For an extensive review, see Babcock et al. (1975, especially pp. 89-189 and pp. 990-1036). The Fourteenth Amendment applies only to actions of states.

Federal Health Manpower Legislation

The Comprehensive Health Manpower Training Act of 1971 and the Nurse Training Act of 1971[17] prohibit federal financial support to any medical health or nursing-training program unless the institution providing the training submits, prior to the awarding of funds, satisfactory assurances that it will not discriminate on the basis of sex and race in the admission of individuals to its training programs. They also provide for non-discrimination in relation to employees working directly with applicants or enrolled students. Responsibility for enforcement rests with OCR. It should also be noted that university health science centers, as major recipients of federal funds, are subject to the requirements of the executive order, and there have been a number of cases of alleged discrimination in academic employment in medical schools.

The National Labor Relations Act and Related Measures

Under certain circumstances, a complaint of discrimination in employment in private higher education on the basis of race, sex, or national origin may be filed with the National Labor Relations Board, which has jurisdiction over the enforcement of the National Labor Relations Act. The power of Congress to regulate labor-management relations is limited by the commerce clause of the United States Constitution, and provisions relating to the jurisdiction of the NLRB are related to that restriction. In general, its jurisdiction is limited to private employers affecting interstate commerce. Private nonprofit universities and colleges are covered, if they have at least $1,000,000 gross annual revenue from all sources (excluding contributions not available for operating expenses because of limitations imposed by the grantor).

Thus far, to the best of our knowledge, there has been only one case involving alleged discrimination in private higher education on which the NLRB has rendered a decision.[18] This is

---

[17]Public Law 92-157, November 18, 1971; and Public Law 92-158, November 18, 1971.

[18]See Bureau of National Affairs (seriatim).

a very recent case in which the Pittsburgh regional office of the NLRB ruled that six full-time faculty members of St. Francis College in Pennsylvania who were members of the Franciscan Order should be excluded from a faculty bargaining unit. The full national board refused to review the case, and the college has announced its intention of appealing the case to the courts ("College to Fight . . . ," 1975).

This discussion of federal and state laws and regulations relating to discrimination in academic employment indicates the complexity of the situation but is by no means an exhaustive account of all the interrelationships involved. Figures 1 and 2 indicate the jurisdictions in which complaints may be filed or cases brought on the basis of sexual or racial discrimination. Because of the paucity of cases before the NLRB, we have not included that agency in the figures. Yet the possibility of complaints filed with the NLRB should be kept in mind. The situation described is not unique to higher education, but applies to employers generally. The discussion also suggests that both Congress and the courts have displayed reluctance to narrow or limit the courses of action open to complainants.

Figure 1. Agencies with which complaints can be filed or cases brought—
sex discrimination in employment in higher education

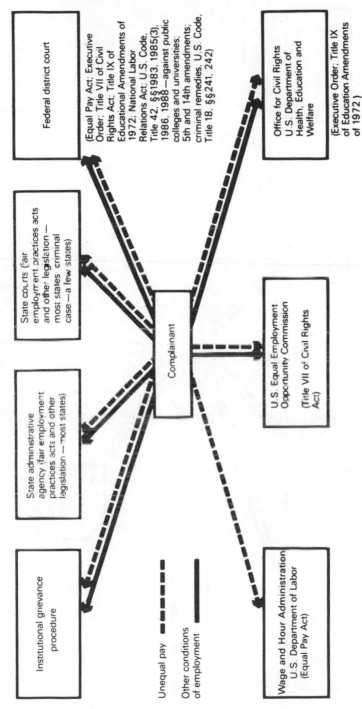

Federal district court

(Equal Pay Act; Executive Order; Title VII of Civil Rights Act; Title IX of Educational Amendments of 1972; National Labor Relations Act; U.S. Code, Title 42, §§1983, 1985(3), 1986, 1988—against public colleges and universities; 5th and 14th amendments; criminal remedies, U.S. Code, Title 18, §§241, 242)

State courts (fair employment practices acts and other legislation — most states criminal case — a few states)

State administrative agency (fair employment practices acts and other legislation — most states)

Institutional grievance procedure

Complainant

Office for Civil Rights U.S. Department of Health, Education and Welfare

(Executive Order; Title IX of Education Amendments of 1972)

U.S. Equal Employment Opportunity Commission

(Title VII of Civil Rights Act)

Wage and Hour Administration U.S. Department of Labor (Equal Pay Act)

Unequal pay

Other conditions of employment

Note: For provisions relating to deferral of action and exhaustion of remedies, see discussion in Section 4.

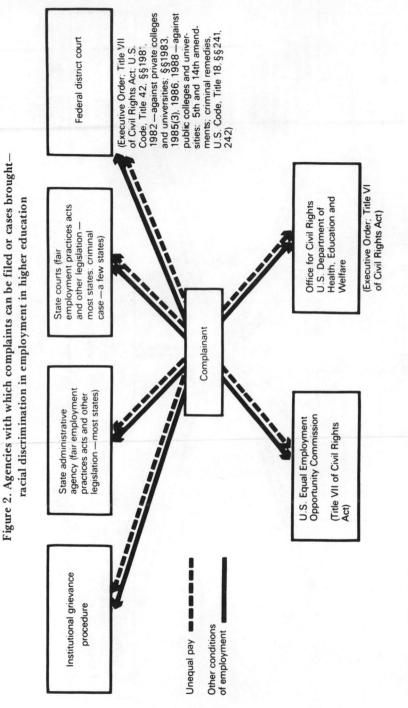

Figure 2. Agencies with which complaints can be filed or cases brought—racial discrimination in employment in higher education

Institutional grievance procedure

Unequal pay ▰▰▰▰▰

Other conditions of employment ▬▬▬▬

State administrative agency (fair employment practices acts and other legislation—most states)

State courts (fair employment practices acts and other legislation— most states; criminal case—a few states)

Federal district court

(Executive Order; Title VII of Civil Rights Act; U.S. Code, Title 42, §§1981, 1982—against private colleges and universities: §§1983, 1985(3), 1986, 1988—against public colleges and universities: 5th and 14th amendments; criminal remedies, U.S. Code, Title 18, §§241, 242)

Complainant

Office for Civil Rights U.S. Department of Health, Education and Welfare

(Executive Order; Title VI of Civil Rights Act)

U.S. Equal Employment Opportunity Commission

(Title VII of Civil Rights Act)

Note: For provisions relating to deferral of action and exhaustion of remedies, see discussion in Section 4.

5

Goals and Timetables

At the heart of the controversy over federal affirmative action regulations are the requirements for the development of goals and timetables in affirmative action plans. Goals and timetables go beyond provisions prohibiting discrimination, requiring the employer to make special efforts to recruit, employ, and promote women and minorities in order to overcome the effects of past discrimination.

There is also a more specific problem arising from apparent conflicts between the *Higher Education Guidelines, Executive Order 11246,* issued by HEW in October 1972, and Revised Order No. 4 of the Department of Labor. The requirements for goals and timetables and the conflict between the *Guidelines* and Revised Order No. 4 can best be made clear by quotations from both of these documents.

Guidelines of October 1972

The distinction between nondiscrimination and affirmative action is well defined in the *Guidelines* (U.S. Department of Health, Education, and Welfare, 1972, pp. 2-3).

> Nondiscrimination requires the elimination of all existing discriminatory conditions, whether purposeful or inadvertent. . . . *Affirmative action* requires the

contractor to do more than ensure employment neutrality with regard to race, color, religion, sex, and national origin. . . . Affirmative action requires the employer to make additional efforts to recruit, employ and promote qualified members of groups formerly excluded, even if that exclusion cannot be traced to particular discriminatory actions on the part of the employer. . . . Revised Order No. 4 requires a contractor to determine whether women and minorities are "underutilized" in its employee work force and, if that is the case, to develop as a part of its affirmative action program specific goals and timetables designed to overcome that underutilization. . . . Underutilization is defined . . . as "having fewer women or minorities in a particular job than would reasonably be expected by their availability. . . ."

If the contractor falls short of its goal at the end of the period it has set, that failure in itself does not require a conclusion of noncompliance. It does, however, require a determination by the contractor as to why the failure occurred. . . .

Nothing in the Executive Order requires that a university contractor eliminate or dilute standards which are necessary to the successful performance of the institution's educational and research functions.

At a later point the *Guidelines* provide more specifically for the development of goals and timetables (ibid., pp. J3-J5):

AVAILABILITY OF WOMEN AND MINORITIES

A unique aspect of equal employment opportunity under the Executive Order is the required compilation of availability data on women and minorities for use as a measure of the contractor's equal employment opportunity. By comparing availability data with current employees, the contractor has an indication of how representative its workforce is of the persons qualified for employment in its institution. . . .

OCR recommends the following procedure for determining availability figures for women and minorities for academic positions: Many disciplinary associations and professional groups have data that show percentages of racial and national origin minorities available in certain fields, and a 1968 study by the Ford Foundation . . . provides percentages of Negroes holding doctorates. To determine the number of women available for senior level positions, the Office recommends that the contractor use data available from the National Register of Scientific and Technical Personnel prepared by the National Science Foundation, and the U.S. Office of Education's annual reports on earned degrees. Another source is the National Research Council of the National Academy of Sciences. . . .

COMPARISON OF CURRENT WORK FORCE WITH AVAILABILITY DATA

The next step for the contractor is to compare the number of women and minorities in its current workforce with their availability in the market from which it can reasonably recruit. This comparison must be by comparable job categories. Whenever the comparison reveals that a hiring unit of the university (a department or other section) is not employing minorities and women to the extent that they are available and qualified for work, it is then required to set goals to overcome this situation.

Goals should be set so as to overcome deficiencies in the utilization of minorities and women within a reasonable time. In many cases this can be accomplished within 5 years; in others more time or less time will be required.

In many institutions the appropriate unit for goals is the school or division, rather than the department. While estimates of availability in academic employment can best be determined on a disciplinary basis, anticipated turnover and vacancies can usually be calculated on a wider basis. While a school, division or college may be the organizational unit which assumes responsibility for setting and achieving goals, departments which have traditionally excluded women or minorities from their ranks are expected to make particular efforts to recruit, hire and promote women and minorities. In other words, the Office for Civil Rights will be concerned not only with whether a school meets its overall goals, but also whether apparent general success has been achieved only by strenuous efforts on the part of a few departments.

It is particularly with reference to this latter paragraph relating to the appropriate organizational unit for goals and timetables that it has become increasingly clear within the last several months that OCR seems to be guided in its enforcement activities by the more stringent requirements of Revised Order No. 4 rather than by its own *Guidelines*.

Revised Order No. 4

Let us therefore turn to some of the more relevant portions of Revised Order No. 4 (*Code of Federal Regulations*, Title 41, Section 60-2):

§ 60-2.11 *Required utilization analysis. . .*
Affirmative action programs must contain the following information:

(a) Workforce analysis which is defined as a listing of each job title as appears in applicable collective bargaining agreements or payroll records (not job group) ranked from the lowest paid to the highest paid within each department or other similar organizational unit including departmental or unit supervision. If there are separate work units or lines of progression within a department, a separate list must be provided for each such work unit, or line, including unit supervisors. . . . For each job title, the total number of incumbents, the total number of male and female incumbents, and the total number of male and female incumbents in each of the following groups must be given: Blacks, Spanish-surnamed Americans, American Indians, and Orientals. The wage rate or salary range for each job title must be given. . . .

(b) An analysis of all major job groups at the facility, with explanation if minorities or women are currently being underutilized in any one or more job groups ("job groups" herein meaning one or a group of jobs having similar content, wage rates, and opportunities). "Underutilization" is defined as having fewer minorities or women in a particular job group than would reasonably be expected by their availability. In making the utilization analysis, the contractor shall conduct such analysis separately for minorities and women.

(1) In determining whether minorities are being underutilized in any job group the contractor will consider at least all of the following factors:

(i) The minority population of the labor area surrounding the facility;

(ii) The size of the minority unemployment force in the labor area surrounding the facility;

(iii) The percentage of the minority work force as compared with the total work force in the immediate labor area;

(iv) The general availability of minorities having requisite skills in the immediate labor area;

(v) The availability of minorities having requisite skills in an area in which the contractor can reasonably recruit;

(vi) The availability of promotable and transferable minorities within the contractor's organization;

(vii) The existence of training institutions capable of training persons in the requisite skills;

(viii) The degree of training which the contractor is reasonably able to undertake as a means of making all job classes available to minorities.

(2) In determining whether women are being underutilized in any job group, the contractor will consider at least all of the following factors:

(i) The size of the female unemployment force in the labor area surrounding the facility;

(ii) The percentage of the female work force as compared with the total work force in the immediate labor area;

(iii) The general availability of women having requisite skills in the immediate labor area;

(iv) The availability of women having requisite skills in an area in which the contractor can reasonably recruit;

(v) The availability of women seeking employment in the labor or recruitment area of the contractor;

(vi) The availability of promotable and transferable female employees within the contractor's organization;

(vii) The existence of training institutions capable of training persons in the requisite skills; and

(viii) The degree of training which the contractor is reasonably able to undertake as a means of making all job classes available to women.

§ 60-2.12 *Establishment of goals and timetables*

(a) The goals and timetables developed by the contractor should be attainable in terms of the contractor's analysis of his deficiencies and his entire affirmative action program. Thus, in establishing the size of his goals and the length of his timetables, the contractor should consider the results which could reasonably be expected from his putting forth every good faith effort to make his overall affirmative action program work. . . .

(b) Involve personnel relations staff, department

and division heads, and local and unit managers in the goal setting process.

(c) Goals should be significant, measurable, and attainable.

(d) Goals should be specific for planned results, with timetables for completion.

(e) Goals may not be rigid and inflexible quotas which must be met, but must be targets reasonably attainable by means of applying every good faith effort to make all aspects of the entire affirmative action program work.

(f) In establishing timetables to meet goals and commitments, the contractor will consider the anticipated expansion, contraction and turnover of and in the work force.

(g) Goals, timetables and affirmative action commitments must be designed to correct any identifiable deficiencies.

(h) Where deficiencies exist and where numbers or percentages are relevant in developing corrective action, the contractor shall establish and set forth specific goals and timetables separately for minorities and women.

(i) Such goals and timetables, with supporting data and the analysis thereof shall be a part of the contractor's written affirmative action program and shall be maintained at each establishment by the contractor. . . .

§ 60-2.23 *Identification of problem areas by organizational units and job titles.*

(a) An in-depth analysis of the following should be made . . .

(1) Composition of the work force by minority group status and sex.

(2) Composition of applicant flow by minority group status and sex.

(3) The total selection process including position

descriptions, position titles, worker specifications, application forms, interview procedures, test administration, test validity, referral procedures, final selection process, and similar factors.

(4) Transfer and promotion practices.

(5) Facilities, company sponsored recreation and social events, and special programs such as educational assistance.

(6) Seniority practices and seniority practices of union contracts. . . .

(b) If any of the following items are found in the analysis, special corrective action should be appropriate.

(1) An "underutilization" of minorities or women in specific job groups.

(2) Lateral and/or vertical movement of minority or female employees occurring at a lesser rate (compared to work force mix) than that of nonminority or male employees.

(3) The selection process eliminates a significantly higher percentage of minorities or women than nonminorities or men.

(4) Application and related preemployment forms not in compliance with Federal legislation.

(5) Position descriptions inaccurate in relation to actual functions and duties.

(6) Tests and other selection techniques not validated as required by the OFCC Order on Employee Testing and other Selection Procedures.

(7) Test forms not validated by location, work performance and inclusion of minorities and women in sample.

(8) Referral ratio of minorities or women to the hiring supervisor or manager indicates a significantly higher percentage are being rejected as compared to nonminority and male applicants. . . .

These provisions make it clear that analyses of "underutilization" must be carried out for each job classification within each organizational unit or department. In addition, § 60-2.13 provides for the establishment of goals and objectives by "organizational units and job groups." There is considerable evidence, based on information relating to OCR's negotiations with the University of California, Berkeley, and negotiations with certain other institutions, that OCR interprets Revised Order No. 4 as requiring the setting of goals and timetables for each department in which underutilization is found. The evidence is less clear that goals and timetables must be set separately for lower faculty ranks and for tenured ranks, but essentially this was done in connection with the Berkeley plan, with OCR's approval.

OCR's interpretation of the data analysis requirements of Revised Order No. 4 in relation to institutions of higher education is set forth in the document that is presented as Table 14 in Appendix A to this report. The requirements call not only for detailed comparisons of utilization and availability pools, department by department, for each racial or ethnic group by sex, but also call for similar detailed analyses in relation to recruitment, selection, placement/assignment, promotion, tenure, transfer (reassignment), salary analysis at initial entry, salary analysis in connection with merit increases and adjustments, fringe benefits, training, voluntary separations, involuntary terminations, and sources of funds (where external to the institution). Retrospective data must be provided relating to recruitment, selection, etc., for the most recent five-year period. The table indicates the number of computations required for institutions with numbers of departments ranging from 25 to 75. The Berkeley campus—a relatively large campus—happens to have 75 departments. This listing shows that the total number of separate analyses would range from 21,000 to 63,000 and that the average number required of each department or organizational unit would be 850. These results should probably be qualified, because retrospective analyses for the last five years are not required—relating, for example, to recruitment when there has been no new hire in a department in the last five years.

There are other respects in which provisions of Revised Order No. 4 are inappropriate in relation to academic employment—for example, the validation of selection tests, which are not used in the hiring of faculty. In addition, under Revised Order No. 14, published in the *Federal Register* on February 14, 1974, Revised Order No. 4 was amended to provide, among other things, that neither women nor minority candidates for employment should be required to possess higher qualifications than those of the least qualified incumbent. Such a provision is especially inappropriate for academic employment, linking, as it does, the qualifications for hiring or promotion to those of the weakest incumbent.

The eight provisions (i to viii) relating to the availability of minorities in the surrounding labor market area under § 60-2.11, and the corresponding provisions relating to the availability of women, have generally been interpreted by both OCR and institutions of higher education as applying to the hiring of nonacademic employees, but not as applying to the hiring of faculty members or other academic employees. In particular, they have been interpreted as not applying to the hiring of faculty members in regular ranks in universities, where the provisions of the *Higher Education Guidelines* referring to relative numbers of persons with advanced degrees have been regarded as superseding the provisions of § 60-2.11 referring to the surrounding labor market area.

In fact, the difficulty arises from the use of the words "the labor market surrounding the facility," and the "immediate labor market area." We have been informed that the Department of Labor does not always interpret the provisions as relating to the immediate labor market area. The correct interpretation relates to the area from which the employer recruits for the particular occupation. In higher education, it may vary from field to field, from specialty to specialty within a field, and from institution to institution. For some faculty members—for example, vocational education teachers in certain occupations in community colleges—the market might be local. For most faculty members in research universities, the market would be national, and in some specialties, the recruitment area would be international.[1]

This point, however, was not made clear in a response of the Office of Federal Contract Compliance to an inquiry from the University of North Carolina. (See the letter of January 17, 1975, from William Friday, president of the University of North Carolina, to former Secretary of Labor, Peter Brennan, and the reply of Philip J. Davis, director of the Office of Federal Contract Compliance, together with excerpts from a memorandum of the University of North Carolina—Appendix B.)

Memorandum of December 1974

By December 1974, controversy over affirmative action issues had become so intense that Peter Holmes, the director of OCR, deemed it advisable to issue a "Memorandum to College and University Presidents," the main theme of which was that preferential hiring of women or minorities was illegal under the executive order. There follow some excerpts from this document:

At the outset, certain general principles should be made clear. Colleges and universities are entitled to select the most qualified candidate, without regard to race, sex, or ethnicity, for any position. The college or university, not the Federal Government, is to say what constitutes qualification for any particular position. No single appointment will be objected to where those not appointed are less well-qualified than the candidate actually selected.

I. RECRUITMENT FOR EMPLOYMENT VACANCIES MUST BE UNDERTAKEN WITHOUT DESIGNATION OR IDENTIFICATION BY RACE, SEX, OR ETHNICITY. . . .

The following case represents an example of an im-

[1] Information provided by William J. Kilberg, solicitor, U.S. Department of Labor.

proper interpretation of the affirmative action obligation:

> For the past four years, the Mathematics Department of X University has been operating under an affirmative action program. Although its goal for hiring women was established at 20 percent over a five-year period, during the past four years, each of four vacancies has been filled by a male. At an annual professional association conference, the department chairman informed a male applying for a fifth vacant position that he could not be given consideration because Federal regulations require the department to fill the position with a woman. . . .

The Mathematics Department must be able to demonstrate clearly that it has adhered to its affirmative action obligation by making a full and good faith effort to recruit and consider women for each of the five vacancies. If the Department is able to make this demonstration, its inability to meet its employment goal would not be deemed a violation of its affirmative action obligation. However, a failure by the Mathematics Department to make a sufficient good faith effort to recruit and consider women and minority candidates for the four earlier openings would constitute a violation of the Executive Order regulations. . . .

III. JOB REQUIREMENTS MUST BE APPLIED UNIFORMLY TO ALL CANDIDATES WITHOUT REGARD TO RACE, COLOR, SEX, RELIGION, OR NATIONAL ORIGIN.

The *Guidelines* stress the need for standardized employment practices that minimize the opportunity for arbitrary and/or discriminatory hiring decisions. It is not intended that affirmative action should result in a dilution of standards in order to attain the objectives of the Executive Order.

The memorandum then gives an example of a small history

department that waived the Ph.D. requirement for women and minorities wishing to apply but retained it for males or non-minorities. It indicates that such a waiver is expressly forbidden and that the history department must either waive the Ph.D. requirement for all applicants or maintain it for all applicants.

IV. A JOB REQUIREMENT WHICH RESULTS IN A DISPROPORTIONATE IMPACT UPON MINORITIES AND/OR WOMEN CAN BE MAINTAINED ONLY IF IT IS JOB-RELATED. . . .

. . . no standards or criteria which have, by intent or effect, worked to exclude women and minorities as a class can be utilized, unless the institution can demonstrate the necessity of such standard to the performance of the job in question. . . .

V. A UNIVERSITY IS REQUIRED TO OBTAIN INFORMATION ON THE RACE, SEX, AND ETHNIC IDENTITY OF APPLICANTS FOR EMPLOYMENT. . . .

The collection and analysis of such data is recognized as an essential means of providing both the institution and the Federal Government with the information necessary to monitor the compliance posture of the institution. . . .

Preserving the anonymity of applicants in the collection of applicant flow data can be accomplished by gathering the requisite race, sex, and ethnic data separately from the application form.

Incidents of June 1975

In mid-June 1975, OCR warned 29 universities that it might withhold their pending federal contracts, totaling some $65 million for the 29 institutions, unless they quickly produced acceptable affirmative action plans or agreed to follow a model approved by the agency. It has been alleged that this action was at least partly stimulated by a suit filed in a federal district court in November 1974 by several women's rights organizations and the National Education Association to compel HEW and the Department of Labor to enforce federal antidiscrimination laws in relation to higher education. The suit called attention to the deficiencies of the enforcement program.

Among the 29 universities, 16 were sent letters on June 11, 1975, asking that they review their programs and consider the model agreement as a possible recourse. Similar letters were to be hand-delivered to five other institutions, it was reported. In addition, eight institutions were issued show-cause orders giving them 30 days to produce an acceptable affirmative action plan. The affirmative action plans of some of these institutions had previously been submitted to OCR, but a compliance review had not been completed within the previous 12 months, as required by Department of Labor regulations.

The letters explained that OCR would not have time, before the fiscal year ended on June 30, to conduct a thorough compliance review and therefore suggested that institutions sign the model agreement. Some of the presidents and chancellors of the institutions involved were "said to be upset because the model agreement was largely based on an affirmative-action agreement that the Office for Civil Rights had recently negotiated with the University of California, Berkeley" (Fields, 1975). The letter called for statistical analyses very much like those specified in Table 14, Appendix A.

The presidents and chancellors were not alone in protesting this action. Some academic women's leaders were quoted as commenting that the decision to press a plan that requires extensive data-gathering but does not stress the hiring of women and minority groups "emphasizes process and not program" (ibid.).

After hurried consultations by representatives of some of the universities and higher education associations with Secretary Caspar W. Weinberger of HEW and Secretary John T. Dunlop of the Department of Labor, 14 universities were given an opportunity to sign a short, revised, Affirmative Action Compliance agreement that enabled them to have their federal contracts approved before June 30. According to OCR, 13 of the universities signed the short agreement, while New Mexico State University worked out a longer agreement with the OCR Dallas office. The agreements provided for further meetings between representatives of the institutions and of OCR, development and submission of revised affirmative action plans 30 days after the meetings, and correction of deficiencies at OCR's request ("Universities Sign . . . ," 1975; and "Universities Given Revised Agreement Form . . . ," 1975).

These developments provide additional evidence that OCR interprets Revised Order No. 4 as requiring the detailed analyses called for in Table 14, as well as specification of goals and time-tables in the manner of the Berkeley plan.

Goals, Quotas, and Qualifications

Federal regulations and guidelines make it clear that goals are different from quotas. Yet there is a legitimate fear that in actual administration, at the campus level or by federal agencies or both, they might come, in fact, to be the same thing. That still remains to be seen. It should be carefully guarded against.[2]

A related issue is how "most qualified" is interpreted. (1) "Most qualified" may be determined on strictly academic grounds alone--knowledge of the subject and ability to teach it and add to it. (2) It may be judged on broader grounds of over-all contributions, including, where appropriate, the ability to serve effectively as "models" and "mentors" to women and minority students. (3) It may be considered loosely as being whatever is most suitable in meeting the established goals. Many variations exist within and among these three major alternatives.

We favor the second alternative. This is also the position of a commission of the American Association of University Professors (AAUP). The report of the Commission on Discrimination of the AAUP expressed this general point of view in the following terms:

> We would go further to say that special efforts to attract persons to improve the overall diversity of a faculty, and to broaden it specifically from its unisex or unirace sameness, seem to us to state a variety of affirmative action which deserves encouragement. . . .

[2] For arguments against goals and timetables, see Hook (1974) and Sea-bury (1972). For discussion generally favorable to goals and timetables, see Hesburgh (1975), Karst and Horowitz (1974), and Sandler (1975).

The argument to the special relevance of race and sex as qualifying characteristics draws its strength from a recognition of the richness which a variety of intellectual perspectives and life experiences can bring to the educational program. It is more than simply a matter of providing jobs for persons from groups which have in the past been unfairly excluded from an opportunity to compete for them; it is a matter of reorganizing the academic institution to fulfill its basic commitment to those who are seriously concerned to maintain the academic enterprise as a vital social force ("Affirmative Action . . . ," 1973, pp. 180-181).

The commission pointed out that a goal is "nothing more or less than an expectation of what an institution has reason to suppose will result under conditions of nondiscrimination, given its standards and recruiting practices, in light of the proportion of those within the field of eligibility and recruitment who are women or members of minority groups" (ibid., pp. 182-183).

The concept of goals and timetables may be more easily applied in some types of institutions than in others. In research universities, in particular, greater weight tends to be given in initial appointments, and even more so in promotions to tenure, to potential research accomplishment and to the closely related potential for innovative and stimulating teaching of graduate students than in other institutions. Highly selective liberal arts colleges also tend to seek these qualities in their faculty appointments and promotions. Thus, the concept of pools of qualified persons becomes somewhat more difficult to apply, especially in appointments or promotions to tenured ranks, in research universities and in selective liberal arts colleges than in most other types of institutions of higher education.

What Proportions Are Sought?

Before making our recommendations on what should be done about goals and timetables, we need to call attention to a source of major misunderstanding that has not as yet been mentioned.

It is frequently implied that the goals of affirmative action will not be achieved until women and members of minority groups are represented in the same proportions as in the total labor force. It is important to recognize that there is nothing in the federal *Guidelines* that implies any such result. The *Guidelines* refer to recent recipients of appropriate degrees, and we may assume that this typically means doctor's degrees for most appointments to regular faculty positions in four-year colleges and universities and master's degrees in two-year colleges.

What the *Guidelines* do imply is that the relative representation of women and minority groups in academic employment should increase as they come to represent a larger proportion of degree recipients. Disparities between their representation in lower and in higher faculty ranks should also be expected to diminish and eventually to disappear.

Should Goals and Timetables Be Retained?

Despite the problems involved in relation to goals and timetables, their abandonment, as a federal requirement, could seriously weaken affirmative action efforts on some college and university campuses by largely removing the impetus to change. On the other hand, on many campuses, federal requirements are by no means the only influence at work. Organized women's groups have become very effective sources of influence for change on a good many campuses, and the many women's caucuses within professional associations are also active, especially in developing information about qualified women candidates. There are also groups that are especially concerned with increasing the relative representation of minority groups. Sometimes there is conflict between these organizations and the women's groups, but often the two groups work together.

It must be recognized, however, that the existence of federal requirements strengthens the capacity of these groups to effect change, and puts direct pressure on institutions. All things considered, the federal government should continue, at least for the immediate future, to call for goals and timetables in affirmative action plans, but there is a need for careful reconsideration of whether rigid application of ratios of pools of qualified persons to existing representation, department by department, yields the most desirable results.

There is no question, however, that much mischief has been done by statements such as that of the anonymous mathematics department chairman cited earlier, to the effect that he could not consider a white male for the one remaining vacancy in his department, because federal requirements forced him to consider only women or members of minority groups. There is a good deal of evidence—most of it anecdotal to be sure—that this kind of thing has been going on, and that in some instances, at least, it represents an easy way out of informing a white male candidate that he is not the best qualified applicant for the position. Beyond that, academic administrative pressure is at least partly to blame. We know of instances, and they are probably not too uncommon, in which chairmen have been informed that they will be allotted a budgetary position provided the individual selected is a woman or member of a minority group.

OCR's directives make it clear that this type of statement or procedure is illegal, but this has not always been fully understood at the level of its regional offices. And it has not been fully understood by academic administrators and faculty members.

The Concept of "Availability Pools" versus "Pools of Qualified Persons"

The use of the word "availability" is misleading. A measure of the relative representation of women or particular minorities among doctorate recipients during the most recent five-year period actually tells us little about how many qualified persons may be available for particular job offers, as the excerpts from the University of North Carolina memorandum in Appendix B make clear. Some may be employed in academic jobs in which they are quite satisfied and which they could not be induced to leave except on the basis of a particularly attractive offer from a prestigious institution. Others may be employed in industry or government—especially in those fields in which job opportunities are available in industry and government—and might not be induced to accept academic employment except on the basis of

an especially attractive offer. In addition, there may be qualified individuals who are not in the pool of recent degree recipients who received their degrees in an earlier period and are
employed in industry, government, or even in academic positions which they might be induced to leave if a desirable offer
came from a prestigious academic institution. Thus, actual availability pools are not susceptible of measurement.

Another complication is that, especially during the period
of rapid enrollment growth in the 1960s, when there were
shortages of qualified applicants for faculty positions in many
fields, candidates who had not completed the requirements for
the doctor's degree were frequently hired as "acting assistant
professors" on the understanding that they would become regular assistant professors upon the granting of the degree. Usually
these were persons who had completed all requirements except
the thesis. Although such appointments are less likely now that
enrollment is growing more slowly and additions to faculty,
especially in some fields, are small or nonexistent, it could be
argued that a doctor's degree is not always an essential requirement for faculty employment, even in universities and four-year
colleges. Indeed, there are some fields—for example, social welfare—in which faculty members are regularly employed in clini-
cal instruction or supervision of "field work" without a doctor's
degree.

This complication needs to be mentioned, because it is
conceivable that OCR's presumption that a doctor's degree is a
generally accepted requirement for employment in a university
or four-year college—through its acceptance of relative representation of women and minorities among recent degree recipients
as an appropriate measure of availability pools—could be chal-
lenged. On the other hand, federal government agencies enforcing affirmative action requirements in academic institutions
clearly need an objective standard that is susceptible of relatively unambiguous measurement. On this basis, a moving average based on numbers of doctor's degrees awarded by race and
sex in the most recent five-year period is a reasonable standard,
at least in relation to appointments at the assistant professor
level.

We believe that what is being measured, however, would be more appropriately described if the term *pools of qualified persons* were used instead of *availability pools*. Even this term is not wholly satisfactory, because not all persons in these pools are equally qualified. But it is less misleading than availability pools, because it does not imply that all persons in the pools are available or that persons not in these particular pools of recent doctoral recipients are not available.

An important aspect of this issue has to do with the validation of selection procedures, to which Revised Order No. 4 refers. Another entire section of the Department of Labor regulations concerns employee-testing and other selection procedures (*Code of Federal Regulations*, Title 41, Section 60-3). This requires that selection tests should be validated—that is, shown to be appropriate as a means of measuring probable employee performance—through analysis of performance of groups of employees performing similar tasks. Are variations in employee performance related to differences in their performance on selection tests administered at the time they were being considered for hiring?

The concept is more readily applicable in an employment situation in which there are large numbers of employees performing similar tasks and in which the performance of those employees can be measured objectively than in other employment situations. Where there are relatively few employees performing a particular type of task, statistically reliable validation results cannot be obtained.

In higher education, selection tests are sometimes used in hiring nonacademic personnel but are rarely, if ever, used in hiring academic personnel. Educational records and any records relating to previous performance in academic employment are the major criteria used in selection of academic personnel at the assistant professor level. Conceivably, at some point a federal agency might require an institution of higher education to validate its use of the doctor's degree as a criterion for employment in regular faculty ranks by measuring the relative performance of faculty members with and without a doctor's degree. In most situations this would be very difficult, because the number of persons with and without doctor's degrees performing similar tasks, especially within a given department, would be likely to be very small. Persons with and without doctor's degrees probably would be carrying out different types of assignments. Those with doctor's degrees would be more likely to be teaching upper-division and graduate courses, and to be spending relatively more time on research, than those without doctor's degrees. Objective measurement of results in academic employment is also difficult and subtle. Thus, validation of requirements for doctor's degrees would be extremely difficult.

Similarly, problems might arise if a court were to decide, along the lines of the decision of the U.S. Supreme Court in *Griggs et al. v. Duke Power Co.* that academic employers could not require doctor's degrees in their selection procedures unless they could demonstrate that the job could not satisfactorily performed without a doctor's degree. There is a statement in that decision, however, that could be significant in relation to a future case involving academic employment:

> In the context of this case, it is unnecessary to reach the question whether testing requirements that take into account capability for the next succeeding position or related future promotion might be utilized upon a showing that such long-range requirements fulfill a genuine business need. In the present case the Company has made no such showing.[3]

The statement implies that a particular requirement—for example, a Ph.D.—might be utilized for appointment at the assistant professor level, even though not always necessary for satisfactory performance at that level, if it could clearly be shown to be necessary for satisfactory performance at the associate professor level.

Thus far, there has been no relevant judicial decision specifically relating to higher education, and there is little evidence that validation of selection standards has been required of aca-

[3]401 U.S.424, 91 S.Ct. 849 (1971).

demic institutions by OCR and other federal agencies, but a case is currently being processed involving the State University of New York, in which the New York State Division of Human Rights has cited the Griggs case to challenge the Ph.D. requirement.

Although we support the concept of goals and timetables, we believe that there is a need for both modification and clarification of federal regulations and guidelines relating to them, particularly with reference to three issues: (1) whether goals and timetables are specified for schools and colleges, groups of related departments, or individual departments, (2) the specification and interpretation of timetables, and (3) the application of affirmative action objectives to appointments and promotions to tenured positions. These issues will be discussed in connection with analyses of how they are actually treated in the affirmative action plans of respondents to our survey.

Among the 100 campus-approved affirmative action plans of our respondent institutions, 62 included specific goals and timetables. The remaining plans usually included directions to schools and departments about methods to be used in developing goals and timetables but had either not reached the stage of specifying them or did not send us appendixes or other documents providing the information necessary for our analysis.

Universities with affirmative action plans were considerably more likely to have spelled out specific goals and timetables (more than two-thirds) than other types of institutions with plans (less than one-half).

In discussing goals and timetables, we shall refer specifically to the plan of the University of California, Berkeley, because it has been the subject of much recent publicity and, apparently, of more discussion between Labor and HEW than any other affirmative action plan in higher education. We shall also refer specifically to the plans of certain other institutions that have granted permission for the use of their names in this connection.

Our attention will be focused primarily on provisions relating to the regular, or ladder, faculty. This, again, is because it is primarily in relation to regular faculty appointments that there is controversy over goals and timetables. Another reason is that regular faculty are invariably covered where goals and timetables have been spelled out for academic employees, whereas lecturers and nonfaculty academic employees are not always covered, even though federal regulations require them to be.

One of the criticisms made of the Berkeley plan by campus groups is that its goals and timetables do not cover lecturers and nonfaculty academic employees. Campus officials have explained that the main reason for this is the difficulty in developing adequate measures of availability pools for these groups and that more time is needed for this effort. It should, however, be pointed out that the Berkeley document did report significant progress in reviewing the status of lecturers and in reclassifying some of them to regular faculty positions.

Schools or Departments?

It will be recalled that the OCR *Guidelines* state that "in many institutions the appropriate unit for goals is the school or division rather than the department." It will also be recalled that OCR appears recently to have been interpreting Revised Order No. 4 as requiring the specification of goals by department.

Among the institutions that provided information on their goals and timetables, nearly all used analyses of underutilization by departments to some extent, but in the determination of goals, there was considerable variety in the breadth or narrowness of their applicability, as the following table indicates:

*Campus sectors for which goals
and timetables were developed*

	Universities	Other institutions
Departments only	15	8
Departments for women; schools or groups of departments for minorities	2	0

(continued on next page)

	Universities	Other institutions
Departments for women; entire university for minorities	2	0
Schools or groups of departments	15	4
Schools or groups of departments for women; entire university for minorities	1	0
Combination; entire campus and departments	3	0
Entire campus or unspecified	3	9
Total	41	21

One aspect of this table that immediately becomes apparent is that several universities decided that broader sectors or the entire university were appropriate in the case of minorities, partly because availability ratios for minorities were extremely small in many individual disciplines and partly because available data were so inadequate that a determination of underutilization by discipline would probably be unreliable.

The Berkeley campus developed goals by departments. The actual percentages of women and minorities among department members were calculated and compared with estimated availability ratios. In nearly all cases, the results indicated that only a small fraction of a minority person would be needed to bring the utilization ratio up to the availability ratio. Only where a full individual (or, let us say, 1.40 persons) was needed was a goal set for that department. Reflecting the larger percentages of women in availability pools, the number of departments needing one additional woman or more was much larger than the number needing members of minorities. The plan's statement of goals resulting from this analysis was as follows:

Goals have been set for 31 of 75 Departments and units in the case of women; 1 Department in the case of blacks; 2 Departments in the case of Asians; and no Departments in the cases of Chicanos and Native Americans (University of California, Berkeley, 1975).

To show how these results were obtained, we have included in Appendix A five sample tables from the Berkeley plan (Tables 15 to 19). They all relate to the social science departments within the College of Letters and Science—the social sciences seemed a good example to choose, because they occupy an intermediate position with respect to availability of both minority groups and women (they do not have as few doctorates in the pool as the physical sciences or as many, relatively, as the humanities in the case of women or education in the case of blacks).[4]

Although the results of the Berkeley procedure were much more favorable to the hiring of women than of minorities, the implications for the hiring of women in the 44 departments or units that were found not to need women were not necessarily appropriate or desirable. These departments cover a wide range, including some of the biological and physical science departments, most of the departments within the school of engineering, a few of the humanities departments, two social science departments (see Table 15), and a large number of professional schools. In some cases, no need was found because the departments had existing female faculty members, but in a number of additional cases, no need was found even though the departments had no women in the ladder faculty ranks, because the availability ratios were very low.

The undesirable implications of the Berkeley procedure can best be appreciated if we consider that universities throughout the nation are competing for persons in extremely limited pools of qualified persons, especially in the cases of minorities and, for women, in such fields as the natural sciences and engineering. In the face of such competition, a university's chances of hiring a woman or minority faculty member would very probably be enhanced if a search were being made in all fields within a given cluster of fields, even though pools of qualified women and minorities were very small in all or most of the individual fields. The result of the Berkeley procedure is to let departments off the hook, or at least to reduce greatly the prob-

[4]The pattern of variation for Asians is somewhat different.

ability that departments found to have no need will undertake vigorous search efforts for women or minority candidates.

When Berkeley's goals for minority groups are compared with those of the other universities, it is found that virtually all the other institutions have developed plans for adding substantially more minority-group members to their faculties. For example, a private university in the South indicated that over the past five-year period, 3.9 percent of the additions to its faculty had been members of minority groups. The university declared its intention of improving upon this performance, but commented that setting "percentage or numerical goals at this time without more information than is currently available seems unwise, even in general terms. Certainly a minimal goal for the next five years would be four to five percent of faculty additions."

The Berkeley procedure also led to an estimated need for minority faculty members that was very small even as compared with the estimated need in the other institutions that used a similar procedure. The reasons for the difference varied, but several illustrations will indicate some of the factors involved. Princeton's plan, for example, projected a need for 11 additional minority faculty members in nontenured positions from 1975-76 to 1980-81, in a much smaller total faculty than Berkeley's. Princeton used essentially the same procedure as Berkeley, but estimated additions of women and minority faculty members whenever the availability and utilization analysis yielded a ratio of 0.50 or more, as contrasted with 1.00 or more in the Berkeley plan (Princeton University, 1975, p. 45).[5]

The projected need for net additions to the faculty at the University of Michigan's Ann Arbor campus under the 1973 affirmative action plan of the university totaled 216 for the period from 1972-73 to 1975-76 (a considerably larger number of additions than was contemplated in the Berkeley plan for a period beginning with 1974-75). Of this total, 28 percent were

[5]OFCC regulations call for establishing a goal "whenever the increase in the number of persons necessary to completely eliminate underutilization is 0.5 persons or greater."

projected to be minority men, 19 percent to be minority women, and 25 percent to be majority women. Part of the explanation for the substantial number of positions projected to be filled by minorities was the fact that the projections anticipated reductions in the number of majority males in an appreciable number of departments (University of Michigan, 1973, p. 45ff). Presumably the reductions reflected anticipated retirements or resignations in most instances. Another factor explaining the difference between the Michigan and Berkeley results was the fact that the projections of the Michigan departments involved elements of judgment, rather than merely mathematical calculations. For instance, "some departments which have no deficiencies based on availability workforce analyses, but which anticipated a reasonable number of openings, have established goals in the hope of improving their profiles" (ibid., p. 35). The plan also pointed out that the projections of the numbers of minorities that could reasonably be hired were probably overly optimistic.

The University of Michigan plan, significantly, was one of the relatively few plans that specified goals for minorities by sex. The majority of plans simply estimated the total number of minority members to be added to the faculty in a given period. We believe that, as data become more readily available on pools of qualified minority women, specific goals should be established for them. These goals for minority women should be within the overall goals for women and, to avoid "counting them out," should apply to clusters of departments or an entire campus.

OCR officials have informed us that they did not characterize the Berkeley plan as their own view of the best possible plan, which other institutions should emulate.[6] Rather, the Berkeley negotiations were the first (in higher education), in their view, that sought to follow the provisions of Revised Order No. 4 in detail. The Berkeley plan is the first and only plan which does, in fact, conform to the full requirements of

[6]Interview of Clark Kerr and Margaret Gordon with Peter Holmes, director, and other OCR officials, May 29, 1975.

that order. It is also clear that the model plan that 29 universities were asked by OCR to adopt in June 1975 closely resembled the Berkeley plan.

Top Berkeley administrators at first objected to department by department analysis, preferring to cluster departments, but persuasion from the federal agencies involved, as well as internal campus pressures, led to the more detailed method of analysis (see Johnson, 1975).

Timetables

Most of the plans of universities that we have examined, with the exception of Berkeley's, set goals for additions of women and minority groups to their faculties for the next three, four, five, or six years. (We are referring here, once again, to those plans that have set specific goals and timetables). These goals and timetables are then revised and updated each year in annual progress reports. In some cases, goals for individual recent years have not been fully achieved, often because a combination of financial stringency and slowing enrollment growth has resulted in smaller additions to the faculty than had been estimated earlier. In other cases, goals have been exceeded. However, in the majority of cases, the data we have obtained are not sufficiently detailed to give much indication of progress in relation to goals.

On the matter of timetables, the Berkeley plan is once again unique. It is at once more sophisticated in its determination of timetables and more questionable in its implications, especially for minority groups. There is an estimate—but only for each department needing more women or minorities—of (1) the number of years required to bring the utilization ratio up to the availability ratio for nontenured, ladder faculty members (instructors and assistant professors, but predominantly the latter) and (2) the number of years required to bring the utilization ratio up to the availability ratio for all ladder faculty, including associate and full professors. The number of years required varies from zero to 16 in the case of nontenured faculty and from 23 to 30 years in the case of all ladder faculty. The differences are explained primarily by differences in anticipated changes in the number of faculty members in individual departments, differences in anticipated ratios of resignations and retirements, and the like. But the overall effect, especially in relation to minority groups, may well be to allow the great majority of departments to relax and cease making any effort to recruit minority-group members. To be sure, the plan is to be updated each year, and conceivably departments that currently have no need may be determined to have a need in some future year, but this is not particularly likely so long as the current narrow basis for determining underutilization is retained.[7]

The critical comments that we have made about the Berkeley plan need to be qualified by pointing out that the Berkeley campus, which in the late 1960s had extremely small proportions of women and minority groups among its faculty members, can point to significant additions of both in the last few years. Among new hires to ladder-rank faculty (instructors, assistant professors, associate professors, and full professors) women accounted for 22 percent in 1972, 23 percent in 1973, and 21 percent in 1974. The actual numbers of women hired were 16 in 1972, 16 in 1973, and 15 in 1974. The corresponding percentages for minorities were 15, 12, and 15 in the three years, respectively. The numbers of minorities hired were 11, 8, and 11, respectively. The rate of new hires is low because enrollment has been relatively stable for a number of years, and because 81 percent of the faculty members now have tenure.[8] In spite of the recent hiring of women, they represented

---

[7]Another respect in which the Berkeley plan is unique is in its use of unpublished data from a faculty survey conducted by the American Council on Education in 1972-73, rather than data on doctoral degrees used by other universities, to determine availability pools for minorities. On the basis of the evidence presented in Section 2 that minorities are increasing their relative representation among recipients of doctor's degrees and that their proportions among doctoral recipients probably now exceed their proportions among faculty members in 1972-73, this method of determining minority-group availability pools is another factor explaining the small "need" for minority-group faculty members that resulted. However, this was a minor factor in explaining the Berkeley results, because the data did not actually differ greatly from the data used by other institutions.

[8]This percentage relates to faculty members in assistant, associate, and full professor ranks.

only 6.5 percent of ladder-rank faculty in April 1974, far below
the overall average for Research Universities I. The proportion
of women among Berkeley ladder-rank faculty members had
declined over the years from 8.3 percent in 1928-29 to 3.6 percent in 1968-69, so that even extensive hiring of women is not
likely to bring their percentage of faculty members up to the
average for universities, or even for Research Universities I, for
many years.

The proportion of minorities (5.5 percent) among Berkeley faculty members, on the other hand, is close to the average
for all institutions of higher education, but slightly more than
one-half of the minority faculty members are of Asian ancestry.

There is another issue that needs to be mentioned in connection with timetables. It will be recalled that the OCR *Guidelines* of October 1972 specified that "goals should be set so as
to overcome deficiencies in the utilization of minorities and
women within a reasonable time. In many cases this can be
accomplished within 5 years; in others more time or less time
will be required."

In practice, the Berkeley plan is the only one, among those
that we have examined, that sets timetables in relation to the
overcoming of deficiencies in utilization, and the timetables,
particularly for "all faculty," turn out to be very long. All the
other plans specify the numbers of women and minorities to be
added within the next three-year or five-year period (or in some
cases a slightly different number of years), or speak of the percentages of new hires that are to consist of women or minorities. The numbers to be added are related to the number of
anticipated vacancies within that specified period, not to the
number needed to overcome any deficiencies completely. In
fact, particularly in those fields in which women and minorities
are rarely represented, there is no possibility whatever of overcoming deficiencies in utilization among total faculty members
in five years, ten years, or, in some extreme cases, a number of
decades. As we have seen, the growth of faculties has slowed
down in recent years and the number of faculty members is
likely to become stationary or to decline slightly in most fields
in most institutions of higher education during the 1980s.

We believe that timetables should not be set for longer than five to ten years ahead. Predictions of vacancies for such periods are likely to be considerably more reliable than for the lengthy periods involved in the Berkeley plan, especially on a department by department basis. Even in a period of slow or no growth for higher education as a whole, there may be unanticipated increases in the demand for faculty members in newly developing fields and unanticipated declines in other fields, as student choices of majors shift.[9]

Furthermore, it should be understood by the federal agencies involved that goals and timetables can only reasonably project the additions of women and minorities to faculties during the period included in the timetable. In some fields and in a substantial proportion of institutions, these additions cannot be expected to bring the total utilization ratios up to the ratios indicated by the pools of qualified persons (that is, to "parity") in a timespan of five to ten years.

Initial Appointments Versus Promotions

Another issue relating to the use of goals and timetables concerns how the concept of pools of qualified persons is interpreted in promotions, as compared with initial appointments. Here again, the Berkeley plan is unique and reflects OCR's interpretation of how Order No. 4 should be applied in relation to promotions. The Berkeley plan, as we noted in Section 3, states that "it is the University's objective that women and minorities will be promoted to the Associate Professor and Full Professor ranks in proportion to those eligible for promotion in the Assistant Professor and Associate Professor ranks respectively in each department." The provision is qualified in a subsequent paragraph which states that "among the persons eligible for promotion, the basis for any promotion decision will, of course, be the individual qualifications of the candidate."

Most of the other affirmative action plans that we have examined refer to the number of women and minorities to be

[9]For a discussion of student sensitivity to changes in the job market in their choices of fields, see Carnegie Commission (1973b).

added to the faculty in a coming three-year or five-year period. They rarely specify their goals by rank or refer to availability pools in relation to promotions. Restricting the availability pool to those who happen to be in the next lower rank could work to the disadvantage of women and minorities, especially in departments from which they are entirely absent or represented in extremely small proportions in the relevant rank. A search that will include outside candidates seems consistent with principles of nondiscrimination in these situations. On the other hand, when women and/or minorities are represented in a relevant rank in a department in more significant proportions, there is no assurance that relative qualifications for promotion will match the sexual and racial composition of those in the rank from which promotion is to occur.

We believe that principles of nondiscrimination should be strictly applied in promotions, as in initial appointments; that an outside search for candidates should be undertaken under some circumstances; and that there should be adequate peer and administrative review of all promotions (including, as a step in the process, review by a faculty committee that includes a majority of members from outside the department involved). In addition, the appropriate campus affirmative action committee should undertake analyses of promotion experience on the campus periodically (especially with reference to departments in which there are few or no women or minorities in the higher ranks).

Recommendation 11: *Goals and timetables should be included in affirmative action plans of colleges and universities. Analyses of current employment patterns of pools of qualified persons should be undertaken for each department, but decisions as to whether goals should be formulated for individual departments, or, as would more usually be appropriate, for groups of related departments or schools, or for the entire campus, should be made only after careful study of the probable overall results for all units and for the campus as a whole. Whatever the decision, the performance of each department in contributing to the achievement of goals and timetables should be subject to periodic review by the campus administration.*

Goals and timetables, as well as strictly nondiscriminatory policies, should relate to appointments to instructor and assistant professor positions. For promotions to tenured ranks, strictly nondiscriminatory policies should be followed, and the experience with promotions in each department should be periodically reviewed to ensure that such policies have been followed. A search for outside candidates for tenured appointments will be appropriate in many situations.

Recommendation 12: *Timetables should be set for periods not exceeding five to ten years. The institution should make a good faith effort to achieve its goals for additions of women and minorities to the faculty during that period.*

As we have seen, it has become increasingly clear that a number of the requirements of Revised Order No. 4 are exceedingly inappropriate in relation to higher education. Because Revised Order No. 4 applies to all covered federal contractors in a large number of industries, it cannot be revised merely to accommodate the needs of higher education, but there is no reason why a special supplement or a set of special interpretations cannot be developed to apply to affirmative action in higher education.

Recommendation 13: *The Department of Labor—in consultation with the Department of Health, Education, and Welfare—should develop a special supplement, or set of interpretations, to Revised Order No. 4 that will be especially appropriate for higher education.*

This document should embody the following principles: (1) goals and timetables, as well as strictly nondiscriminatory policies, should relate to entry-level academic appointments (instructor and assistant professor in the case of faculty appointments) and should be based on data relating to degrees awarded in the most recent five-year period; (2) institutions should be free to formulate goals and timetables for groups of departments, or schools and colleges or for the campus as a whole, rather than for individual departments, when they deem it appropriate; (3) proportions of women and minorities among faculty members should not be regarded as adequate if unduly concentrated in certain schools or departments; (4) timetables should not exceed five to ten years, and institutions should be expected to make a good faith effort to achieve projected additions of women and minorities in that period—not necessarily to achieve "parity"; (5) appointments and promotions to tenured positions should be made on the basis of strictly nondiscriminatory procedures, and institutions should be expected to provide evidence that experience with such appointments and promotions in each department is periodically reviewed by the administration to ensure that nondiscriminatory procedures have been followed; (6) the existing eight requirements relating to local labor market conditions in § 60-2.11 should be interpreted as relevant only to nonacademic employment and not to most academic positions; and (7) any provision that women or minority candidates should not be required to have higher qualifications than those of the "least qualified incumbent" should be declared inapplicable to academic employment.

Regulations and guidelines of the Department of Health, Education, and Welfare relating to enforcement of the executive order should be revised to reflect the provisions of the special supplement or set of interpretations to Revised Order No. 4.

Data requirements should be revised to reflect the modified provisions. Institutions should be expected to compile annually and keep available detailed data—on a departmental basis for each racial and selected ethnic group and for each job classification—on utilization, pools of qualified persons (based on data supplied by OCR), recruitment, selection, promotions, salaries and separations. Separate data should not be required on placement/assignment, tenure, transfer (reassignment), fringe benefits, or training, because (1) they would overlap with other required data or (2) are not particularly relevant to academic employment or (3) in the case of fringe benefits, are usually uniform for large groups of employees and do not need to be provided on a detailed departmental basis.[10]

[10]In this paragraph, we are referring to the data requirements outlined in Table 14, Appendix A.

Recommendation 14: *The special supplement to Revised Order No. 4 and accompanying changes in HEW regulations should give explicit recognition to the need for increasing the supply of qualified women and minorities by requiring institutions involved in doctoral and professional education to include a supply plan, along the lines of our Recommendation 1. The regulations should also give explicit recognition to an institution's progress from year to year in adding women and minorities to faculties.*

Recommendation 15: *When an institution can demonstrate that its proportions of women and minorities among faculty members and other academic employees approximate pools of qualified persons and are well distributed throughout the institution, it should be exempted from requirements calling for continuous reassessment of goals and timetables and from detailed reporting requirements relating to academic employment.[11] It should, however, be required to continue to pursue nondiscriminatory policies and to maintain relevant records that will be available on request. Any evidence of a significant diminution in proportions of women and minorities would call for a new compliance review.*

An appropriate proportion is likely to be achieved sooner for majority women than for minorities, and thus the relaxation of requirements might relate first to majority women.

[11]This does not mean that it should be exempt from reporting on form EEO-6, but that it should be exempt from continuously reporting data on applicants, selection, etc., as called for in Table 14.

6

Deficiencies in the Administration of Federal Programs

Observers of federal affirmative action tend to agree on the inadequacy of the staff of OCR, and also of EEOC and of OFCC, in relation to higher education. The most frequently expressed criticisms concern preparation of the OCR staff to deal with the intricate problems and difficulties of interpretation of nondiscrimination and affirmative action in faculty employment. They also relate to the seriously inadequate size of the staff when viewed against the large number of colleges and universities affected by the provisions.

Inadequacy of Staff

According to Vetter (1974), the "government employees who work in the program are poorly trained and seem to have little knowledge or understanding of higher education."[1] He also notes that only a very small proportion of these employees have been connected with institutions of higher education in faculty,

[1] Vetter's paper provided background information for the policy statement recently approved by the Administrative Conference of the United States, for which it was prepared (see Appendix B). However, Vetter's paper represents only his own views and not the official views of the Administrative Conference.

consultative, or administrative positions, and that there have been many staff vacancies and minimal special training for beginning employees.[2]

Other observers also commented on the inadequacy of the staff in relation to the magnitude and difficulty of the problems of enforcement. However, the size of the regional staff has been enlarged considerably in the last few years. According to the U.S. Commission on Civil Rights (1975a, p. 210), in July 1974 there were 142 authorized positions, of which 123 were filled, in the regional offices. The authorized levels varied from a high of 18 positions in the New York, San Francisco, and Chicago offices, to a low of 9 positions in the Seattle office.

Another criticism that has been made frequently is that policies followed by regional representatives have varied from region to region, and that some have been much more stringent in the standards applied before affirmative action plans have been approved than have others.

In addition, some of the early demands on universities were crude and inappropriate. For example, one of nine reported demands made of the University of Michigan in 1970 was that it must "achieve a ratio of female employment in academic positions at least equivalent to availability as determined by the number of qualified female applicants" (Bazell, 1970). President Robben W. Fleming protested this requirement as "unworkable because it ignores the quality of applicants and lends itself to artificially increasing the number of women who apply." Early in 1971, it was reported that the university and HEW had reached agreement and that HEW had conceded, among other things, that, in addition to the percentage of applications, other factors should be considered ("U. of Michigan, HEW Agree," 1971). This incident occurred, of course, well before the publication of the October 1972 *Guidelines*.

Although plans have been underway to increase the rela-

---

[2]The official civil service job description for professional staff members of OFCC, and apparently also for staff members of other agencies concerned with civil rights questions, calls for past experience in community service. Persons with experience in higher education administration are not likely to meet this requirement.

tive authority of the regional offices, they have not been fully implemented. While decentralization of authority would probably help to speed up the processing of affirmative action plans and complaints, the problem of the quality of staff in the regional offices remains, as well as the need for reasonable uniformity in interpretations and actions.

Slightly more than one-half of the responses to our survey of affirmative action policies included comments relating to federal personnel with whom the institutions had had contact. Only about 30 percent of the comments from universities and a much smaller percentage of those from other institutions were favorable. Samples of comments, both favorable and critical, are the following:

> *Private research university—Northeast.* Our relationships with the Region II office of HEW (New York) have been close and friendly. Though we have not always thought that the staff of the regional office understood or approved of _____'s mission, they have almost always appeared to be reasonable and thoughtful.

> *Public research university—Middle West.* The University's relationship with various federal agencies responsible for the administration of laws and Executive Orders governing affirmative action/equal opportunity matters has been excellent. This includes experiences with federal agencies during the period of time in which this University was subject to pre-award requirements in the area of campus construction, and the resulting implications for minority manpower utilization.

> *Private research university—South.* We have also found that federal representatives vary markedly in their competence and ability to conduct a proper and thorough investigation. Few if any of them possess an understanding of the University as an institution nor are they sensitive to the crucial distinctions between

industrial and educational organizations. Each new agent must be indoctrinated before he or she is able to perceive the nature of the promotion system. . . . So serious has been this problem that we are considering an invitation to DHEW, and EEOC, and the Labor Department to co-sponsor a training seminar on University operations for their agents responsible for higher education. However the standardized procedures of the EEOC are more acceptable than the ad hoc nature of DHEW's investigations. In the past, DHEW has threatened us with termination of funds before we received a copy of the complaint being investigated. However, DHEW allows a greater degree of flexibility in approach to the resolution of complaints.

Public research university—Middle West. Much depends on the agency involved and the experience of the agency specialist. For the most part, regional agencies cannot make quick decisions, must clear with Washington on very minor things. (Long time frame on conciliation or investigation of cases). Agents poorly trained, conflicting opinions on important matters between EEOC and HEW.

Private research university—West. Two major problems in dealing with federal agencies have been a lack of understanding of educational institutions and the differing and highly personalized interpretations of the laws and regulations by individual compliance officers. . . .

Another demand was that we replace our Asian faculty in the School of Engineering with blacks. When the compliance officer was asked how we were to find qualified black engineers, he said to "advertise in the soul stations."

Public research university—West. While the personnel from the Regional Office have been conciliatory and willing to assist us in developing our affirmative action program, it has been difficult to explain to them the special character of the personnel practices in our kinds of universities. It has been difficult for them to understand the highly specialized character of a university faculty, that such a faculty is not interchangeable. . . .

The preoccupation of the Office for Civil Rights that each and every unit responsible for hiring should meet affirmative goals clearly has created in the minds of faculty the notion of quotas and reverse discrimination as well as the potential lowering of standards.

Interestingly, we could discern no clear regional pattern in the location of institutions with favorable or unfavorable reactions, so reactions were perhaps more a matter of the particular regional representatives with whom institutions had contact.

Recommendation 16: *The Council recommends that the Department of Health, Education, and Welfare give special emphasis to the development within OCR of an adequate and highly qualified staff that is knowledgeable about the special characteristics of academic employment. This staff should be largely centered in the Washington office, and negotiations relating to academic employment in institutions of higher education that hire in a national market should be conducted by officials of the Washington office, rather than by regional officials. A larger staff will be needed in the transitional period than will be required after institutions have made substantial progress in implementing affirmative action.*

Delays and Backlogs of Cases

One persistent criticism of OCR's administration of affirmative action in higher education relates to the long delays in the processing of compliance reviews and complaints, the tiny proportion of cases in which affirmative action plans have received final approval, and the resulting involvement of institutions in negotiations over periods of several years.

According to the U.S. Commission on Civil Rights (1975a, p. 277), OCR ignored for years the requirement that preaward reviews be conducted of all contractors whose contracts would amount to $1 million or more. "During fiscal year 1973, no such reviews were conducted." In fact, charges the commission, OCR's reviews have been exclusively in response to complaints.

Data relating to the processing of affirmative action plans are somewhat conflicting, but the general pattern is consistently one in which very few affirmative action plans have received final approval. A compilation prepared by OCR in December 1973 showed that "of a total of 201 affirmative action plans submitted to the agency's 10 regional offices, 18 had been officially accepted, and 14 rejected, leaving 169 still to be acted on" (Fields, 1974a, p. 8). The very small proportion of acceptances is confirmed by the results of our survey.

OCR's style of enforcement has involved protracted negotiations with institutions of higher education, characterized by extreme reluctance to impose any penalty beyond delays in the awarding of contracts or the allocation of funds. The heart of the difficulty may be the severity of the penalties of actually withholding funds or, in more extreme cases, declaring an institution ineligible for future contracts.

According to the U.S. Commission on Civil Rights (1975a, p. 278), OCR's policy has been to refrain from declaring a prospective contractor in noncompliance unless there is extensive supporting evidence in the context of a hearing. In practice, no formal hearing has ever been held, and, until very recently, a show-cause order had been issued in only one case (the University of Washington).[3] A number of additional show-cause orders were issued in the late spring of 1975, as we noted in Section 5.

The report of the U.S. Commission on Civil Rights (1975a, pp. 281-305) includes extensive documentation of the protracted negotiations of OCR with four campuses—the University of California at Berkeley, the University of Washington, the University of Michigan, and Harvard University.

[3]Technically, a show-cause order was issued in the Berkeley case, but on the same day (February 18, 1975) its affirmative action plan was approved by OCR.

According to the commission's report (p. 281), OCR files indicate that the first compliance review of the Berkeley campus took place on June 11, 1970, shortly after the filing of a sex discrimination complaint by the Women's Equity Action League. Actually, it does not appear that a thorough review was initiated until June 1971. The Civil Rights Commission's report carries the story through March 7, 1974, when a conciliation agreement was reached between the campus and OCR, although the agency continued to regard the campus affirmative action plan as unacceptable, and the conciliation agreement was based on a commitment by the campus to develop an acceptable plan by September 30, 1974. Subsequent developments involved serious criticism by OCR of a number of inadequacies in the plan submitted in September 1974. The campus developed revisions in the following months, and on February 18, 1975, Peter Holmes, director of OCR, announced acceptance of the revised plan, declaring Berkeley's plan "one of the best affirmative action plans negotiated with a major institution in the country" (Kadonaga, 1975b, p. 1). On April 10, the decision of the Secretary of Labor not to "assume jurisdiction" over the Berkeley plan was announced.

The case histories of the other three campuses summarized by the Commission on Civil Rights are similar with respect to the complexity and duration of negotiations. Although OCR can be criticized for allowing these important cases to drag on so long, the summaries also show that the campuses, for whatever reasons, were very slow in developing affirmative action plans that came anywhere near approaching compliance with the *Guidelines*.

The record of the 10 regions is uneven. Vetter (1974) cites data on affirmative action plans processed from November 16, 1971, to December 31, 1972, showing that the percentage of cases receiving interim or final approval ranged from a high of 44 percent in the Dallas region to 3 percent in the New York area and zero in the Atlanta, Chicago, and Kansas City regions.

OCR's record in handling individual and class complaints has also been characterized by delays, but they do not seem as extreme as those associated with compliance reviews. According to the Commission on Civil Rights (1975a, p. 308), OCR received 358 complaints under the executive order in fiscal year 1973. Of these, 20 were referred to EEOC, 201 were investigated, and 179 were resolved. A total of 137 were not investigated. At the close of the fiscal year, therefore, 159 cases were not resolved. These data may not present the entire picture, however, because there have been numerous complaints about lengthy delays in acknowledging complaints. Unacknowledged complaints are probably not reflected in the agency's records.

In November 1974, several women's rights organizations and the National Education Association filed suit in a federal district court in Washington, D.C., to compel HEW and the Department of Labor to enforce federal antidiscrimination laws in relation to higher education. Spokeswomen·for the plaintiffs explained that "even though some 350 complaints invoking the Executive Orders and 200 Title IX complaints have been filed with HEW, the government has in 'repeated and continuing derogation' of its duty done little about proven and alleged violations." The complaint also charged that "the government has neglected to encourage, review or criticize affirmative action plans in educational institutions under the Executive Orders," and that it has never referred a case to the Justice Department for legal action ("Women Sue HEW. . . . ," 1974, p. 3).

In response to the item in our mailed questionnaire to colleges and universities asking for "additional comments relating to your negotiations with federal agencies," the most frequently expressed criticism was that federal agencies are excessively slow in responding to institutions submitting affirmative action programs or other required documents. About 30 percent of the universities and several smaller institutions expressed this type of complaint. Examples of their comments are the following:

> *Private research university—Northeast.* [Our] experience of having to wait over a year for a response from HEW does not seem to be unique. Operating with an affirmative action plan that has not been deemed adequate by the government retards the progress and implementation of workable affirmative action policies.

Public doctoral-granting institution—South. As of this date, we have received no official response to our plan from HEW other than a confirmation that the plan has been received. We are now well into the second year of implementation as we await word from the Office for Civil Rights.

Private research university—Middle West. The University filed a basic plan September 1971. In December of 1971 a Progress Report was submitted. A Progress Report was submitted in June of 1972. In January of 1973 an Amendment to the plan was filed. In June of 1974 an updated plan was filed with new goals. . . . Our plan has not been accepted, rejected, or conditionally accepted.

Liberal arts college—Northeast. . . . the College was required to file an affirmative action plan with respect to both administrative and staff employees. That plan was filed (date July 1973) and has yet to be acknowledged, much less accepted, by OCR.

Private doctoral-granting institution—Middle West. Our affirmative action plan was submitted in duplicate to the Regional Office. . . . The Regional Office forwarded one copy to the Washington Office with the recommendation that it be approved. The Washington Office requested some modifications. Deadline, 30 days. It was revised as requested and resubmitted. That was July, 1971. To date we have had no word either as to acceptance or rejection of the revision.

These problems of delays and inadequate enforcement procedures are not unique to higher education. A report prepared by the General Accounting Office and released by the Comptroller General of the United States (1975) charged that some compliance agencies were reluctant to initiate enforcement actions and that their conciliation negotiations with contractors exceeded Department of Labor time limits. The report also charged that most compliance agencies were not reviewing an adequate proportion of the contractors for which they were responsible. The detailed discussion in the report related chiefly to the Department of Defense and the General Services Administration. In addition, the report indicated that the Comptroller had advised the Department of Labor that Revised Order No. 4 "also seems to be in violation of the basic principles of Federal procurement law . . . in that a contractor can be defaulted . . . for its failure to submit an 'acceptable' affirmative plan despite the fact that these regulations do not seem to contain any *definite* minimum standards and criteria apprising the prospective bidders of the basis upon which their compliance with the EEO [equal employment opportunity] requirements will be judged" (ibid., p. 3).

Too Many Cooks?

One of the most persistent and widespread complaints of campus administrations is that there are too many federal agencies involved in the enforcement of antidiscrimination and that a particular campus may be involved simultaneously with several federal or state agencies, sometimes relating to the same issues or the same complaints. This can require a heavy involvement of personnel and very substantial expense for the college or university in defending its case in all of the areas involved. The problem is not, of course, confined to higher education.

Some supporters of affirmative action policies strongly oppose proposals that would limit the number of federal agencies in which complaints could be filed. They argue that, if a woman or member of a minority group is met with indifference by representatives of one agency, the grievant has the option of turning to some other agency. In practice, it is highly questionable whether so many options are actually advantageous. Given the serious backlog of cases, particularly at EEOC, redress in actuality is not likely to be available for as long as several years. A reasonable argument can be advanced that centralizing responsibility for the processing of complaints of discrimination in a single federal agency, for example, EEOC, and providing that agency with adequate staff to handle the complaints, would actually greatly speed up the handling of complaints, as well as eliminate wasteful costs associated with overlapping jurisdictions. We have been informed by legal experts that in very few other areas of federal law or policy does a similar right to bring a complaint in multiple jurisdictions exist.

The option of filing a complaint with a state fair employment practice commission would continue regardless of any change in federal policies, as would some of the options of going directly to court.

The power of the Secretary of Labor to review certain types of important decisions relating to colleges and universities under the executive order creates another complication, recently exemplified in the Berkeley case. Once OCR approved Berkeley's plan on February 18, 1975, the OFCC in the Department of Labor had 45 days to decide whether or not to intervene. Two days later, Phillip Davis, director of OFCC, was quoted as having "heard about HEW's approving the plan only after HEW and the University announced the decision at a press conference." "We were caught by complete surprise," Davis added (Kadonaga, 1975a, p. 1).

The Secretary of Labor, however, decided on April 10, 1975, not to assume jurisdiction over the Berkeley plan. Yet the Berkeley campus did face for a time, as others may later, the prospect of a second set of separate negotiations and a second set of separate decisions about many major and minor items.

Another type of problem involving alleged conflict of jurisdiction is exemplified by a court case brought by the University of Maryland in June 1974. The university filed suit against OCR, charging that its investigators improperly interfered in a federal court suit involving an allegation of sex discrimination. The suit asked for an injunction ordering the civil rights office not to pursue its own investigation of the faculty member's complaint until her court case was decided. The university also charged that OCR demanded that it settle the case, despite the fact that "OCR has made no substantive responses to 'voluminous statistical data and other information' on its employment practices that the university already has submitted to the agency" (Fields, 1974b, p. 1).

Although not expressed as frequently as criticism about delays, a complaint that too many federal agencies were involved or a suggestion that the number of agencies be reduced characterized the responses of one-fifth of the universities and of several smaller institutions. Still others urged greater consistency among the policies and procedures of federal agencies and/or a single set of guidelines. Among some of the comments along these lines were the following:

> *Private research university—South.* .... the complexity of compliance activities by the various enforcement agencies has resulted in duplication of effort and lengthy delays in the resolution of complaints. In recent years, as many as three different federal agencies have visited our campus to investigate a single complaint. Cooperation with these agencies requires voluminous documentation and substantial investments of time.

> *Private doctoral-granting institution—South.* Since the May, 1973 HEW compliance review, we have undergone another review by the Wage and Hour Division of the Labor Department covering much of the same material.

> *Public doctoral-granting institution—Southwest.* The multiplicity of federal agencies involved leads to frequently duplicating and overlapping requirements which sometimes are in direct conflict and at other times lead to excessive demands being placed upon the university.

> *Private comprehensive university—Middle West.* Currently several federal agencies have regulatory authority for affirmative action, i.e., IRS, the Department

of Labor, HEW. Unless some way is found to reconcile this diverse approach we will stay wedded to confusion.

Recommendation 17: *The Department of Labor should continue to delegate responsibility for enforcement of affirmative action requirements in higher education to the Department of Health, Education, and Welfare. The Department of Labor's involvement should be confined to (1) final approval of regulations and guidelines developed by HEW within the general framework of Department of Labor regulations, (2) periodic review by the Department of Labor of HEW's policies and performance in relation to enforcement vis-à-vis higher education, and (3) occasional modification of the Department of Labor's general policies and requirements on the basis of such reviews or other indications of needs for changes. The Secretary of Health, Education, and Welfare should have final authority to approve affirmative action plans and to impose sanctions on institutions.*[4]

Recommendation 18: *All the federal agencies involved in nondiscrimination and affirmative action matters in higher education should cooperate in developing coordinated guidelines. Along with the development of these coordinated guidelines, requirements for the provision of data should be unified and simplified. Wherever possible, federal agencies should develop procedures for sharing data instead of requiring separate reporting to each agency.*

Role of EEOC

From time to time, proposals have been made in Congress and elsewhere that enforcement of federal nondiscrimination policies, or at least the handling of complaints, should be concentrated in the Equal Employment Opportunity Commission.

---

[4]In practice, this is essentially the relationship that has prevailed, but legally the Secretary of HEW does not have final authority for certain important decisions.

Any proposal to concentrate the handling of complaints in the EEOC is inevitably controversial in the light of the enormous backlog of cases that has developed. In June 1975, it was reported that the backlog of unprocessed complaints filed with EEOC totaled 90,000 ("An Industry Man Takes Over . . . ," 1975). The number of complaints filed with EEOC increased enormously after the agency was given the power to bring cases against private employers to court under the 1972 legislation. The enforcement staff has been greatly increased since then, and EEOC is reported to have been involved in 12,000 conciliation proceedings and 300 court cases in fiscal year 1975, but no great inroads are being made on the backlog.

Proposals have been made that EEOC's backlog of cases could be brought under control if the agency were given the power to issue cease and desist orders.[5] Experts believe that many complaints could be settled promptly if the agency had that power, because many employers would abide by the commission's orders and not proceed into court. A bill introduced by Congressman Augustus Hawkins and others in 1971, which passed the House but not the Senate, gave the commission such power.[6] Under its provisions, if unable to secure an acceptable conciliation agreement, the commission shall "issue and cause to be served upon the respondent a complaint stating the facts . . . together with a notice of hearing . . . not less than five days after the serving of such complaint." The bill goes on to provide:

> If the Commission finds that the respondent has engaged in an unlawful employment practice, the Commission shall state its findings of fact and shall issue and cause to be served on the respondent and the person or persons aggrieved . . . an order requiring the respondent to cease and desist from such unlawful employment practice and take such affirmative action, including reinstatement or hiring of employ-

[5] See, for example, Powell (1975, p. 20).
[6] H.R. 1746, January 22, 1971.

ees, with or without back pay . . . as will effectuate
the policies of this title. . . . Such order may further
require such respondent to make reports from time to
time showing the extent to which he has complied
with the order.

The bill also provided (1) that the proceeding could at any
time be ended by agreement between the commission and the
parties for the elimination of the alleged unlawful employment
practice, and (2) that the commission could petition the U.S.
court of appeals within the relevant circuit for the enforcement
of its order, in which case the court would take jurisdiction, but
the findings of the commission with respect to questions of fact
(if supported by substantial evidence) would be conclusive. In
the case of a commission cease and desist order that had not
been taken into court, either party would have the right to seek
review in a court of appeal. On the other hand, where the commission had petitioned the relevant circuit court for an enforcement order, the findings of the court would be final, except
that there would be a right of appeal to the U.S. Supreme
Court.

Apart from the problem of a backlog of cases, there have
been allegations from time to time that administration of EEOC
was ineffective. This situation may well improve under the new
chairman, Lowell W. Perry, who took office in June 1975.

An additional argument in favor of making EEOC the
agency chiefly responsible for processing complaints of discrimination in employment in higher education is that provisions of
state fair employment practice acts tend to be very similar to
Title VII (though there are variations from state to state in
enforcement powers), and the EEOC maintains close relationships with state and local fair employment practice agencies in
enforcement procedures.

Recommendation 19: *The Council recommends the concentration of authority for processing complaints relating to discrimination in employment in higher education with the Equal Employment Opportunity Commission, along with such additions*

to the commission's staff as may be necessary to process such complaints. OCR should continue to refer all individual complaints to EEOC and should also refer class complaints to EEOC except in special circumstances in which they are closely associated with compliance investigations.

It is also recommended that Title VII of the Civil Rights Act of 1964 be amended to authorize the EEOC to issue cease and desist orders, along the lines of the provisions of H.R. 1746 (1971).

The Equal Employment Opportunity Coordinating Council (EEOCC) should play a much more decisive role than it now does in coordinating federal agency involvement in cases relating to higher education. Procedures should be developed for ensuring that a complaint would not be processed by two or more agencies simultaneously but would be referred to a single agency.

The Secretary of HEW should be invited to attend EEOCC meetings whenever problems under his jurisdiction are discussed.[7]

In addition, we believe that Title IX of the Education Amendments should be amended to make it clear that its provisions do not apply to employment, either in elementary and secondary education or in higher education. The legislative history of Title IX indicates clearly that its primary purpose was to eliminate discrimination on the basis of sex in policies relating to students. Now that employment in educational institutions is

[7]Section 715 of Title VII provides that the council should be composed of the Secretary of Labor, the chairman of the Equal Employment Opportunity Commission, the Attorney General, the chairman of the United States Civil Service Commission, and the chairman of the United States Commission on Civil Rights.

Recommendation 19 relates only to employment in higher education. It does not relate to matters involving students.

For recommendations going considerably beyond Recommendation 19, and calling for a new and comprehensive agency to protect the job rights of women and minorities, see U.S. Commission on Civil Rights (1975b). Although some of the recommendations in that report are consistent with ours, others are not.

covered by Title VII of the Civil Rights Act, there is no need for additional legislation banning discrimination in employment. The concentration of complaints of discrimination in employment with the EEOC would be strengthened by removing applicability to employment from Title IX.

Recommendation 20: *Title IX of the Education Amendments of 1972 should be amended to make it clear that the title does not make specific provision for nondiscrimination in employment, but respects the employment provisions of Title VII of the Civil Rights Act and of the executive order.*

Equal Pay Issues

The problem of overlapping jurisdictions is particularly complex in relation to equal pay issues. As we have seen, the Equal Pay Act of 1963 relates only to sex discrimination in pay, but provisions of several other federal laws (especially Title VII and Title IX), as well as the executive order prohibit discrimination in pay and in conditions of employment, on the basis of sex, race, or both. Most of the state fair employment practice acts have provisions banning discrimination in compensation on the basis of sex, race, religion, or national origin, and many of the states also have equal pay acts that prohibit sexual discrimination in pay.

Complaints of employment discrimination brought before EEOC frequently involve allegations of unequal pay, along with other types of discrimination, and complaints on unequal pay are often filed both with the Wage and Hour Administration and the EEOC, where sex-based discrimination is involved. Complaints of discrimination in pay may also be filed with OCR.

Our recommendation for concentrating the processing of complaints relating to employment discrimination with EEOC would help to reduce overlapping responsibilities, as would amendment of Title IX to eliminate any application to employment. There would still be the problem of overlapping jurisdiction between the Wage and Hour Administration and EEOC on cases of sex discrimination in compensation not amenable to a clearcut solution. Because EEOC cases often combine charges of discrimination in compensation with other complaints, and because, under the Equal Pay Act, the Wage and Hour Administration of the Department of Labor can handle only sexual discrimination and not racial discrimination in pay, it is not appropriate to propose that EEOC refer all complaints of salary discrimination to the Wage and Hour Administration. On the other hand, because the Wage and Hour Administration and other agencies within the Department of Labor are concerned with wage analysis, there is a case for referring any special analyses of salary structures that are required in the processing of EEOC cases to the Wage and Hour Administration, as is now done to a certain extent.

Similar statements can be made about the relationship between OCR and the Wage and Hour Administration in connection with salary analyses needed under the executive order.

Another problem is that academic salary structures are not comparable with the white-collar and blue-collar wage schedules that are usually involved in cases handled by the Wage and Hour Administration. Similarly, compensation for professional and managerial workers in other sectors of the economy involves analytical problems different from those involved in wage analyses relating to workers requiring less specialized educational qualifications. There have been suggestions (for example, Lester, forthcoming) to the effect that the Wage and Hour Administration develop a special set of guidelines for professional and administrative workers –first brought under the jurisdiction of the Equal Pay Act in 1972–but we are not certain that this can be satisfactorily accomplished.

The enlarged role for the Equal Employment Opportunity Coordinating Council that we have recommended should lead to closer cooperation among the agencies most directly involved with salary discrimination. In general, we believe that both EEOC and OCR should refer any extensive salary analyses that are required in connection with EEOC cases or with compliance reviews of OCR under the executive order to the Wage and Hour Administration. There are indications, however, that that division needs to add personnel with specialized knowledge of academic salary relationships and professional and administrative salary structures in other sectors of employment.

Recommendation 21: *Because complaints filed with EEOC charging salary discrimination usually also involve allegations of other types of employment discrimination that cannot clearly be separated from salary discrimination, EEOC should have jurisdiction over such complaints, but should refer any special salary analyses that need to be conducted to the Wage and Hour Administration.*

The Office for Civil Rights should refer salary analyses conducted in connection with affirmative action compliance procedures to the Wage and Hour Administration of the Department of Labor. The staff of WHA should be increased to include persons familiar with academic salary relationships and with salary relationships in professional and managerial employment generally.[8]

Institutional Expenditures for Affirmative Action

Our affirmative action survey did not ask specific questions about expenditures for affirmative action programs, partly because we doubted that those expenditures could be unambiguously identified. For example, are travel expenses of women and minority candidates brought to an institution for interview to be included, but not travel expenses of majority males? The costs of detailed data collection are among the more important affirmative action expenses, and yet it can be argued that many institutions of higher education had inadequate record-keeping practices, and that the more detailed data developed under affirmative action programs can contribute to more effective management. Maintaining an affirmative action staff is another of the major expenses associated with affirmative action programs, especially in large institutions, and in this connection the costs are relatively clearcut.

The complaints of many of our respondents relating to the

---

[8]As in Recommendation 16, the need for additional staff may be temporary.

costs of affirmative action tended to concern primarily the expenses for detailed data collection and reporting to numerous government agencies. We have already recommended that the requirements for data collection be simplified and coordinated and that federal agencies share data to the greatest extent possible.

There remain questions of how universities and colleges are meeting the overall costs associated with affirmative action. Information that we have obtained from the statewide University of California system is illuminating in this respect, although we have no way of knowing how representative it may be.

In its 1973-74 allocation from the state, there was included for the first time in the budget of the University of California an item of $250,000 for affirmative action expenditures.[9] This was used to develop pilot programs on all nine campuses and in the office of the president, with the funds being spent for affirmative action staff members and for expenses in connection with recruitment and advertising, training and development, and monitoring and evaluation of the program. In 1974-75, in recognition of the fact that the budgetary item of $250,000 was seriously inadequate, and after efforts to get the state to increase this amount failed, the board of regents allocated an additional $1,000,000 for affirmative action expenditures. However, the university estimated that the actual costs exceeded the allocation of $1,250,000 by an additional $3,000,000 that was being diverted from existing resources. These resources included faculty and staff time, record-keeping, data collection, computer-program time, etc.

According to memoranda made available to us, the affirmative action program of the university in 1973-74 and 1974-75 was concerned with only the most urgent aspects of affirmative action and included the following functions:

• Creation of administrative units at the campus level and in

[9]We are indebted to Gloria L. Copeland, assistant vice-president, University of California, for supplying this information on the financing of affirmative action expenditures.

the office of the president to direct, coordinate, and monitor affirmative action efforts

- Recruitment and selection of academic personnel, principally through the use of funds for advertising and travel expenditures
- Recruitment and selection of staff (nonacademic) personnel, principally through advertising and travel with emphasis on outreach to minority communities
- Training and development of staff personnel
- Establishment of data bases on the composition of the workforce, of the applicant flow, and of transfer and promotion activities relative to minorities and women
- Employee counseling programs
- Informational seminars for supervisors
- Workshops for training in skills in language, typing, etc.
- On-the-job training for craft skills

In the university's budget request to the state for 1975-76, a total of $2,842,500 was sought for affirmative action, inclusive of the $250,000 already in the budget. The legislature approved an additional $250,000, over and above the $250,000 that had been in the budget since 1973-74, but the additional amount was deleted by Governor Edmund G. Brown, Jr., who has been quoted on several occasions to the effect that what is needed to achieve affirmative action objectives is determination and effort, not additional expenditures.

One of the projects for which the university sought funds in its 1975-76 budget request, in the amount of $310,000, was a program for the development of academic personnel through the provision of funds to support research by junior faculty members (instructors and assistant professors). The funds would be made available for summer research stipends, computer time, laboratory assistants, etc.

In view of the financial stringency faced by many public and private institutions of higher education, the problem of obtaining funds for affirmative action expenditures is difficult. It can be argued that the federal government, in imposing affirmative action obligations on colleges and universities, should provide some financial support to assist institutions in carrying out these obligations. The question is, what is the most appropriate way of providing this assistance?

Universities are permitted to recover indirect costs associated with research from federal contracts. The percentage of the contract funds recoverable varies according to the actual expenditures and accounting practices of the institution. Annual negotiations are carried out between each institution and the U.S. Department of Health, Education, and Welfare (regardless of which federal departments may be furnishing funds for individual contracts), in which the universities estimate the magnitude of indirect costs associated with research, and in which an agreement is reached as to the percentage which may be added to contract budgets for indirect costs.

There are some legitimate indirect costs that cannot usually be included in direct project expenditures in contract budgets. These include staff time involved in preparing contract proposals and negotiating with federal officials, and they frequently include clerical assistance that is provided by permanent university personnel and not charged directly against contract budgets. In some cases, also, costs of providing space for special project personnel are not included in project budgets —often because inclusion of such costs might increase the total budget to the point of jeopardizing its approval. Space is somehow provided in university buildings, and such costs as janitorial service are not charged to the project budget.

Nevertheless, funds for indirect costs received by an institution are not necessarily allocated wholly, or even partly, to cover such indirect expenses, but are sometimes used for special purposes that cannot easily be financed from regular university funds. An additional complication is that state universities frequently face a situation in which the state government captures some portion of these funds, usually through deductions from the stage budgetary allocation to the institution, for the perfectly legitimate reason that some of these costs were actually being met from state appropriations.

Again, we have obtained some specific information relating to the University of California.[10] Currently, overhead allowances in the university's federal contracts amount to 34.2 percent of "modified total direct costs." The term "modified" relates particularly to the fact that costs of any special equipment needed for the project are not included. Of the total amount of overhead funds received by the university, 50 percent must be turned over to the state, which deducts that amount from the university budget. The other half is retained by the president's office and is allocated to special projects approved under the Regents' Opportunity Fund—projects for which the university would have difficulty obtaining funds through its state budget. Some of these funds have been allocated for aid to disadvantaged students.

One way in which universities with federal contracts have been able to cover some of the special costs of affirmative action is through the negotiation of larger allowances for indirect costs in their federal contracts. The maximum proportion of affirmative action costs that can be recovered in this manner is determined by the proportion of the university's total budget for educational and general expenses that is accounted for by the research budget. For research universities, this proportion is likely to range from 15 to 30 percent. Another possibility, which would not be dependent on the size of the research budget, would be for Congress to recognize that it is placing a financial burden on institutions of higher education through federal affirmative action regulations. Thus, it would be reasonable to reimburse institutions directly for a portion of this financial burden—in much the same manner as the federal government reimburses institutions for a small fraction of federal student aid allocations to cover costs of administering student aid programs.

To the extent that a percentage of affirmative action costs are recovered through allowances for indirect costs of research

[10]We are indebted to August G. Manza, Berkeley Campus Research Officer, for this information.

projects, this will not really help institutions except in some individual cases, because the total research budgets of the federal agencies are usually fixed. Thus there would need to be appropriations increases specifically to cover these costs. Such an increase should be over and above the increase that the Council recommended in its recent report, *The Federal Role in Postsecondary Education.* There the recommendation was that federal allocations for research to universities and colleges should increase along with the gross national product.

Recommendation 22: *Since federal policies permit inclusion of a small portion of the costs of affirmative action programs as indirect costs, Congress should supplement federal agencies' research budgets to reflect these new indirect costs. Congress should also consider appropriating funds to meet a fraction of the cost of record-keeping and administration associated with affirmative action.*

State governments and private donors should be receptive to requests from colleges and universities for special budgetary allocations or private gifts to aid in meeting the costs of affirmative action programs.

A Special Task Force

Several of the recommendations that we have made in Sections 5 and 6 could be made more precise and detailed if a special task force, with persons drawn from higher education and from women's and minority groups, were appointed to provide advice on the revision of regulations, guidelines, and data requirements recommended in this report. One of the problems with the development of federal affirmative action policies is that there has been too little consultation with appropriate and knowledgeable groups in the formulation of policies and regulations. We have considered the possibility of recommending advisory committees for several of the federal agencies involved but have rejected it on the ground that there are many such advisory committees to federal agencies and that few of them are very effective. An ad hoc task force, charged with the responsibility for developing a report within a limited period of time, on the other hand, could be very useful in contributing to the implementation of some of our recommendations.

Recommendation 23: *The Secretary of Labor, the Secretary of Health, Education, and Welfare, and the chairman of the Equal Employment Opportunity Commission should act jointly to appoint a special task force, including persons drawn from institutions of higher education, women's groups, and minority groups to advise them on the revision of regulations, guidelines, and data requirements recommended in this report.*

Confidentiality of Personnel Records

One of the most difficult and sensitive problems associated with cases involving charges of discrimination has to do with whether and to what extent universities and colleges may be required to make confidential personnel records available to state or federal officials in the course of their investigations or to courts considering charges of discrimination. The problem is not unique to higher education, nor is it a new problem. It has arisen in the past in cases involving, for example, dismissals of faculty members on grounds of inadequate performance.

The confidentiality of personnel records is especially important to faculty members and administrators in higher education, because confidential evaluations by faculty members of a candidate for appointment or promotion play a very important role in the selection and promotion process. If a faculty member becomes fearful that his confidential evaluation of a graduate student, a colleague, or a faculty member in another institution whose work is familiar to him may fall into the hands of a government official or a court, he is likely to become reluctant to express himself frankly in such letters or memoranda.

Several well-known research universities have resisted demands of OCR officials for access to confidential personnel records, sometimes unsuccessfully and sometimes with partial success. In some cases, a compromise has been worked out in which records have been made available after expunging the names of authors of letters of evaluation.

The policies of federal agencies vary on this issue. Section 709(e) of Title VII of the Civil Rights Act of 1964 provides that "it shall be unlawful for any officer or employee of the Commission to make public in any manner whatever any information obtained by the Commission pursuant to its authority under this section prior to the institution of any proceeding under this title involving such information." Department of Labor regulations under Executive Order 11246 also include provisions intended to restrict disclosure of confidential information.

On the other hand, a complainant may have great difficulty in proving discrimination without access to his or her confidential personnel records and those of other candidates who were considered for the same appointment or promotion. The difficult problem of weighing the rights of complainants against the rights of institutions is increasingly becoming an issue in which court decisions will play the crucial role.

The leading case on this issue involved a professor at the University of New Mexico who was terminated after filing a charge of discrimination with the state Human Rights Commission. Eventually, EEOC conducted an investigation of the complaint in which the university was asked to disclose the personnel files of all current members of the complainant's department and all faculty members who had been terminated during the previous few years. The university resisted, the commission issued a subpoena for the files, and the university went to court to contest the demand for the files. However, the decision went against the university in both the federal district court and the Tenth Circuit Court. Both parties to the action had stipulated that the records in question were confidential and extremely sensitive. The circuit court rejected this claim, citing the statutory prohibition against the release by EEOC of information obtained in the course of its investigations. The court held that the request for the documents was neither irrelevant, unreasonable, nor arbitrary, and the subpoena was enforced without modification.[11] One or two other recent federal court decisions

[11]*Equal Employment Opportunity Commission v. University of New Mexico* (Dist. Ct., New Mexico, 1973; and 10th Cir. Ct., 1974). We are in-

are not entirely consistent with this decision. But legal experts tend, on the whole, to believe that it will not be possible for universities to refuse access to confidential files in the face of the conflicting rights of complainants to have records made available to federal and state agencies and the courts.

debted to Michael R. Smith, assistant to vice-chancellor Ira M. Heyman, University of California, Berkeley, for information on this case.

7

Grievances and Enforcement Procedures

The probability that OCR's failure to issue show-cause orders and to go beyond mere delays in allocation of federal funds to campuses may be related to the severity of the penalty involved in actual withholding of contracts or, in extreme cases, debarment from future contracts.

The Question of Sanctions

This consideration points up a basic dilemma in the federal compliance program that is not unique in relation to higher education, but may in some circumstances present particular difficulties in higher education. For the most part, research funds have been involved, and the cases that have received the greatest attention have been those of highly prestigious research universities that rank near the top in amounts of federal research funds received annually. In awarding these research funds, the federal government is purchasing a desired service, and in some situations, the campus involved may be uniquely qualified, by virtue of both highly specialized faculty expertise and unique and valuable equipment, to furnish the service.

Beyond considerations relating to individual research projects is the possibility of longer-run damage to valuable research resources. Withholding of research funds would in many cases result in layoffs of nontenured research personnel, as well as restriction of training opportunities for advanced graduate students.

An additional complication is the question of whether it is equitable to penalize particular research institutes or groups when the "underutilization" of women or minority groups may be found chiefly in teaching departments that have no connection with the research group. True, the institution as a whole suffers in terms of prestige when it loses large amounts of federal funds, but the primary loss is borne by the affected research groups. Are there alternative penalties that might be effective and more appropriate?

A related point is that it is the research universities that receive large amounts of federal contract and grant funds. Thus, use of this sanction tends to affect these universities and to have relatively little force in relation to other institutions. In the case of minorities, as we have seen, relative participation on faculties may be even more sparse in most other types of institutions than in Research Universities I. Thus development of more even-handed sanctions, not as a replacement for withholding of federal contract and grant funds, but as a more generally applicable type of penalty, might make for more effective enforcement.

On the premise that "OCR should not be dependent so exclusively on the extreme sanctions of termination, cancellation and debarment," Vetter (1974) has proposed that the agency should have at its disposal a system of graduated sanctions. In addition, the agency should not be able to impose any sanction without an opportunity for a prior hearing. The sanction might appropriately take the form of a monetary fine in some cases, but in other cases the penalty might be an order geared to the particular violation:

> Depending upon circumstances, sanctions for demonstrated violations have one or more of three functions to perform: (1) to deter violations of the regulations generally, by the respondent and others, (2) to compel a respondent to conform a continuing cause of conduct to the requirements of the program, (3) to

make whole injured persons. A dispute might arise over an institution's recruiting practices, an example of (2) above. If those are shown to fall short of compliance with the institution's obligations under the Executive Order, the indicated remedy is the equivalent of an injunction. On the other hand, if an institution fails in a few individual instances to perform its commitment to advertise openings, an illustration of (1), a monetary penalty, the equivalent of a fine, might be appropriate. Finally, it may be desirable in some cases to provide remedies for individuals—i.e., a promotion or grant of tenure.

Before arriving at a recommendation, we need to point out that the use of the federal spending power to enforce certain policies has a long history, dating back at least to the 1920s, and that it has played an important role in the implementation of many policies deemed in the national interest. To some degree, this use of the federal spending power has been in connection with grants-in-aid to the states, as in the public assistance program, under which the states are required to enforce certain standards, such as uniform administration throughout the state and the right of an individual to appeal an adverse administrative decision, subject to possible withdrawal of federal funds. The withholding of federal funds has also been used effectively in some cases in the enforcement of school desegregation in the South, but, in addition, school districts have been taken to court to enforce desegregation.

Executive Order 11246 does not have the legal background of an act of Congress, as do the provisions enforced by the EEOC and other agencies, discussed in Section 4, but it does have the backing of several court decisions up to the level of the federal courts of appeals, to the effect that it has legitimacy equivalent to a set of regulations resulting from legislative enactment. It is therefore not appropriate to suggest changes on the ground of lack of legitimacy of the executive order.

A major question in this connection is whether the relevant rules and regulations under the executive order could be modified for higher education alone. The GAO report (Comptroller General, 1975), cited earlier, indicates that the problem of reluctance to withhold contracts relates to the entire federal contract compliance program. On the other hand, this council can speak only in relation to higher education. Just as a special supplement or set of interpretations could be issued in relation to the enforcement of Revised Order No. 4 in higher education, there could also be a set of interpretations relating to sanctions under the executive order that would be applicable to higher education. The political question of whether such a special supplement or set of interpretations could be seriously considered within the Departments of Labor and HEW without encountering demands for similar treatment from other sectors of the economy is one which lies outside of our terms of reference.

Recommendation 24: *A special supplement or set of interpretations under the executive order should be developed to provide for a more flexible set of sanctions for noncompliance with affirmative action enforcement requirements in higher education. The provisions for withholding of federal-contract funds should be retained for use in cases in which milder sanctions have failed to have any effect. There should be strict requirements for "show-cause" orders and the holding of hearings before any sanction is imposed.*[1]

The Secretaries of Labor and of Health, Education, and Welfare should take joint action to appoint a special advisory committee, including legal and constitutional experts, to draw up specific recommendations for appropriate penalties.

Internal Grievance Procedures

Many colleges and universities have long had grievance procedures for members of the academic senate, in the form of a right of appeal to a standing or special ad hoc faculty committee. These procedures apply primarily to cases involving dismissal of faculty members with tenure or of nontenured faculty

---

[1] In practice, contracts have been delayed without a hearing, even though technically this is not the correct procedure.

members before the expiration of their current contracts. The procedures tend to follow the standards developed by the AAUP (American Association of University Professors, 1973, pp. 6-7).

In recent years, under the impact of actual or potential unionization, and under the impact of civil rights pressures, grievance procedures have been developed for nonacademic employees in a good many institutions. Frequently, especially on large university campuses, the group that has, until very recently, been left out has consisted of nonsenate or nonfaculty academic employees. One of the results of the development of affirmative action plans, however, has been the establishment of grievance procedures that will protect these academic employees.

The great majority of our respondents, especially among universities, have the traditional provisions for appeal by a faculty member faced with dismissal. Under the impact of affirmative action, most universities, but a smaller proportion of other institutions, have developed or are in the process of developing grievance procedures for nonfaculty academic employees and for nonacademic employees. However, where faculty unionization has developed—as we have seen, primarily in state colleges and public two-year colleges—grievance procedures tend to be included in collective bargaining agreements and in some cases call for binding arbitration as the final step.

There is considerable variety in patterns of coverage of various groups of employees. For example, among the 55 universities for which we have some information about grievance procedures for *academic* employees, 10 have only the traditional grievance procedures for faculty members (right of appeal to a committee of the academic senate or its equivalent), 10 have a single set of procedures available to all academic employees, and 21 have or are developing separate procedures for faculty members and for nonfaculty academic employees. Another 14 have or are developing a single set of procedures, along with a separate procedure for faculty members filing grievances not related to charges of discrimination. In one of the 21 cases with separate procedures, a faculty member apparently has a choice between appealing to a committee of the academic senate or using the broader grievance procedure available to all academic employees.

Some institutions have established separate channels for handling grievances alleging discrimination; others have integrated discrimination complaints into the normal grievance process. One-half of the universities and about one-third of other institutions for which we have relevant information provide for the processing of complaints of discrimination through internal grievance procedures.

Certain features of all grievance procedures for both academic and nonacademic employees are common to nearly all the plans we have examined. The first step consists of an informal approach to the head of the department or other employment unit, while the second step consists of the filing of a formal complaint in writing with that same individual. (These steps are not likely to be spelled out in traditional provisions relating to faculty members, because most of the cases involve either failure to promote to tenure or the initiation of steps to dismiss a tenured faculty member. In these types of cases, the department has usually been involved at an earlier stage.) If the complainant is not satisfied with the results of these first two steps, he or she may then file a complaint with the chief campus officer or with some other high administrative official. In some cases the complaint is to be filed with an affirmative action officer.

From this point on, procedures differ considerably. On a few university campuses, the complaint must be investigated by one or more administrative officials before there is a right of appeal to any other body. In some cases affirmative action committees serve as appeal bodies in grievance cases. In others, the affirmative action officer is a member of the hearing committee, conducts a preliminary investigation before the hearing is held, or in other ways plays a crucial role in the grievance process.

Where the grievance process for handling discrimination complaints differs from that for handling other grievances, or where nonfaculty academic and/or nonacademic employees share a common grievance procedure with the faculty, the com-

position of the hearing board is likely to differ from the traditional all-faculty committee. In six universities and in six other
institutions for which we have relevant information, nonfaculty
members as well as faculty members are included on the hearing
board. Furthermore, nine universities and four other institutions require that women and members of minority groups, if at
all possible, be included on hearing panels.

Two of the procedures we have examined deviate from the
general pattern in different ways. At Michigan State University,
any faculty member, other university employee, or student may
file a complaint on grounds of discrimination with a special
board that includes (1) three undergraduate students, (2) one
graduate student, (3) three faculty members selected through
academic senate procedures, (4) a representative of administrative and professional employees, (5) a representative of a nonacademic employees association, and (6) a representative of a
union local that apparently represents some of the nonacademic
employees. At the conclusion of its hearings the board is
empowered to render a decision and order. The order may specify the action or actions that "must be taken by the charged
individual or organization to remedy the violation of the University policy against discrimination."[2] This is in contrast with
the typical provision under which the hearing officer or committee makes a recommendation to the chief campus officer.

Beyond that, there is an appeal by either party to a special
appeal board. Each party has a right to designate a member of
the appeal board, and the two members thus designated are
required to attempt to agree on a third member, who need not
be chosen from the university community. If they cannot agree,
the chief campus officer must then request the American Arbitration Association to designate the third member, and this
member's fees and expenses will be paid by the university. The
actions taken by the appeal board are to be "reported to the
President of the University who shall in turn share these with

[2]The order must be consistent with policies of the board of trustees affecting job security and academic freedom. In addition, any recommendation
for the payment of money must be referred to the board of trustees.

the Board of Trustees." There is no mention of any right of the president or board of trustees to review the decision. Thus, this procedure not only involves broader representation on the initial board than any other we have examined, but also in its final stage, unlike more typical grievance procedures, amounts to binding arbitration. Depending on the nature of the complaint, a faculty member may have the alternative of appealing to the usual academic senate committee.

The other somewhat atypical procedure is found at the University of California (statewide) and applies only to complaints of nonfaculty academic employees involving discrimination. (Faculty members have the usual right of appeal to a committee of the academic senate). A nonfaculty academic employee with a grievance has the right to elect whether to have the appeal heard by a university hearing officer, a university hearing committee, or a nonuniversity hearing officer. A university hearing officer or committee is appointed by the chief campus officer from a panel of employees of the university (in practice the panel consists of faculty members with arbitration experience). If the grievant elects a nonuniversity hearing officer, the local office of the American Arbitration Association is asked to furnish a list of five names. The two parties have the right of alternatively striking names, and the person whose name remains becomes the nonuniversity hearing officer. However, whether the case is heard by a university hearing officer or committee or by a nonuniversity hearing officer, the report takes the form of a recommendation to the chief campus officer, who has the right to reverse the ruling. The procedure is very similar to one that has been in existence for nonacademic employees over a longer period.

Clearly, the more broadly representative committees that have developed within the framework of affirmative action programs are likely to have greater appeal to most women and minority-group members with complaints of discriminatory treatment than the traditional faculty procedure under which the complaint is heard by a committee of the academic senate, for the latter type of committee is likely to consist chiefly or exclusively of white male faculty members.

Some of the grievance procedures that have developed under the impetus of affirmative action have carefully framed provisions relating to the conduct of hearings, the right to be represented by counsel in the case of both parties, and the like. Others do not, but those that lack such provisions tend to be in an early stage of development. Traditional procedures for faculty members also include detailed provisions on the conduct of hearings in many cases.

As yet, relatively little information is available on experience under the newer types of grievance procedures, partly because many of them are of quite recent origin.

Among our respondents, there were six that provided copies of collective bargaining agreements that included grievance procedures applicable to faculty members. Of these, two were state colleges, three were community colleges, and one was a large campus of the State University of New York (providing the collective bargaining agreement for the entire SUNY system). Four of the agreements, including SUNY's, called for binding arbitration as the final step in the grievance procedure. In addition, there were two institutions that were not unionized but that provided for arbitration as the last step in the grievance procedure—one of these was a private doctoral-granting university and the other was a public two-year college. We have also indicated that the Michigan State University grievance procedure calls for what amounts to binding arbitration as the final step.

Increasingly, the right of appeal under an internal grievance procedure has come to be recognized as an essential aspect of adequate personnel policies. In the context of affirmative action in higher education, effective internal grievance procedures, moreover, should greatly reduce the number of complaints that are filed with state or federal agencies or that wind up in court.

The Council believes that every institution of higher education should develop grievance procedures that are available to all of its employees, although it may be quite appropriate to have different procedures for academic and nonacademic employees. We also believe that appropriate administrative or affirmative action officers should consult with all affected groups on the campus in the development of new grievance procedures specifically designed to meet the needs of affirmative action programs. Although faculty members are likely to wish to retain the traditional privilege of appeal to a committee of the academic senate, there is a case for an alternative right of appeal to a more broadly representative group for faculty members in cases involving alleged discrimination, along with a right of appeal to such a group for nonfaculty academic employees.

A more controversial issue is whether grievance procedures should provide for binding arbitration. There is also the question as to whether federal regulations should require academic institutions to develop grievance procedures, and, if so, whether those procedures should provide for resort to binding arbitration as a final stage.

Those who have been following debates on affirmative action issues in higher education are familiar with the fact that there have been several proposals that, as an alternative to processing faculty complaints of discrimination through government agencies and the courts, parties be given the option of submitting a case that cannot be settled by internal procedures to arbitration. In effect, these proposals call for arbitration as the final step in the grievance procedure. Others have argued against any general resort to arbitration.[3]

Where collective bargaining enters the scene, the question of whether a provision for binding arbitration should be included in the collective bargaining agreement will be settled, of course, by negotiation. A special committee of the AAUP submitted a report that was cautiously favorable to arbitration of faculty grievances in 1973, but which concluded on a warning note ("Arbitration of Faculty Grievances . . . ," 1973):

> Arbitration can be a useful device for resolving some kinds of disputes and grievances that arise in academic life. Especially when collective bargaining is

[3]For excellent discussions of the applicability of arbitration procedures, see Lester (1974, pp. 96-101), who is in favor of arbitration, and Vetter (1974), who is opposed. A brief statement in favor of arbitration may also be found in Fleming (1974).

practiced, resort to arbitrators who are sensitive to the needs and standards of higher education may be the preferred way to avoid deadlocks or administrative domination. But arbitration is not a substitute for careful procedures that respect the autonomy of the faculty and administration in their respective spheres. A system of collective bargaining that routinely resorts to arbitration is an abdication of responsibility. This is especially true of the faculty's primary responsibility to determine who shall hold and retain faculty appointments.

A critical question in relation to both grievance procedures and arbitration is whether federal agencies and the courts will respect decisions resulting from those procedures, as they have generally in cases involving arbitration under collective bargaining agreements. In a careful review of the issues and relevant court decisions Aaron (1972) concluded that the doctrine of exhausting internal procedures first should not be applied by the courts in Title VII cases, pointing out that there are significant differences between the processes of arbitration under a collective bargaining agreement and the protection of rights established by a statute.[4]

It is our view that arbitration deserves careful consideration, in the course of developing grievance procedures, as one means of solving disputes locally and quickly. Arbitration processes must, of course, meet standards of due process, and decisions cannot be contrary to law. Appeal to the courts should be possible claiming violation of due process, but the courts should otherwise defer to the arbitration process. Use of private arbitration can, of course, greatly reduce resort to the courts.

Recommendation 25: *The Council recommends that all institutions of higher education develop one or more sets of grievance*

---

[4]Aaron's article, however, was apparently written prior to the 1972 amendments, which gave EEOC the right to take private employers to court.

procedures that will be available to all of its employees, or to academic and nonacademic employees separately. In the development of grievance procedures, institutions should consult with all concerned groups on the campus. All grievance procedures should provide for hearings in which normal principles of due process are observed.[5]

Whether federal regulations should require grievance procedures is a matter of controversy. The *Higher Education Guidelines* issued by HEW in October 1972 urged "the development of grievance procedures for all employees, academic and nonacademic alike," but did not require them (see Appendix B). The Title IX regulations approved by the White House in May 1975 went further and required grievance procedures without specifying their details. We believe that there are strong arguments in favor of a federal regulation requiring institutions of higher education to have grievance procedures. With the federal government as fully involved as it is in the enforcement of nondiscrimination and affirmative action, a policy that provides for appeal to an internal grievance procedure as a matter of right seems appropriate. We also believe that federal policies should encourage, though not necessarily always require, complainants to exhaust internal grievance procedures. In practice, under our recommendations, this would be a matter for the EEOC or, on equal pay matters, the Wage and Hour Administration. These agencies might best use their discretion over whether or not to delay assuming jurisdiction over a complaint case, depending on a judgment as to whether the internal grievance procedures were likely to be adequate and equitable.

We do not believe that the federal government, at this point, should attempt to dictate the details of internal grievance procedures. Not only are there many variations in institutional grievance procedures, but in many colleges and universities they are still in the process of formulation or in a very early state of operation. There is a need for lengthier experience under exist-

---

[5] As a guide to appropriate due process provisions, see, for example, American Association of University Professors (1973, pp. 6-7).

ing and developing grievance procedures, as well as evaluative research on their results, before any attempt should be made by the federal government to stipulate particular procedures.

Whether mandatory grievance procedures for higher education would require amendments to existing legislation is not entirely clear. We believe that the coordinated federal regulations that we have recommended in relation to higher education should provide for mandatory grievance procedures. It would then be a matter for Congress to determine whether such a requirement is consistent with existing legislation, especially Title VII and the Equal Pay Act.

Recommendation 26: *The coordinated federal regulations that we have recommended should include a requirement that all institutions of higher education develop internal grievance procedures for all employees, if they do not already have them. At least for the present, however, the federal government should not attempt to stipulate the precise form those grievance procedures should take, except to require that generally accepted standards of due process be observed.* [6]

Federal agencies empowered to investigate complaints should encourage complainants to exhaust internal remedies before formally filing a complaint with the federal agency, where grievance procedures are deemed to be adequate and equitable. This may require changes in federal legislation, especially Title VII of the Civil Rights Act.

Nevertheless, it is important to recognize that grievance procedures cannot feasibly provide any protection to persons who have not been hired, i.e., to outsiders as opposed to insiders. Thus, the right to file a complaint or to initiate a private action in court will continue to be vital for those who believe they have been discriminated against in hiring.

For all the reasons given above, we have one final recommendation:

[6]The requirement should specifically refer to AAUP standards for due process (see the preceding footnote).

Recommendation 27: *The federal government, no later than 1980, should undertake a comprehensive review of affirmative action requirements and of mechanisms of enforcement to determine what, if any, requirements and mechanisms are still needed and in what segments of higher education. The presumption should be in favor of disengagement as soon as reasonably possible, at first perhaps for certain types of institutions and for majority women, because of the probability that the supply of qualified majority women will increase relatively rapidly and parity will be achieved more quickly for them than for minorities.*

8

Who Should Have
What Responsibilities?

Implementation of the recommendations in this report calls for action by (1) institutions of higher education, (2) Congress, and (3) federal agencies. This final section outlines which of these bodies should have responsibility for carrying out each recommendation. Most of the recommendations addressed to the federal government could be implemented by executive action and would not require action by Congress.

Institutions of Higher Education

All Colleges and Universities

- Development and implementation of strictly nondiscriminatory employment policies in accordance with recommendations in Section 3
- Development and implementation of grievance procedures for all academic and nonacademic employees

All Colleges and Universities with Federal Contracts of $50,000 or More and Employing 50 or More Persons

- Development and implementation of affirmative action policies in accordance with recommendations in Sections 3, 5, and 7

All Colleges and Universities with Doctoral and Professional Programs

- Development and implementation of a supply plan designed to provide maximum opportunities for women and minorities to participate on a basis of equal opportunity in graduate and professional education

- Development and implementation of policies that will provide equal opportunity for graduate and professional students with family responsibilities

Congress

- Adoption of amendments to Title VII of the Civil Rights Act of 1964 (1) granting the Equal Employment Opportunity Commission the power to issue cease and desist orders and (2) encouraging the EEOC to respect internal grievance procedures of colleges and universities, when those procedures conform to normal standards of due process
- Appropriating funds for temporary additions, including persons knowledgeable about academic employment, to the staffs of EEOC, the Office for Civil Rights in HEW, and the Wage and Hour Administration and the Office of Federal Contract Compliance in the Department of Labor
- Augmentation of research funds flowing to institutions of higher education to permit inclusion of a portion of affirmative action costs in allowances for indirect costs of research projects, and appropriations of funds to cover a fraction of affirmative action costs that cannot be covered under research contracts
- Adoption of an amendment to Title IX of the Education Amendments of 1972, making it clear that the title does not make specific provision for nondiscrimination in employment, but respects the employment provisions of Title VII of the Civil Rights Act and of the executive order

Federal Agencies

U.S. Department of Labor

- Development (in consultation with HEW) of a special supplement or set of interpretations to Revised Order No. 4 appropriate for higher education
- Additions to the staffs of the Wage and Hour Administration and the Office of Federal Contract Compliance of persons knowledgeable about academic employment

U.S. Department of Health, Education, and Welfare

- Revision of *Higher Education Guidelines* of October 1972 (1) to conform with the special supplement to Revised Order No. 4 and (2) to require institutions subject to the executive order to develop and implement grievance procedures
- Additions to the staff of the Office for Civil Rights of persons knowledgeable about academic employment
- Centralization of decisions, especially those relating to colleges and universities that hire in a national market, in the Washington office
- Referral of all individual and class complaints of discrimination in employment to the Equal Employment Opportunity Commission
- Referral of salary analyses to the Wage and Hour Administration of the Department of Labor
- Implementation of policies requiring the National Center for Educational Statistics to collect and publish promptly (in cooperation with the National Research Council and the Equal Employment Opportunity Commission) data on the sexual and racial characteristics of degree recipients and of academic employees; and of policies requiring OCR to make such data available to colleges and universities covered by the executive order as rapidly as possible

Equal Employment Opportunity Commission

- Additions to its staff of persons knowledgeable about academic employment
- Referral of salary analyses to the Wage and Hour Administration of the Department of Labor
- Deferral of investigation of complaints, for a reasonable period, when an internal grievance procedure is in process, and dismissal of the charge, after appropriate investigation, if due process has been observed in the grievance procedure and the complaint has been found to be without basis

Equal Employment Opportunity Coordinating Council

- Development and implementation of policies ensuring referral of individual and class complaints to a single agency, in accordance with our recommendations

U.S. Department of Labor and U.S. Department of Health, Education, and Welfare

- Negotiation of an arrangement under which the Secretary of HEW will have final responsibility for approval of affirmative action plans and imposition of sanctions relating to institutions of higher education, subject to overall policy determination and periodic policy review by the Secretary of Labor
- Appointment of a special task force of legal experts to develop a plan for graduated sanctions to be applied in the enforcement of affirmative action in higher education[1]

U.S. Department of Labor, U.S. Department of Health, Education, and Welfare, and Equal Employment Opportunity Commission, in Consultation with Other Appropriate Agencies

- Development of a coordinated set of regulations or guidelines relating to nondiscrimination and affirmative action in higher education, including simplified and unified data-reporting requirements
- Appointment of an ad hoc task force to advise on the development of coordinated regulations and data-reporting requirements (to include persons drawn from higher education, women's groups, and minority groups)

---

[1] Recommendations for changes made by such a task force would have to be approved by the White House, as well as the Secretary of Labor.

Appendix A

Statistical Tables

Table 6. Women as a percentage of new doctorate teachers in
institutions of higher education, by type, 1967-1973

Employing institution	1967	1968	1971	1972	1973
Group I	4.4	10.0	15.0	15.4	27.8
Group II	12.8	13.7	16.4	18.5	25.2
Group III	13.7	12.9	18.3	19.6	22.5
Group IV	9.3	10.8	13.9	15.6	17.9
Group V	10.7	12.2	15.0	15.8	18.4
All universities	10.7	12.2	15.5	16.9	20.6
Group VI	22.1	10.0	16.0	28.8	27.2
Group VII	19.4	16.4	19.1	17.4	21.1
Group VIII	17.6	16.9	17.1	18.0	21.6
Group IX	16.1	16.1	16.6	18.6	18.1
Group X	28.1	22.7	22.4	20.3	20.4
All four-year colleges	19.0	16.7	17.9	18.8	20.1
Two-year colleges	27.0	23.7	21.3	26.0	22.2
Elementary and secondary schools	35.8	29.5	29.4	26.4	26.6
All educational institutions	14.7	14.5	17.3	18.5	20.8

Note: Computed from doctorate record file data, National Research Council, Washington. The classification of institutions is based on quality measures developed by Cartter and others.

Source: Cartter and Ruhter (1975, p. 11).

Table 7. Percentage of new doctorate teachers hired,
by employing institution and sex, 1967-1973

Employing institution	1967	1968	1971	1972	1973
	Men				
Group I	5.6	4.3	2.7	2.3	2.0
Group II	11.3	10.8	8.7	8.3	6.1
Group III	12.1	11.8	8.7	8.9	8.0
Group IV	18.5	17.3	15.7	14.6	12.9
Group V	14.6	14.2	13.3	14.1	12.5
All universities	62.2	58.5	49.0	48.3	41.5

Table 7

Employing institution	1967	1968	1971	1972	1973
Men					
Group VI	2.4	2.5	1.8	1.6	1.8
Group VII	8.5	8.8	8.9	8.8	9.0
Group VIII	9.0	9.0	11.6	11.0	11.7
Group IX	11.5	14.5	17.4	17.6	20.0
Group X	3.2	4.1	4.8	5.6	6.4
All four-year colleges	34.5	38.9	44.5	44.5	48.9
Two-year colleges	1.3	1.3	3.1	3.8	5.7
Elementary and secondary schools	2.0	1.4	3.3	3.4	3.9
Total	100.0	100.0	100.0	100.0	100.0
Women					
Group I	1.5	2.8	2.2	1.9	2.9
Group II	9.6	10.2	8.2	8.3	7.9
Group III	11.2	10.4	9.3	9.6	8.9
Group IV	11.0	12.5	12.1	11.8	10.7
Group V	10.1	11.8	11.3	11.7	10.7
All universities	43.5	47.7	43.2	43.2	41.1
Group VI	3.9	1.6	1.6	2.8	2.6
Group VII	11.8	10.3	10.1	8.1	9.2
Group VIII	11.2	10.9	11.4	10.6	12.2
Group IX	12.9	16.5	16.5	17.7	16.9
Group X	7.3	7.1	6.7	6.2	6.3
All four-year colleges	47.0	46.5	46.3	45.5	47.2
Two-year colleges	2.9	2.5	4.1	5.9	6.2
Elementary and secondary schools	6.6	3.3	6.5	5.4	5.5
Total	100.0	100.0	100.0	100.0	100.0

Note: Computed from doctorate record file data, National Research Council, Washington. The classification of institutions is based on quality measures developed by Cartter and others.

Source: Cartter and Ruhter (1975, p. 2).

Table 8. Colleges and universities included in Carnegie Council sample, and number that responded

Campus	Number of campuses in Carnegie classification	Number in sample	Sample as percent of total	Institutions in sample responding	
				Number	Percent
Total	2,122	207	10	132	64
Public	1,221	98	8	66	67
Private	901	109	12	66	61
Research Universities I	52	32	62	26	81
Public	30	19	63	15	79
Private	22	13	59	11	85
Research Universities II	40	19	48	17	89
Public	27	11	41	11	100
Private	13	8	62	6	75
Doctoral Universities, I and II	81	22	27	17	77
Public	51	12	24	9	75
Private	30	10	33	8	80
Comprehensive Universities and Colleges	453	36	8	20	56
Public	308	19	6	13	68
Private	145	17	12	7	41
Liberal Arts Colleges I, private	144	26	18	16	62
Liberal Arts Colleges II, private	547	35	6	18	51
Two-Year Colleges, public	805	37	5	18	49

Note: For definition of types of institutions, see Appendix B. Public liberal arts colleges, private two-year colleges, and specialized institutions were excluded from the survey.

Source: Carnegie Council Survey of Affirmative Action Policies.

Table 9. Number receiving doctoral degrees in 1973, by citizenship and racial/ethnic identification

Citizenship	White Caucasian	Black[a]	Asian[b]	Latin[c]	Native American	All Other	Minority total	Grand total
U.S. citizens	26,400	760	320	228	148	12	1,468	27,868
Non-U.S. citizens, immigration visas	826	56	1,067	23	0	12	1,158	1,984
Non-U.S. citizens, other visas	1,817	160	1,042	96	1	46	1,345	3,162
Total (citizenship and ethnicity known)	29,043	976	2,429	347	149	70	3,971	33,014
Citizenship and ethnicity unknown	—	—	—	—	—	—	—	713
Total	29,043	976	2,429	347	149	70	3,971	33,727

Note: Data adjusted for partial response.

[a]Includes 12 individuals who indicate White, Indian, or other mixtures.

[b]Includes South Asians, to the extent these people so identified themselves.

[c]Includes Puerto Ricans, Spanish-Americans and Mexican-Americans.

Source: National Research Council/National Academy of Sciences (1974, p. 8).

Table 10. Racial/ethnic groups identified in the comprehensive roster of
doctoral scientists and engineers, by academic year of doctorate

Period of Ph.D. graduation	U.S. total	All minorities		Racial/ethnic group				
		Number	Percent	Black	Asian	Latin	Native American	Other
1930-1934	5,750	89	1.7	18	59	12	0	0
1935-1939	7,335	110	1.5	39	49	22	0	0
1940-1944	8,768	189	2.2	51	100	36	0	2
1945-1949	9,889	441	4.5	118	234	73	0	16
1950-1954	25,482	886	3.5	156	612	95	12	11
1955-1959	27,909	1,265	4.5	270	829	111	18	32
1960-1964	39,423	2,582	6.5	257	2,007	253	21	44
1965-1969	66,795	5,365	8.0	508	4,275	431	30	121
1970-1972	53,478	3,736	7.0[a]	443	2,822	374	25	72
Total	244,829	14,663	6.0	1,860	10,987	1,412	106	298

[a]This decline from 1965-1969 was probably attributable to poorer coverage of foreign doctoral recipients in the 1970-1972 cohort.

Source: National Research Council/National Academy of Sciences (1974a, p. 19).

Table 11. Doctoral recipients, by sex and field, 1967-68 and 1972-73

Field	Men		Women	
	1967-68	*1972-73*	*1967-68*	*1972-73*
Total				
Number	19,201	27,562	2,813	6,066
Percent	100.0	100.0	100.0	100.0
Physical sciences	22.8	17.6	8.2	6.2
Mathematics	4.8	4.0	1.7	2.0
Physics and astronomy	7.2	5.6	1.2	0.9
Chemistry	8.6	6.1	4.9	3.0
Earth sciences	2.2	2.0	0.4	0.4
Engineering	14.7	11.9	0.5	0.7
Life sciences	16.5	15.2	18.1	14.4
Biological sciences	11.2	9.7	16.0	11.9
Agricultural sciences	3.5	3.6	0.2	0.6
Medical sciences	1.8	1.7	1.9	1.8
Environmental sciences	0	0.3	0	0.1
Social sciences	14.3	16.9	19.4	20.5
Psychology	5.8	6.3	11.8	11.8
Economics and econometrics	3.7	3.4	1.3	1.0
Political science, international relations	2.6	2.9	2.3	1.9
Other	2.1	4.4	4.0	5.7
Arts and humanities	12.7	13.8	24.9	25.5
History	3.3	3.8	3.5	3.0
English and American language and literature	3.5	3.2	9.0	8.5
Other language and literature	2.7	2.1	7.9	6.9
Other	3.2	4.7	4.5	7.2
Professional fields	n.a.	4.6	n.a.	3.3
Business administration	2.2	2.8	0.4	0.4
Social work	n.a.	0.3	n.a.	0.5
Home economics	n.a.	0.0	n.a.	0.7
Other	n.a.	1.5	n.a.	1.6
Education	16.7	19.8	28.4	29.4

Sources: National Research Council/National Academy of Sciences (1969 and 1974b).

Table 12. Average salaries of full-time faculty members on 9-10 month contracts, by control and type of institution, rank, and sex, 1974-75, and percentage increases since 1972-73

Public institutions

Type and rank	Average salary, 1974-75		Differ-ence	Percentage increase since 1972-73	
	Men	Women		Men	Women
All public institutions	$16,166	$13,697	$2,469	12.6	12.2
Professors	21,177	19,173	2,004	9.8	8.4
Associate professors	16,492	16,011	481	12.4	11.3
Assistant professors	13,614	13,123	491	11.1	11.0
Instructors	14,155	12,363	1,792	24.4	18.1
Universities	17,099	13,445	3,654	9.9	9.4
Professors	22,219	20,044	2,175	7.6	10.7
Associate professors	16,687	15,824	863	11.8	9.7
Assistant professors	13,733	13,005	728	9.0	9.7
Instructors	10,887	10,406	481	9.7	10.8
Other four-year institutions	15,576	13,540	2,036	13.6	10.3
Professors	19,979	19,168	811	13.1	7.3
Associate professors	16,160	15,881	279	12.2	11.3
Assistant professors	13,404	12,980	424	12.5	11.3
Instructors	11,069	10,594	475	12.9	10.3
Two-year institutions	15,462	14,034	1,428	18.6	16.5
Professors	18,976	17,739	1,237	11.1	12.0
Associate professors	16,907	16,780	127	15.3	14.4
Assistant professors	14,017	13,806	211	13.1	13.2
Instructors	15,538	13,836	1,702	24.8	20.9

Private institutions

Type and rank	Average salary, 1974-75		Differ-ence	Percentage increase since 1972-73	
	Men	Women		Men	Women
All private institutions	$15,358	$12,086	$3,272	7.0	8.7
Professors	20,427	17,040	3,387	8.4	9.4
Associate professors	15,149	13,677	1,472	7.9	9.6
Assistant professors	12,570	11,647	923	3.2	9.4
Instructors	10,262	9,701	561	8.3	7.9

Table 12

	Average salary, 1974-75		Differ-	Percentage increase since 1972-73	
Type and rank	Men	Women	ence	Men	Women
Universities	$18,350	$13,929	$4,421	9.9	8.7
Professors	23,751	20,435	3,316	9.6	10.8
Associate professors	16,937	15,810	1,127	9.3	11.4
Assistant professors	13,882	12,934	948	10.0	7.4
Instructors	11,302	10,841	461	8.5	11.7
Other four-year institutions	13,994	11,782	2,212	6.2	10.1
Professors	17,957	16,164	1,793	8.4	8.8
Associate professors	14,290	13,081	1,209	7.9	9.8
Assistant professors	12,046	11,294	752	0.1	10.3
Instructors	10,077	9,586	491	7.9	9.3
Two-year institutions	10,661	9,694	967	12.7	1.0
Professors	13,014	12,359	655	27.4	22.5
Associate professors	12,310	11,829	481	10.8	7.6
Assistant professors	10,684	10,624	60	9.1	7.0
Instructors	9,608	8,758	850	15.4	-4.2

Source: Jacobson (1973, p. 1); and "Faculty Salaries Shown Rising" (1975, p. 5).

Table 13. Affirmative action committees in affirmative action plans of respondent institutions

Carnegie classification	Number with committees	Number with affirmative action plans	Percent with committees
Research Universities I	19	24	79
Research Universities II	8	15	53
Doctoral-Granting Universities	11	15	73
Comprehensive Universities and Colleges	12	15	80
Liberal Arts Colleges I	7	12	58

(continued on next page)

Table 13 *(continued)*

Carnegie classification	Number with committees	Number with affirmative action plans	Percent with committees
Liberal Arts Colleges II	4	7	57
Two-Year Institutions	6	8	75
Total	67	96[a]	70

[a]This number is smaller than the total number with affirmative action plans (see Table 4), because a few institutions with plans did not provide copies of their plans, and it was therefore impossible to determine whether the plan included provision for a committee.

Source: Carnegie Council Survey of Affirmative Action Policies.

Table 14. Analyses of academic employment required of colleges and universities by current Department of Labor regulations as interpreted by OCR

1. *Utilization analysis*
   a. *Definition:* Comparison of percent of minorities and women in the contractor's work force with percent of minorities and women in the relevant external labor market.
   b. *Level of detail:* As of a given date, a separate analysis for each (7) racial/ethnic and sex category (black, Spanish-surnamed, Asian, Native American, other minority, women) for each (10) job classification (e.g., at a minimum: full professor, associate professor, assistant professor, instructor, lecturer, researcher, research assistant, teaching assistant, university extension staff, other teaching and research staff), for each (25-75) department or other organizational unit.
   c. *Number of separate availability pools to be identified (number of separate analyses):* 1,750-5,250
2. *Recruitment analysis*
   a. *Definition:* Comparison of percent of minorities and women in pool of persons being considered for a position (i.e., persons recruited plus persons who applied independently) with percent of minorities and women in the relevant external labor market.
   b. *Level of detail:* For each racial/ethnic and sex category (7), for each job classification (10) in each department or other organizational unit (25-75) where a new hire(s) has been made during a specified period of time (e.g., 5 years).
   c. *Number of recruitment analyses required:* 2,800-8,400

Table 14

---

3. *Selection analysis*
   - a. *Definition:* Comparison of percent of minorities and women selected for a type of position with percent of minorities and women in pool of persons being considered for such positions. (May overlap with promotion analysis depending on nature of "applicant" pool.)
   - b. *Level of detail:* For each racial/ethnic and sex category (7), for each job classification (10) in each department or other organizational unit (25-75) where a new hire(s) has been made during a specified period of time (e.g., 5 years).
4. *Placement/assignment analysis*
   - a. *Definition:* Qualitative assessment of the specific positions/work responsibilities to which persons are assigned to determine whether any pattern of less favorable placement or assignment for women and minorities exists.
   - b. *Level of detail:* For each racial/ethnic and sex category (7), for each job classification (10) in each department or other organizational unit (25-75) where a new hire(s) has been made during a specified period of time (e.g., 5 years).
   - c. *Number of placement/assignment analyses required:* 2,800-8,400
5. *Promotion analysis*
   - a. *Definition:* Comparison of percent of minorities and women promoted with percent of minorities and women eligible for promotion.
   - b. *Level of detail:* For each racial/ethnic and sex category (6), for each job classification (7) in each department or other organizational unit (25-75) where promotions have occurred during a specified period of time (e.g., 5 years). (May overlap with selection analysis depending on nature of "applicant" pool.)
   - c. *Number of promotion analyses required:* 1,750-5,200
6. *Tenure analysis*
   - a. *Definition:* Comparison of percent of minorities and women granted tenure with percent of minorities and women eligible for tenure. (May overlap with promotion analysis depending on tenure granting policy.)
   - b. *Level of detail:* For each racial/ethnic and sex category (6), for each job classification (7) in each department or other organizational unit (25-75) where tenure decisions have occurred during a specified period of time (e.g., 5 years).
   - c. *Number of tenure analyses required:* 700-2,100
7. *Transfer (reassignment) analysis*
   - a. *Definition:* Qualitative assessment of each transfer (reassignment) action (i.e., positive, negative, or neutral) and for each

(continued on next page)

Table 14 *(continued)*

type of transfer, a comparison of the percent of minorities and women transferred (reassigned) with the percent
of minorities and women eligible for transfer (reassignment).

h. *Level of detail:* For each transfer (reassignment) action during a special period of time, a determination of the qualita-
tive impact of each transfer (reassignment) and a
comparison by job classification (10) and department or other organizational unit (25-75) by race/
ethnic and sex category (7) of the persons transferred (reassigned) and the persons eligible for transfer (reassignment).

c. *Number of transfer analyses required:* 700-2,100

8. *Salary analysis* (initial entry)

a. *Definition:* Comparison of the average salary at initial entry granted
to women and minorities with the average salary at ini-
tial entry granted to non-minority males.

b. *Level of detail:* As of a given date, for a specified period of time, a
separate analysis for each (7) racial/ethnic and sex
category for each (10) job classification, for each
(25-75) department or other organizational unit.

c. *Number of salary analyses required:* 1,750-5,250

9. *Salary analysis* (merit increase/adjustments)

a. *Definition:* Comparison of the average salary increase granted to
women and minorities with the average salary increase
granted to non-minority males.

b. *Level of detail:* As of a given date, for a specified period of time, a
separate analysis for each (7) racial/ethnic and sex
category, for each (10) job classification, for each
(25-75) department or other organizational unit.

c. *Number of salary increase analyses required:* 1,750-5,250

10. *Fringe benefit analysis*

a. *Definition:* Comparison of the nature and level of fringe benefits
provided to women and minorities with the nature and
level of fringe benefits provided to non-minority males.

b. *Level of detail:* As of a given date, a separate analysis for each (7)
racial/ethnic and sex category, for each (10) job
classification, for each (25-75) department or other
organizational unit.

c. *Number of fringe benefit analyses required:* 1,750-5,250

11. *Training analysis*

a. *Definition:* Qualitative assessment of each training program toward
career development (positive, negative, neutral) and for
each training program a comparison of the percent of
minorities and women participating with percent of
minorities and women in the work force of the contractor for whom each such training program would be
appropriate.

Table 14

b. *Level of detail:* For each training program/activity conducted over a specified period of time, a determination of the qualitative impact on career development of each such program and a comparison by relevant job classifications and organizational units by race/ethnic and sex category (7) of the percent of women and minorities participating in such training program/ activity with the percent of minorities and women for whom such training would be relevant.

c. *Number of training analyses required:* 175-350

12. *Separation analysis* (voluntary)

a. *Definition:* Comparison of the percent of minorities and women voluntarily terminating employment with percent of minorities and women in the contractor's work force.

b. *Level of detail:* For each racial/ethnic and sex category (7), for each job classification (10) in each department or other organizational unit (25-75) where a separation has occurred during a specified period of time (e.g., 5 years).

c. *Number of separation analyses required:* 1,750-5,250

13. *Termination analysis* (involuntary)

a. *Definition:* Comparison of percent of minorities and women involuntarily terminating employment with percent of minorities and women in the contractor's work force.

b. *Level of detail:* For each type of involuntary termination (e.g., nonrenewal of contract; dismissal for cause; routine layoff), for each racial/ethnic and sex category (7), for each job classification (10) in each department or other organizational unit (25-75) where a termination has occurred during a specified period of time (e.g., 5 years).

c. *Number of termination analyses required:* 700-2,100

14. *Source of funds analysis* (currently under discussion; *not* yet *required*)

a. *Definition:* Comparison of percent of minorities and women receiving salaries from funds provided by external funding sources ("soft money") with percent of minorities and women in the contractor's work force.

b. *Level of detail:* As of a given date, a separate analysis for each (7) racial/ethnic and sex category, for each (25-75) department or organizational unit.

Analytic Summary:

Total number of analyses required: 21,000-63,000

Total number of analyses required of each department or other organizational unit: 850

(continued on next page)

Table 14 *(continued)*

In addition to the analytic requirements set forth above in items (1)-(13), Department of Labor regulations as currently interpreted require a second (in-depth) level of analysis when and if any of the comparisons made in items (2)-(13) reveal a disparate effect on women or minorities. Such second level analyses are designed to identify the factors of the employment decision-making process, the use of which has created the disparate effect or impact. In most cases, the provisions of 41 CFR 60-3 would apply to those factors identified by the second-level analysis.

Source: Office for Civil Rights, U.S. Department of Health, Education, and Welfare.

Table 15. Sample table from the Berkeley plan: for women in the College of Letters and Sciences, departments of social sciences

Unit	Total headcount	Headcount women	Proportion of women in unit	Availability	Hires to parity	Department goal	Department timetable[a]	
Economics	29	1	0.0345	0.0507	+0.46			
Geography	10	1	0.1000	0.0575	-0.43			
Sociology	26	3	0.1154	0.1791	+1.65	+1.65	0 NT	21 AF
Anthropology	33	5	0.1515	0.2327	+2.68	+2.68	0 NT	26 AF
History	52	2	0.0385	0.1136	+3.90	+3.90	8 NT	27 AF
Political science	39	1	0.0256	0.0914	+2.56	+2.56	11 NT	30 AF
Psychology	37	4	0.1081	0.2096	+3.75	+3.75	0 NT	26 AF

[a]NT refers to nontenured faculty; AF refers to all regular faculty.

Source: University of California (1975).

Table 16. Sample table from the Berkeley plan: for blacks in the College of Letters and Sciences, departments of social sciences

Unit	Total headcount	Headcount blacks	Proportion of blacks in unit	Availability	Hires to parity	Department goal	Department timetable
Economics	29	0	0	0.0082	+0.23		
Geography	10	0	0	0.0000	+0.00		
Sociology	26	3	0.1154	0.0254	−2.91		
Anthropology	33	2	0.0606	0.0150	−1.50		
History	52	0	0	0.0169	+0.87		
Political science	39	0	0	0.0082	+0.31		
Psychology	37	0	0	0.0100	+0.36		

Source: University of California (1975).

Table 17. Sample table from the Berkeley plan: for Asians in the College of Letters and Sciences, departments of social sciences

Unit	Total headcount	Headcount Asians	Proportion of Asians in unit	Availability	Hires to parity	Department goal	Department timetable
Economics	29	1	0.0345	0.0164	−0.53		
Geography	10	0	0	0.0171	+0.17		
Sociology	26	0	0	0.0169	+0.43		
Anthropology	33	0	0	0.0200	+0.66		
History	52	1	0.0192	0.0169	−0.13		
Political science	39	0	0	0.0247	+0.96		
Psychology	37	0	0	0.0060	+0.22		

Source: University of California (1975).

Table 18. Sample table from the Berkeley plan: for Chicanos in the College of Letters and Sciences, departments of social sciences

Unit	Total headcount	Headcount Chicanos	Proportion of Chicanos in unit	Availability	Hires to parity	Department goal	Department timetable
Economics	29	0	0	0.0000	+0.00		
Geography	10	0	0	0.0000	+0.00		
Sociology	26	0	0	0.0028	+0.07		
Anthropology	33	0	0	0.0100	+0.33		
History	52	1	0.0192	0.0000	−1.00		
Political science	39	0	0	0.0000	+0.00		
Psychology	37	0	0	0.0000	+0.00		

Source: University of California (1975).

Table 19. Sample table from the Berkeley plan: for Native Americans in the College of Letters and Sciences, departments of social sciences

Unit	Total headcount	Headcount Native Americans	Proportion of Native Americans in unit	Availability	Hires to parity	Department goal	Department timetable
Economics	29	0	0	0.0066	+0.19		
Geography	10	0	0	0.0000	+0.00		
Sociology	26	0	0	0.0038	+0.07		
Anthropology	33	0	0	0.0000	+0.00		
History	55	0	0	0.0056	+0.28		
Political science	35	0	0	0.0082	+0.31		
Psychology	37	0	0	0.0056	+0.20		

Source: University of California (1975).

Appendix B

Selected Documents

**LETTER FROM CLARK KERR
AND QUESTIONNAIRE TO INSTITUTIONS
INCLUDED IN THE COUNCIL'S SURVEY
OF AFFIRMATIVE ACTION POLICIES**

Carnegie Council on Policy Studies in Higher Education

CLARK KERR
CHAIRMAN

2150 SHATTUCK AVENUE   BERKELEY, CALIFORNIA 94704   (415)849-4474

The Carnegie Council is preparing a report on affirmative action policies, which will have two major purposes: (1) to provide information on the progress made by institutions of higher education in developing their own affirmative action policies, and (2) to recommend modifications in the way in which federal affirmative action programs are administered. In general, we support the goals of affirmative action, but believe the present situation is unnecessarily complicated and confused because of the involvement of too many federal agencies in enforcement, the lack of understanding of the special characteristics of academic employment by some enforcement officials, and the need for penalties that are more appropriate than the withholding of federal funds--a penalty so severe that it has never actually been used.

In order to develop adequate information on the affirmative action policies of colleges and universities, we are conducting a survey of a representative sample of about 200 institutions drawn from the Carnegie Commission classification of institutions of higher education. Your institution is included in our sample, and we hope very much that you will provide the requested information. To minimize the burden of responding, we are requesting that, rather than fill in a lengthy questionnaire, you send us the following documents, to the extent that they are available:

1. Your academic personnel manual, or other documents providing information on the following:

    a. Policies, if any, relating to recruitment procedures;

    b. Policies relating to review procedures for faculty appointments and promotions;

    c. Policies especially relevant to employment opportunities for married women, such as provisions for part-time appointments and promotion to tenure on a part-time basis, and anti-nepotism rules;

    d. Grievance procedures for academic personnel.

AN ACTIVITY OF THE CARNEGIE FOUNDATION FOR THE ADVANCEMENT OF TEACHING

-2-

2. <u>A copy of your affirmative action plan</u>, if any, together with your responses to the questions on the brief enclosed questionnaire relating to the status of your affirmative action plan under federal affirmative action policies.

3. <u>A copy of your catalogue</u> for each of the years 1968 and 1974.

4. <u>Data</u> on changes in the relative representation of women and minority groups on your faculty, preferably by rank, if readily available.

In the case of multi-campus institutions, our sample includes individual campuses rather than system-wide offices. We realize that in some cases, e.g., academic personnel manuals, the relevant documents may relate to the multi-campus system, whereas in other cases, e.g., affirmative action plans and catalogues, the relevant documents may relate to your individual campus. We hope that you will send us the appropriate documents, whether they relate to your campus or to the entire system.

Our plans call for analyzing and reporting the data for major groups of institutions within the Carnegie classification--e.g., research universities, other doctoral granting institutions, etc. We do not plan to reveal data for individual institutions, even though some of the documents we have requested are official publications.

We hope very much that you will provide the requested information. We believe that our proposed report can play a constructive role, not only in providing more adequate information on academic personnel policies that are relevant to affirmative action issues, but also in developing constructive recommendations for modifications in federal enforcement policies.

We should like to have your response by April 15, 1975, if possible. Please mail the documents and the completed questionnaire to

> Dr. Margaret S. Gordon
> Carnegie Council on Higher Education
> 2150 Shattuck Avenue
> Berkeley, California 94704

> Sincerely,

> Clark Kerr

Enclosure

QUESTIONNAIRE RELATING TO THE STATUS
OF YOUR AFFIRMATIVE PLAN

1. When was your affirmative action plan first approved by you (the president or chief campus officer)? _____

2. Has your affirmative action plan been submitted to the Office for Civil Rights in the Department of Health, Education, and Welfare? _____

3. Has your affirmative action plan been approved by that Office? _____

4. Were modifications requested or demanded before the plan was approved? _____

5. If so, we request that you briefly summarize the modifications that were requested, or agreed upon after negotiations:

_____

_____

_____

_____

_____

6. Additional comments relating to your negotiations with federal agencies:

_____

_____

_____

_____

7. Suggestions, if any, relating to federal affirmative action policies:

_____

_____

_____

BRIEF SUMMARY OF CARNEGIE COMMISSION
CLASSIFICATION OF INSTITUTIONS
OF HIGHER EDUCATION

This classification includes all institutions listed in the U.S. Office of Education's *Advance Report on Opening Fall Enrollment in Higher Education: Institutional Data, 1970*. When a campus of a multicampus institution is listed separately, it is included as a separate institution in our classification. In a few instances, the Office of Education includes all campuses of an institution in a single listing, and in such cases the institution is treated as a single entry in our classification. Our classification includes 2,827 institutions, compared with the Office of Education total of 2,565 for 1970. The difference is explained by the fact that, *for purposes of obtaining the total number of institutions,* we have treated each campus as an institution, whereas the Office of Education treats multicampus systems as single institutions.

1. Doctoral-Granting Institutions

1.1 Research Universities I. The 50 leading universities in terms of federal financial support of academic science in at least two of the three academic years, 1968-69, 1969-70, and 1970-71, provided they awarded at least 50 Ph.D.'s (plus M.D.'s if a medical school was on the same campus) in 1969-70. Rockefeller University was included because of the high quality of its research and doctoral training, although it did not meet these criteria.

1.2 Research Universities II. These universities were on the list of the 100 leading institutions in terms of federal financial support in at least two out of the above three years and awarded at least 50 Ph.D.'s (plus M.D.'s if a medical school was on the same campus) in 1969-70, or they were among the leading 50 institutions in terms of the total number of Ph.D.'s (plus M.D.'s if on the same campus) awarded during the years from 1960-61 to 1969-70. In addition, a few institutions that did not quite meet these criteria, but that have graduate programs of high quality and with impressive promise for future development, have been included in 1.2.

1.3 Doctoral-Granting Universities I. These institutions awarded 40 or more Ph.D.'s in 1969-70 (plus M.D.'s if on the same campus) or received at least $3 million in total federal financial support in either 1969-70 or 1970-71. No institution is included that granted fewer than 20 Ph.D.'s (plus M.D.'s if on the same campus), regardless of the amount of federal financial support it received.

1.4 Doctoral-Granting Universities II. These institutions awarded at least 10 Ph.D.'s in 1969-70, with the exception of a few new doctoral-granting institutions that may be expected to increase the number of Ph.D.'s awarded within a few years.[1]

2. Comprehensive Universities and Colleges

2.1 Comprehensive Universities and Colleges I. This group includes institutions that offered a liberal arts program as well as several other programs, such as engineering and business administration. Many of them offered master's degrees, but all lacked a doctoral program or had an extremely limited doctoral program. All institutions in this group had at least two professional or occupational programs and enrolled at least 2,000 students in 1970. If an institution's enrollment was smaller than this, it was not considered comprehensive.

2.2 Comprehensive Universities and Colleges II. This list includes state colleges and some private colleges that offered a liberal arts program and at least one professional or occupational program such as teacher training or nursing. Many of the institutions in this group are former teachers colleges that have recently broadened their programs to include a liberal arts curriculum.

[1] In all cases the term *Ph.D.* also includes the Ed.D. and other doctor's degrees.

Private institutions with fewer than 1,500 students and public institutions with fewer than 1,000 students in 1970 are not included even though they may offer a selection of programs, because they were not regarded as comprehensive with such small enrollments. Such institutions are classified as liberal arts colleges. The enrollment differentiation between private and public institutions was made because the public state colleges are experiencing relatively rapid increases in enrollment and are likely to have at least 1,500 students within a few years even if they did not in 1970. Most of the state colleges with relatively few students were established quite recently.

3. Liberal Arts Colleges

3.1 Liberal Arts Colleges I. These colleges scored 5 or above on Astin's selectivity index[2] *or* they were included among the 200 leading baccalaureate-granting institutions in terms of numbers of their graduates receiving Ph.D.'s at 40 leading doctoral-granting institutions from 1920 to 1966 (National Academy of Sciences, *Doctorate Recipients from United States Universities, 1958-1966*, 1967, Appendix B).

3.2 Liberal Arts Colleges II. These institutions include all the liberal arts colleges that did not meet our criteria for inclusion in the first group of liberal arts colleges. Again, the distinction between "liberal arts" and "comprehensive" is not clear-cut for some of the larger colleges in this group and is necessarily partly a matter of judgment.

In addition, many liberal arts colleges are extensively involved in teacher training, but future teachers tend to receive

---

[2] Astin's selectivity index is based on National Merit Scholarship Qualifying Test Scores for all students who took the NMSQT in 1964, classified according to the college of their first choice. From these distributions of scores, it was possible to estimate both the mean and the standard deviation of the scores of students actually entering each college by making certain adjustments in the data. For additional details, see Appendix C of Alexander W. Astin, *Predicting Academic Performance in College* (The Free Press, New York, 1971).

their degrees in arts and sciences fields, rather than in education.

4. Two-Year Colleges and Institutes

5. Professional Schools and Other Specialized Institutions
(Not covered in the Carnegie Council Survey of Affirmative Action Programs)

Source: Carnegie Commission (1973a). It should be noted that the enrollment data used in developing the classification were for 1970. The statement to the effect that state colleges classified as Comprehensive Universities and Colleges II are experiencing rapid increases in enrollment has not been as true in the last few years as it was when the classification was originally developed.

SELECTED PARAGRAPHS FROM U.S. CODE, TITLE 42

Subchapter 1.—Generally

§ 1981. *EQUAL RIGHTS UNDER THE LAW*

All persons within the jurisdiction of the United States shall have the same right in every State and Territory to make and enforce contracts, to sue, be parties, give evidence, and to the full and equal benefit of all laws and proceedings for the security of persons and property as is enjoyed by white citizens, and shall be subject to like punishment, pains, penalties, taxes, licenses, and exactions of every kind, and to no other. (R. S. § 1977.)

Derivation

Act May 31, 1870, ch. 114, § 16, 16 Stat. 144.

§ 1982. *PROPERTY RIGHTS OF CITIZENS*

All citizens of the United States shall have the same right, in every State and Territory, as is enjoyed by white citizens thereof to inherit, purchase, lease, sell, hold, and convey real and personal property. (R. S. § 1978.)

Derivation

Act Apr. 9, 1866, ch. 31, § 1, 14 Stat. 27.

§ 1983. *CIVIL ACTION FOR DEPRIVATION OF RIGHTS*

Every person who, under color of any statute, ordinance, regulation, custom, or usage, of any State or Territory, subjects, or causes to be subjected, any citizen of the United States or other person within the jurisdiction thereof to the deprivation of any rights, privileges, or immunities secured by the Constitution and laws, shall be liable to the party injured in an action at law, suit in equity, or other proper proceeding for redress. (R. S. § 1979.)

Derivation

Act Apr. 20, 1871, ch. 22, § 1, 17 Stat. 13.

§ 1985. *CONSPIRACY TO INTERFERE WITH CIVIL RIGHTS*
(3) *DEPRIVING PERSONS OF RIGHTS OR PRIVILEGES*

If two or more persons in any State or Territory conspire or go in disguise on the highway or on the premises of another, for the purpose of depriving, either directly or indirectly, any person or class of persons of the equal protection of the laws, or of equal privileges and immunities under the laws; or for the purpose of preventing or hindering the constituted authorities of any State or Territory from giving or securing to all persons within such State or Territory the equal protection of the laws; or if two or more persons conspire to prevent by force, intimidation, or threat, any citizen who is lawfully entitled to vote, from giving his support or advocacy in a legal manner, toward or in favor of the election of any lawfully qualified person as an elector for President or Vice President, or as a Member of Congress of the United States; or to injure any citizen in person or property on account of such support or advocacy; in any case of conspiracy set forth in this section, if one or more persons engaged therein do, or cause to be done, any act in furtherance of the object of such conspiracy, whereby another is injured in his person or property, or deprived of having and exercising any right or privilege of a citizen of the United States, the party so injured or deprived may have an action for the recovery of damages, occasioned by such injury or deprivation, against any one or more of the conspirators. (R. S. § 1980.)

Derivation

Acts July 31, 1861, ch. 33, 12 Stat. 284; Apr. 20, 1871, ch. 22, § 2, 17 Stat. 13.

Section Referred to in Other Sections

This section is referred to in section 1986 of this title; title 28 section 1343.

§ 1986. *SAME; ACTION FOR NEGLECT TO PREVENT*

Every person who, having knowledge that any of the wrongs conspired to be done, and mentioned in section 1985 of this title, are about to be committed, and having power to prevent or aid in preventing the commission of the same, neglects or refuses so to do, if such wrongful act be committed, shall be liable to the party injured, or his legal representatives, for all damages caused by such wrongful act, which such person by reasonable diligence could have prevented; and such damages may be recovered in an action on the case; and any number of persons guilty of such wrongful neglect or refusal may be joined as defendants in the action; and if the death of any party be caused by any such wrongful act and neglect, the legal representatives of the deceased shall have such action therefor, and may recover not exceeding $5,000 damages therein, for the benefit of the widow of the deceased, if there be one, and if there be no widow, then for the benefit of the next of kin of the deceased. But no action under the provisions of this section shall be sustained which is not commenced within one year after the cause of action has accrued. (R. S. § 1981.)

Derivation

Act Apr. 20, 1871, ch. 22, § 6, 17 Stat. 15.

§ 1988. *PROCEEDINGS IN VINDICATION OF CIVIL RIGHTS*

The jurisdiction in civil and criminal matters conferred on the district courts by the provisions of this chapter and Title 18, for the protection of all persons in the United States in their civil rights, and for their vindication, shall be exercised and enforced in conformity with the laws of the United States, so far as such laws are suitable to carry the same into effect; but in all cases where they are not adapted to the object, or are deficient in the provisions necessary to furnish suitable remedies and punish offenses against law, the common law, as modified and changed by the constitution and statutes of the State wherein the court having jurisdiction of such civil or criminal cause is held, so far as the same is not inconsistent with the Constitution and laws of the United States, shall be extended to and govern the said courts in the trial and disposition of the cause, and, if it is of a criminal nature in the infliction of punishment on the party found guilty. (R. S. § 722.)

Derivation

Acts Apr. 9, 1866, ch. 31, § 3, 14 Stat. 27; May 31, 1870, ch. 114, § 18, 16 Stat. 144.

References in Text

In the original "this chapter and Title 18" reads "this title and of title 'Civil Rights', and of title 'Crimes'," meaning titles XIII, XXIV, and LXX of the Revised Statutes.

Federal Rules of Civil Procedure

Effect of Rule 69 on this section, see note by Advisory Committee under said Rule, Title 28, Appendix, Judiciary and Judicial Procedure. Execution, see Rule 69.

Federal Rules of Criminal Procedure

Scope and application, see Rules 1 and 54, Title 18, Appendix, Crimes and Criminal Procedure.

RECOMMENDATIONS OF THE ADMINISTRATIVE CONFERENCE OF THE UNITED STATES, ADOPTED JUNE 5-6, 1975

Recommendation 75-2: Affirmative Action for Equal Opportunity in Nonconstruction Employment

Executive Order 11246, which concerns equal employment opportunity, applies to all contractors with the Federal government. Pursuant to this executive order, the Department of Labor has promulgated one set of regulations prohibiting discrimination and requiring affirmative action to govern contractors in the construction industry, and another set of such regulations to govern all other contractors.

A study of the application of the nonconstruction regulations to university faculty employment practices illustrates that the use of a single set of regulations for all nonconstruction employment can fail to take adequate account of important special circumstances of major employment categories. With respect to university faculty employment, for example, the regulations as applied have generated difficulties arising from failure to take account of the limited supply of qualified personnel in various disciplines, the nonquantifiability of standards for academic personnel, the diversity of institutional needs fulfilled by academic personnel (e.g., research, teaching, public service), and the concept of peer review in academic employment practices. It seems evident that difficulties of the sorts experienced in the application of the nonconstruction regulations to academic employment in higher education will be encountered in their application to other employment categories as well.

The study further suggests that contract cancellation is in many cases too severe or impracticable as the primary sanction for noncompliance with equal employment opportunity regulations; in practice, cancellation is rarely used. The more common sanction, as in the field of higher education employment, is the declaration of nonresponsibility of an employer. Unlike the procedures leading to other sanctions, such as debarment of a contractor or cancellation of a contract, no opportunity for prior hearing is afforded in connection with a declaration of nonresponsibility. The provision of an opportunity for hearing before imposition of any sanction under the contract compliance program will tend to assure the fairness and reliability of administrative determinations and to encourage responsible and consistent application of policy.

Recommendation

1. The Department of Labor, in consultation with the compliance agencies, should promptly commence a review of the contract compliance program applicable to nonconstruction contractors to determine whether regulations more closely adapted to the characteristics of specific occupations or industries are required, considering especially (1) variations in the susceptibility of types of employment to uniform or quantifiable methods of evaluating and predicting performance and (2) variations in policies of recruitment and advancement and in other personnel practices.

2. The Department of Labor should develop a system of graduated sanctions for breach of the obligation contained in the equal employment opportunity clause of government contracts, and should seek legislation to this end as may be necessary.[1]

3. A sanction, including that of declaration of nonresponsibility on equal employment opportunity grounds made prior to the award of a contract, should not be imposed except after opportunity for a hearing (whether evidentiary or informal) at which the validity of the claim of breach, or assertion of nonresponsibility, and the appropriateness of the proposed sanction may be placed in issue.

4. In performing its responsibilities for contract compliance in higher education the Department of Health, Education, and Welfare should (a) provide regional office staffs with uniform and clearly defined policies (b) recruit and assign staff who are familiar with institutions of higher education for adminis-

---

[1] In this connection the Department should consider Conference Recommendation 71-9: Enforcement of Standards in Federal Grant-in-Aid Programs, and Recommendation 72-6: Civil Money Penalties as a Sanction.

tration of the program in higher education, (c) consult widely with representatives of higher education institutions and other interested groups in developing and administering its compliance rules and policies, and (d) strengthen coordination of its administration of regulations applicable to higher education with other agencies having overlapping responsibilities, in particular the Equal Employment Opportunity Commission and the Wage and Hour Administration of the Department of Labor.

EXCERPTS FROM HIGHER EDUCATION GUIDELINES
OF OCTOBER 1972

Recruitment

In both academic and nonacademic areas, universities must recruit women and minority persons as actively as they have recruited white males. . . .

An expanded search network should include not only the traditional avenues through which promising candidates have been located. . . . In addition, to the extent that it is necessary to overcome underutilization, the university should search in areas and channels previously unexplored. . . .

Hiring

Once a nondiscriminatory applicant pool has been established through recruitment, the process of selection from that pool must also carefully follow procedures designed to ensure nondiscrimination. In all cases, standards and criteria for employment should be made reasonably explicit, and should be accessible to all employees and applicants. . . .

In hiring decisions, assignment to a particular title or rank may be discriminatory. For example, in many institutions women are more often assigned initially to lower academic ranks than are men. . . . Where there is no valid basis for such differential treatment, such a practice is in violation of the Executive Order. . . .

In the area of academic appointments, a nondiscriminatory selection process does not mean that an institution should indulge in "reverse discrimination" or "preferential treatment" which leads to the selection of unqualified persons over qualified ones. Indeed, to take such action on grounds of race, ethnicity, sex or religion constitutes discrimination in violation of the Executive Order. . . .

Antinepotism Policies

Policies or practices which prohibit or limit the simultaneous employment of two members of the same family and which have an adverse impact upon one sex or the other are in violation of the Executive Order. For example, because men have traditionally been favored in employment over women, anti-nepotism regulations in most cases operate to deny employment opportunity to a wife rather than to a husband.

If an institution's regulations against the simultaneous employment of husband and wife are discriminatory on their face (e.g., applicable to "faculty wives"), or if they have in practice served in most instances to deny a wife rather than a husband employment, . . . they should be altered or abolished in order to mitigate their discriminatory impact. . . .

Institutional regulations which set reasonable restrictions on an individual's capacity to function as judge or advocate in specific situations involving a member of his or her immediate family are permissible where they do not have the effect of denying equal employment opportunity to one sex over the other.

Placement, Job Classification, and Assignment

. . . In academic employment, minorities and women have sometimes been classified as "research associates," "lecturers" or similar categories of employment which do not carry with them the benefits and protections of regular academic appointment, and from which promotion is rare, while men with the same qualifications are appointed to regular faculty positions. Such sex- or minority-segregated classification is discriminatory and must be eliminated. In addition, appropriate remedies must be afforded those persons previously assigned to such classifications. . . .

Salary

The Executive Order requires that universities adhere carefully to the concept of equal pay for equal work. . . .

An institution should set forth with reasonable particularity criteria for determining salary for each job classification and within each job classification. These criteria should be made available to present and potential employees.

Back Pay

Back pay awards are authorized and widely used as a remedy under Title VII of the Civil Rights Act of 1964, the Equal Pay

Act, and the National Labor Relations Act. Universities, like other employers, are subject to the provisions of these statutes.

This means that evidence of discrimination that would require back pay as a remedy will be referred to the appropriate Federal enforcement agency if the Office for Civil Rights is not able to negotiate a voluntary settlement with a university. . . .

Grievance Procedures

As of March 1972 and pursuant to the provisions of the Equal Employment Opportunity Act of 1972, the Equal Employment Opportunity Commission has jurisdiction over individual complaints of discrimination by academic as well as nonacademic employees of educational institutions.

Pursuant to formal agreement between OCR and EEOC . . . individual complaints of discrimination will be investigated and remedied by EEOC. Class complaints, groups of individual complaints or other information which indicates possible institutional *patterns* of discrimination . . . will remain subject to investigation by OCR. In such cases, retrospective relief for individuals within such classes or groups will remain within the jurisdiction of EEOC.

Where an employer has established sound standards of due process for the hearing of employee grievance, and has undertaken a prompt and good faith effort to identify and provide relief for grievances, a duplicative assumption of jurisdiction by the Federal Government has not always proven necessary. We therefore urge the development of sound grievance procedures for all employees, academic and nonacademic alike, in order to ensure the fair treatment of individual cases where discrimination is alleged, and to maintain the integrity of the employer's internal employment system. . . .

Development of Affirmative Action Programs

Effective affirmative action programs shall contain, but not necessarily be limited to, the following ingredients:

1. *Development or reaffirmation of the contractor's equal employment opportunity policy:* Each institution should have a

clear written statement over the signature of the chief administrative officer which sets forth the institution's legal obligation and policy for the guidance of all supervisory personnel, both academic and nonacademic, for all employees and for the community served by the institution. . . .

2. *Dissemination of the policy:* Internal communication of the institution's policy in writing to all supervisory personnel is essential to their understanding, cooperation and compliance. All persons responsible for personnel decisions must know what the law requires, what the institution's policy is, and how to interpret the policy and implement the program within the area of their responsibility. Formal and informal external dissemination of the policy is necessary to inform and secure the cooperation of organizations within the community, including civil rights groups, professional associations, women's groups, and various sources of referral within the recruitment area of the institution. . . .

3. *Responsibility for implementation:* An administrative procedure must be set up to organize and monitor the affirmative action program. 41 CFR 60-2.22 provides that an executive of the contractor should be appointed as director of EEO programs, and that he or she should be given "the necessary top management support and staffing to execute the assignment." . . . This should be a person knowledgeable of and sensitive to the problems of women and minority groups. Depending on the size of the institution, this may be his or her sole responsibility and necessary authority and staff should be accorded the position to ensure the proper implementation of the program.

In several institutions the EEO officer has been assisted by one or more task forces composed in substantial part of women and minority persons. This has usually facilitated the task of the EEO officer and enhanced the prospects of success for the affirmative action program in the institution.

4. *Identification of problem areas by organizational units and job classifications:* . . .

5. *Internal audit and reporting systems:* . . .

6. *Publication of affirmative action programs:* . . .

CORRESPONDENCE BETWEEN WILLIAM FRIDAY,
PRESIDENT OF THE UNIVERSITY OF NORTH CAROLINA,
AND THE DEPARTMENT OF LABOR
AND EXCERPTS FROM ACCOMPANYING
MEMORANDUM OF THE UNIVERSITY

THE UNIVERSITY OF NORTH CAROLINA

General Administration

P. O. BOX 2688
CHAPEL HILL 27514

January 17, 1975

The Honorable Peter Brennan
Secretary of Labor
Washington, D. C. 20500

Dear Mr. Secretary:

The sixteen constituent institutions of The University of North Carolina have
sought to produce acceptable written affirmative action plans, consistent with
the provisions of Executive Order 11246 and in service of felt moral and ethical
imperatives. In that connection, we have benefited from a constructive relationship with Mr. William Thomas and his associates in the Office for Civil Rights,
Region IV, Department of Health, Education, and Welfare. We anticipate, as
a consequence of recent conferences with those officials, that agreement on
acceptable written plans can be achieved in the near future. In the interim,
the constituent institutions of the University are proceeding with implementation
of the current drafts of their respective written plans, and significant progress
in the effort to achieve greater representation of women and members of racial
minority groups within the employee complements is being realized.

A potential impediment to final agreement derives from a disagreement between
the University and the Office for Civil Rights concerning the correct interpretation and application of certain provisions of Title 41, Part 60-1, Public Contracts
and Property Management, as issued by the Secretary of Labor. Accordingly,
at a meeting held on December 17, 1974, between representatives of the University
and representatives of the Office for Civil Rights, Region IV, it was agreed that
we might appropriately seek from your office interpretive guidance on the subject.
I concurrently address copies of this correspondence to Mr. Peter Holmes,
Director, Office for Civil Rights, and to Mr. William Thomas, Director, Office
for Civil Rights (Region IV).

Attached herewith is a statement of the issue as we perceive it and our
suggestions concerning a resolution of the question which, we believe, will
serve constructively the interests of all who are involved in the substantial
effort to achieve greater equity in the employment context for persons who

The Honorable Peter Brennan
Page Two
January 17, 1975

previously have suffered disadvantage because of their race, color, religion, sex or national origin.

We earnestly solicit your assistance in clarifying and imparting reasonable substance to those rather cryptic administrative provisions identified.

Cordially,

William Friday

Attachment

cc: Mr. Peter E. Holmes
Mr. William H. Thomas

EXCERPTS FROM UNIVERSITY OF NORTH CAROLINA
MEMORANDUM, JANUARY 17, 1975

... There is disagreement between the University and the Office for Civil Rights concerning the meaning, intent and proper application of those regulatory provisions which treat the matter of "availability." The Office for Civil Rights asserts that "availability" means the general "existence" of a pool of individuals who possess the requisite qualifications for employment within the labor area determined to be pertinent. The University contends, however, that "availability" should be construed to mean the realistically probable access of the contractor to and the potential employability by the contractor of persons who possess the requisite qualifications for employment within the labor area determined to be pertinent.

The importance of this difference in perception is substantial. A hypothetical example will serve to illustrate the conceptual and practical difficulties and potential inequities which attend the interpretation espoused by the Office for Civil Rights. Assume that the faculty of the mathematics department of a university consists of 19 males (95 percent) and 1 female (5 percent). A determination of the sufficiency or insufficiency of current "utilization" of females within the department is to be achieved by postulating a norm based on the "availability" of females who possess the requisite qualifications. Assuming, for purposes of discussion, that the possession of an earned doctoral degree in mathematics is one established valid prerequisite to consideration of an individual for employment in the department and that the labor market for the department is national in scope, the initial basic parameters of the theoretical pool can be ascertained. Assume, further, that as of the analysis date reliable data establish that 250 women in the United States hold earned doctorates in mathematics and thereby comprise 10 percent of the total pool of persons holding such degrees. At what point in the progressive refinement of this raw statistic may any realistic and useful conclusions be drawn about the sufficiency or insufficiency of the university's employment of females? The directives, both informal and formal, of the Office for Civil

Rights indicate that no further refinement necessarily need be undertaken for purposes of measuring the contractor's past compliance with affirmative action mandates and establishing remedial hiring goals. Thus, as we understand the obligations posited by the Office for Civil Rights, in the hypothetical situation suggested the university would be deemed deficient in its utilization of females as members of the mathematics department to the extent of 100 percent and, thus, would have a corresponding obligation to double the representation of women on the faculty of the mathematics department.

Whether viewed as a method for measuring past derelictions (i.e. "deficiency," with its connotations of misfeasance or nonfeasance), or, correspondingly, for positing remedial goals (with attendant substantial expectations and inducements), the objectionable aspects and consequences of such a simplistic analysis are immediately apparent. A superficial inquiry of that type says virtually nothing of utility about the actual "availability to the contractor" (either past or present or prospective) of qualified and employable individuals of various races and both sexes . . .

A realistic "availability analysis" would not stop with the raw data apparently deemed sufficient by the Office for Civil Rights. With reference to the hypothetical situation suggested previously, we point out one predictable anomalous consequence of such a truncated inquiry. All of the university-level institutions in the United States presumably are engaged, more or less simultaneously, in the production of affirmative action programs which include availability analyses, inter alia, for departments of mathematics. Under the analytical approach apparently prescribed by the Office for Civil Rights as applied in the hypothetical context suggested, all such institutions would be obligated to achieve at least a 10 percent representation of women in their respective mathematics department faculties. To assume that any such mathematically perfect pro rata distribution of the available pool of female mathematicians will occur pursuant to the separate, uncoordinated and self-interested efforts of all participating institutions is to court delusion of the most extreme variety. Thus, a large number of the subject institutions are foreordained not to achieve the "remedial" goals predicated on found "deficiencies" in their past performance.

A refinement of the raw data, in service of a realistic assessment of "availability," should include at least the following:

A. Availability to the general higher education community
   1. Female mathematicians available for academic employment . . .
   2. Female mathematicians representing pertinent subspecialties who are available for academic employment . . .
   3. Female mathematicians qualified for and interested in academic employment who currently are unemployed . . .
   4. Female mathematicians currently engaged in academic employment who could be induced to change their situs of employment . . .
B. Availability to the particular higher education institution
   1. The consonance of specific characteristics of particular employment opportunities with the qualifications and interests of potential candidates . . .
   2. Comparative and competitive financial inducements . . .
   4. Living environment . . .
   5. Individual mobility . . .

U.S. DEPARTMENT OF LABOR
EMPLOYMENT STANDARDS ADMINISTRATION
Office of Federal Contract Compliance
WASHINGTON, D.C 20210

MAR 7 1975

Mr. William Friday, President
University of North Carolina
General Administration
Post Office Box 2688
Chapel Hill, North Carolina 27514

Dear Mr. Friday:

This is in response to your letter to Secretary Drennan
requesting resolution of an apparent disagreement with the
Regional Office of the Office of Civil Rights, Department
of Health, Education and Welfare. The disagreement concerns the proper method to use in accordance with Revised
Order No. 4 to determine availability and consequently
deficiencies and goals.

We concur that percentages of graduates who are minorities
and females would give only rough estimates of availability.
From the point of view of the Office of Federal Contract
Compliance (OFCC), such figures are not by themselves
sufficient because they do not meet the requirements of
section 60-2.11 of Revised Order No. 4. This section sets
out eight (8) factors that must be considered in determining
availability of minorities and eight (8) similar factors
that must be used in determining availability of women.
Education is only one of the factors and is insufficient
as an availability estimate in and of itself. All factors
in section 60-2.11 must be considered.

A contractor may develop its own method of computing availability as long as it considers all the items listed in
section 60-2.11 and does not otherwise violate Revised Order
No. 4. Section 60-2.11 does recognize that the factors
listed constitute a minimum. In using additional factors,

however, contractors may not make adjustments that would reflect the results of individual or institutionalized discrimination. Using factors (assumptions) in computing availability which are in themselves discriminatory either on their face or in operation, e.g. have an adverse effect upon women or minorities, could result in figures that show no underutilization or deficiencies and hence would permit continuation of the underutilization. As an example, take the assumption that most women do not want to travel in their work. Let us say that your experience as an employer shows that only one (1) out of ten (10) of your female employees has been desirous of travel. Therefore, with regard to positions involving travel, you adjust the availability figures by taking only 10 percent of the otherwise qualified women. Your result is a showing of no underutilization and consequently no goal is required. However, there are a number of problems in this process. The first one is that your own experience with female employees may not have been representative. It might be that your experience merely reflects your expectations. The same results are obtained from looking at the larger employment scene. Few women are in traveling jobs. If these types of assumptions are used in arriving at availability figures, all you are doing is reflecting the status quo and perpetuating underutilization and discrimination. In this example few women have had the opportunity to travel in their work because it has been socially unacceptable, not because there is any sex linked qualification required in a traveling job. A contractor may not base its analysis only upon its own recruitment and employment experience. A contractor's experience would directly reflect its own efforts and attitudes. This could be good or bad, but it would not necessarily be representative.

You raised the possibility of adding a disclaimer to the utilization and availability analysis. We do not see where this would solve anything. In the first place, a contractor has an obligation to come up with the most accurate and realistic availability data possible. Then, the contractor must commit itself to making every good faith effort to meet its goal. Any disclaimer would not mean that the contractor has any less of a burden to produce an acceptable workforce analysis and it would not mean that less of a good faith effort is required. If a contractor wishes to explain

the limitations of the figures in its program, that is
acceptable. However, such an explanation does not mean
that a contractor has any less of an obligation to produce
the best analysis possible and overcome shortcomings in the
data.

You questioned the need for ultimate goals when those goals
will be constantly changing as future conditions change. We
are aware that availability is a changing factor and that
goals will therefore require constant adjustment. For this
reason Revised Order No. 4 requires at least annual updating
of the affirmative action program. A major goal of our program is to improve the availability of women and minorities
for the better jobs. Contractors have an obligation to assist
in the improved availability through training and other means.
As the effects of discrimination are eliminated, we expect
availability to increase. And, as more minorities and women
are qualified and available for better jobs, we expect this
fact to be reflected in the contractor's goals and workforce.

In summary, we agree that availability figures should reflect
real availability as nearly as possible. There is no point
in overestimating availability for then goals would be un-
realistically high. Underestimating availability would result
in perpetuating the current underutilization of minorities
and women. As a minimum in determining availability, all of
the factors listed in section 60-2.11 of Revised Order No. 4
must be considered.

I hope we have been of assistance.

Sincerely,

PHILIP J. DAVIS
Director

Reprinted from Summer 1973 AAUP Bulletin

AFFIRMATIVE ACTION IN HIGHER EDUCATION: A REPORT BY THE COUNCIL COMMISSION ON DISCRIMINATION

The Report which follows was presented in April, 1973, to the Council and to the Fifty-ninth Annual Meeting.

The Council Committee on Discrimination has been directed to formulate a position on the role of affirmative action in the elimination of discriminatory practices in academic recruiting, appointment, and advancement. In doing so, we begin with the premise that discrimination against women and minorities in higher education is both reprehensible and illegal, and reaffirm the emphatic condemnation of such practices by the AAUP.

More particularly, it is to the specific meaning and implications of affirmative action that our concern is directed, and especially to the question of so-called "preferential" or "compensatory" treatment of women and minorities. Because the phrase "affirmative action" has been assigned such extraordinarily different meanings by different persons and agencies, however, we mean to set the tone for this Report at the beginning by stating our own position as to what it must mean consistent with the standards of the AAUP. It is that affirmative action in the improvement of professional opportunities for women and minorities must be (and readily can be) devised wholly consistent with the highest aspirations of universities and colleges for excellence and outstanding quality, and that affirmative action should in no way use the very instrument of racial or sexual discrimination which it deplores.

The plans which we commend are those which are entirely affirmative, i.e., plans in which "preference" and "compensation" are words of positive connotation rather than words of condescension or *noblesse oblige*—preference for the more highly valued candidate and compensation for past failures to reach the actual market of intellectual resources available to higher education. The Committee believes that the further improvement of quality in higher education and the elimination of discrimination due to race or sex are not at odds with each other, but at one. What is sought in the idea of affirmative action is essentially the revision of standards and practices to assure that institutions are in fact drawing from the largest marketplace of human resources in staffing their faculties, and a critical review of appointment and advancement criteria to insure that they do not inadvertently foreclose consideration of the best qualified persons by untested presuppositions which operate to exclude women and minorities. Further, faculties are asked to consider carefully whether they are requiring a higher standard and more conclusive evidence of accomplishment of those women and minorities who are considered for appointment and advancement. What is asked for in the development of an affirmative action plan is not a "quota" of women or blacks, but simply a forecast of what a department or college would expect to occur given the *non*discriminatory use of *proper* appointment standards and recruiting practices—with the expectation that where the forecast turns out to be wide of the mark as to what actually happens, the institution will at once make proper inquiry as to why that was so. In essence, it is measures such as these which the Committee believes to be required by the Office for Civil Rights of HEW of universities using federal funds, and we do not see that there is in such requirements anything which the AAUP should find inconsistent with its own goals. Indeed, there may be more reason for concern that affirmative action of this kind which is critical to the abatement of discrimination may fail to be pursued with vigor than that it may be pursued too zealously. At the present moment, the politics of reaction are a greater source for concern than the possibility that affirmative action might lend itself to heavy-handed bureaucratic misapplication.

1. Defining the Criteria of Merit

"Excellence" and "quality" are not shibboleths with which institutions of higher learning may turn away all inquiry. Rather, they are aspirations of higher education which are thought to be served by seeking certain attributes and skills in those to be considered for academic positions. Some of these appear almost intuitively to be clearly related to certain standards customarily used by universities, others less obviously so but nonetheless determined by experience to "work," and still others are not infrequently carried along largely by custom and presupposition. Where a long period of time has passed since any serious study has been made to review the effects and the assumptions of stated or unstated standards of appointment and advancement (or where no study was ever made, but the standards were simply adopted on the strength of common custom and plausible hypothesis), it would be reasonable in any case to expect a conscientious faculty to reconsider the matter from time to time. When the use of certain unexamined standards tends to operate to the overwhelming disadvantage of persons of a particular sex or race who have already been placed at a great disadvantage by other social forces (not exclusive of past practices within higher education itself), it is even more reasonable to expect that an institution of higher learning would especially consider its standards in light of that fact as well: to determine whether it is inadvertently depriving itself of a larger field of potential scholars and teachers than simple economy requires, even while compounding the effects of prior discrimination generally.

We cannot assume uncritically that present criteria of merit and procedures for their application have yielded the excellence intended; to the extent that the use of certain standards has resulted in the exclusion of women and minorities from professional positions in higher education, or their inclusion only in token proportions to their availability, the academy has denied itself access to the critical mass of intellectual vitality represented by these groups. We believe that such criteria must thus be considered deficient on the very grounds of excellence itself.

The rationale for professional advancement in American higher education has rested upon the theoretical assumption that there is no inherent conflict between the principles of intellectual and scholarly merit and of equality of access to the academic profession for all persons. In practice, this access has repeatedly been denied a significant number of persons on grounds related to their membership in a particular group. In part, this denial of access has resulted from unexamined presuppositions of professional fitness which have tended to exclude from consideration persons who do not fall within a particular definition of the acceptable academic person. This is in part, but only in part, a function of the procedures through which professional academics have been sought out and recognized within the academy. Insofar as few are called, the range of choice must necessarily be a narrow one, and those fewer still who are chosen tend to mirror the profession's image of what it *is*, not what it should or might be. Beyond procedural defects, however, the very criteria by which professional recognition is accorded have necessarily tended to reflect the prejudices and assumptions of those who set them, and professional recognition and advancement have generally been accorded those who most closely resemble the norm of those who have in the past succeeded in the academy.

It is therefore incumbent upon the academic community, as the first test of equal opportunity, to require something more: that the standards of competence and qualification be set independently of the actual choices made, ostensibly according to these standards; for otherwise, a fatal circularity ensues, in which the very standards of fitness have no independent parameters other than survival itself.

Where a particular criterion of merit, even while not discriminatory on its face or in intent, nonetheless operates to the disproportionate elimination of women and minority group persons, the burden upon the institution to defend it as an appropriate criterion rises in direct proportion to its exclusionary effect. Where criteria for appointment or promotion are unstated, or so vaguely framed as to permit their arbitrary and highly subjective application in individual cases, the institution's ability to defend its actions is the less. While we do not mean to suggest that criteria for academic appointment and advancement be reduced to an easily quantifiable set of attributes or credentials, all of which might be possessed uniformly by a large number of persons otherwise wholly unsuited to the position in question, we are convinced that a reluctance or inability to explicate and substantiate the criteria and standards employed generally and in a given instance does nothing to dispel the notion that something more than chance or intuition has been at work.

2. The Critical Review and Revision of Standards for Academic Appointment and Advancement

The range of permissible discretion which has been the norm in reaching professional judgments offers both a hazard and a valuable opportunity to the academic community. The hazard stems from the latitude for the operation of tacit and inadvertent or explicit prejudices against persons because of race or sex, and their consequent exclusion on indefensible grounds when the standards are clearly met; the opportunity stems from the possibility for broadening the internal criteria for choice in accordance with a general notion of excellence, and hence expanding that notion.

As faculty members keenly aware from our own experience that it may not be possible to verify every consideration taken into account or to experiment wildly, we cannot, of course, urge an abandonment of common sense or common experience. Nor, frankly, have we learned of anything in the specifics of the HEW Guidelines which does so. Rather, what is called for is a review to determine whether we have taken too much for granted in ways which have been harmful, to an extent that institutions themselves may not have known, and a consideration of alternatives which would be neither unreasonable nor unduly onerous in the avoidance of inadvertent discrimination and unwarranted exclusion. Specifically, the review and revision of criteria for academic appointment and advancement should be sensitive to the following considerations:

(a) The greater the effect of a given standard in diminishing the opportunity of women and minorities for possible appointment, the greater the corresponding responsibility to determine and to defend the particular standard as necessary and proper. The disqualification of larger percentages of women and minorities by standards which are only hypothetically related to professional excellence may, understandably, invite skepticism and inquiry.

(b) Standards which may serve valid professional and institutional interests, but which are more exclusionary than alternative standards sufficient to serve those interests, should be reconsidered in light of the less exclusionary alternatives. For instance, an institution-wide antinepotism rule is doubtless connected with a legitimate interest to avoid conflicts of loyalties among faculty members, but its exclusionary effect is far broader than a rule that requires faculty members to excuse themselves from participating in particular decisions involving family members, and in practice the exclusionary effect of overly broad antinepotism rules has overwhelmingly disabled a far greater proportion of women than men from consideration for academic appointment. The AAUP has already called for the curtailment of such rules.

(c) Criteria adopted to limit the field of eligible candidates largely (if not exclusively) for reasons of administrative convenience or out of past habits especially need to be reconsidered. For example, candidates may be sought only from those few graduate programs which in the past have provided the majority of the institution's staff; or application may be limited only to those who have had prior teaching experience. To the extent that such a policy of presumed efficiency excludes persons who may be equally excellent, the interest of economy should be carefully weighed against the tendency of the standard to disqualify a disproportionate number of women and minority persons.

(d) The overall excellence of a given department may be better assured by considering its existing strengths and weaknesses and, accordingly, varying the emphasis given to different kinds of individual qualification for appointment from time to time, rather than applying a rank-order of standards of fitness identically in every case. The failure to consider appointments in terms of a balance of qualities within a department may in fact result in less overall excellence than otherwise. Exactly as excellence of a *total* department is the goal, consideration of different kinds of skills and interests in different persons becomes important in order to maintain that kind of excellence and to liberalize the emphasis given to the appointment of persons stronger in certain respects than those in which the department is already very notable.

We would go further in this observation. An institution which professes to be concerned with many things must not only indicate by its appointment practices that it means what it declares, it must act consistently with that declaration thereafter in the advancement, salary, and respect for the appointee. It is unacceptable and hypocritical to make an appointment of a candidate based on a belief that that candidate, whose strongest assets are different from those of the existing faculty, is appointed precisely because his or her strengths are valued in what they add to the quality of the department, and thereafter nonetheless treat that person as less valuable when it comes to subsequent consideration in respect to salary, tenure, and similar considerations.

(e) The consideration of diversity of characteristics among the faculty of a given department or institution may be relevant to excellence and to affirmative action in an even larger and even more important sense. Ordinarily, an institution would never think to list a narrow range of "age" as a categorical criterion of eligibility for academic appointment, precisely because it is a wholly inappropriate means of categorically eliminating great numbers of people who may be as well qualified or better qualified than others. To restrict eligible candidates as a general and categorical matter to persons between, say, thirty-five and fifty years old would be thrice wrong: it unduly narrows the field of excellent people by an exclusionary standard which may work against the achievement of the highest quality of faculty obtainable; it is discriminatory and unfair to the well-qualified persons whom it categorically excludes; it may weaken the faculty in the particular sense of staffing it in a flat and homogeneous manner, depriving it of perspectives and differences among persons of more diverse ages.

It is nonetheless true that a characteristic which may be indefensible when used as a categorical standard of ineligibility is neither inappropriate nor invidious when it is taken into consideration affirmatively in choosing between two or more other-wise qualified persons, when it is related to securing a larger diversity than currently exists within the faculty. As between two otherwise well-qualified persons, a general concern for balance and the subtler values of diversity from the heterogeneity of younger and older faculty members has quite commonly found expression in resolving a preference between two candidates for a given position—never as a reflection upon, or as an "exclusionary" device against, the one, but as a relevant factor in light of the existing composition of the faculty.

The point may be generalized: meeting a felt shortage of tenured professors by preferring a more experienced and senior person; broadening the professional profile within a department, most of whose faculty secured their degrees from the same institution, by preferring in the next several appointments well-qualified persons of a different academic graduate exposure or professional background; leavening a faculty predominantly oriented toward research and publication with others more interested in exploring new teaching methods, and vice-versa. It is useless to deny that we believe such considerations are relevant, as indeed we familiarly and unselfconsciously take them into account all the time, and rightly so; never in lieu of seeking the "best qualified person," but as contributing to a sensible decision of what constitutes the best qualified person in terms of existing needs and circumstance.

As we do not think this Association would disapprove conscientious efforts by academic faculties to register an affirmative interest, as they often have, in the positive improvement of their departments in the several ways we have just illustrated, but rather that this Association would (and does) regard those efforts as wholly conducive to fairness and quality, we do not see any sufficient reason to be less approving in the affirmative consideration of race or sex. We would go further to say that special efforts to attract persons to improve the overall diversity of a faculty, and to broaden it specifically from its unisex or unirace sameness, seem to us to state a variety of affirmative action which deserves encouragement. A preference in these terms, asserted affirmatively to enrich a faculty in its own experience as well as in what it projects in its example of mutually able men and women, and mutually able blacks and whites, seems to us to state a neutral, principled, and altogether precedented policy of preference.

The argument to the special relevance of race and sex as qualifying characteristics draws its strength from a recognition of the richness which a variety of intellectual perspectives and life experiences can bring to the educational program. It is more than simply a matter of providing jobs for persons from groups which have in the past been unfairly excluded from an opportunity to compete for them; it is a matter of reorganizing the academic institution to fulfill its basic commitment to those who are seriously concerned to maintain the academic enterprise as a vital social force. The law now requires the elimination of discriminatory practices and equality of access for all persons regardless of race or sex; moral justice requires an end to prejudice and an increase of opportunities for those who have been denied them in the past by prejudice; enlightened self-interest requires that an institution reexamine its priorities where standards of merit are concerned, to revitalize the intellectual life of the community through the utilization of heretofore untapped resources. Most important, insofar as the university aspires to discover, preserve, and transmit knowledge and experience not for one group or selected groups, but for all people, to that extent it must broaden its perception of who shall be responsible for this discovery, preservation, and transmission. In so doing, it broadens the base of intellectual inquiry and lays the foundation of more human social practices.

(f) It is far from clear that every qualification we may associate with excellence in teaching and research is in fact as important as we are inclined to view it, or that our predisposition to certain qualities we habitually associate with significant scholarship is as defensible as we may earnestly suppose. There is, as we have noted, a certain circularity in the verification of standards insofar as professors may discern "excellence" in others who resemble themselves, and thus, by their appointment and advancement decisions, generate the proof that merit is the function of those resemblances. It is also far from clear that some degree of frank experimentation in academic appointment would not yield significant information in terms of how a faculty decides what is to be taught, or what is an appropriate or interesting subject for research and publication. It is surely not impossible, for instance, to question whether what is not taught and what is not researched is at least as much a function of parochialism and endless circularity of education-and-teaching as it is a function of wise perspective in determining what is truly important. The point need not be labored, however, for the professional literature concerned with higher education has itself repeatedly expressed these same concerns.

Nevertheless, the point has relevance to an affirmative action plan in the following sense. An institution appropriately concerned with its own continuing development may well wish to involve a component of experimentalism in its own staff policies deliberately reserving discretion to depart from standards and criteria it generally employs precisely as a means of determining whether there may be important scholarly and educational functions to be served by standards different from those it ordinarily applies. The selection of some faculty "out of the ordinary" is itself very much a part of an institution's continuing concern with excellence in this sense. The preference for candidates who bring to a particular position certain differences of experience and background which the university may very properly be reluctant to adopt as a general matter in advance of any opportunity to determine what kind of difference they may make, but which it needs to take into account in order to have that opportunity, is neither invidious to others nor irrelevant to a university's legitimate aspirations. This consideration, while it exists quite apart from the need for an affirmative action plan in the improvement of equal opportunity for women and minorities, may nevertheless affect and help to broaden the design of that plan.

3. The Review and Revision of Academic Recruitment Policies

It must be obvious that even the most conscientious review and revision of eligibility, appointment, and advancement standards can have little effect in the shaping of academic faculties independent of recruiting practices. Even supposing that all of the preceding concerns for excellence, diversity, and experimentalism are nominally composed in the standard of a department or institution, they may yield very little if the manner in which the department goes about the business of finding qualified persons is itself so confined that in fact only a very few qualified persons are likely to turn up, and these not necessarily the best qualified. Additionally, it is now abundantly clear that certain conventional ways of locating possible candidates may operate to the disproportionate exclusion of women and minorities from equal opportunity for consideration—not necessarily as a consequence of willful discrimination but as a practical matter nonetheless. It is natural, for instance, that members of an appointments committee would seek names of possible candidates from acquaintances at other institutions—and that the resulting suggestions may substantially understate the availability of interested, qualified women and minority persons in a number of ways. For example, the institution from which the references are sought may be one which has proportionately fewer women or minority persons among its graduates or graduate students than other institutions. Or, the acquaintances providing the reference may act on presuppositions respecting the interest, qualification, or availability of women and minorities, and thus underrepresent them in their references.

Even if we were to assume, therefore, that there is no *willful* discrimination against women and minorities in the easy custom of recruiting by personal inquiry and reference, still the consequence of exclusion by inadvertence is grossly unfair—and altogether inconsistent with the development of excellence in higher education.

The call for affirmative action plans provides an occasion we believe is long overdue—to re-examine recruiting practices and patterns, and to revise them with the specific ambition of broadening the field of persons whose interest and qualifications the institution should want to know of and correspondingly providing them an opportunity to express their interest. In our view, this is an area in which we should be particularly concerned with "under-utilization" of qualified women and minority persons, i.e., that customary and unexamined parochialism in recruiting practices seriously understates the availability of persons fully qualified according to an institution's own standards, and that they do so disproportionately with respect to women and minority persons.

The Committee does not think it feasible to blueprint the particular ways in which each discipline, department, or institution can best proceed consistent with reasonable economy—for the means of reaching larger numbers of qualified candidates differs considerably from discipline to discipline. In nearly all cases, however, it may be necessary to assess academic staffing needs more in advance of the time when the appointment is itself to be made, i.e., to provide greater lead-time in order that new ways of locating additional qualified persons can be given a chance to work successfully. In some disciplines, moreover, it may be feasible through national professional associations to enlist the aid of a national service, readily providing a point of contact between interested candidates and available positions, vastly improving the field of available candidates with very little expense or time to a given department. For more than a decade, the Association of American Law Schools has provided a directory and registry for those interested in law teaching, for instance, and its use by a great number of law schools is now exceedingly well established. Similarly, many of the disciplinary associations in the humanities and social sciences operate professional registers and employment information bulletins, which provide a mutually satisfactory opportunity for prospective applicants and employers to make themselves known to one another. Far from being regarded as introducing an unhelpful and inefficient element in recruiting, such services should be seen as contributing to the efficiency and quality of academic staffing.

Finally, given the procedural inequity of past recruiting practices which have not only worked with discriminatory effect against women and minorities but which may well have had an additional effect of discouraging their interest in considering an academic career, we believe that a highly principled argument for preference and compensation may be made which bears on the generation of the pool of candidates to be considered. Since good evidence exists to support the claim that overwhelmingly there has been an initial skewing of the candidate pool in traditional search and recruitment procedures, it may reasonably be argued that equity itself now requires a certain "preference" whose effects are "compensatory" in the special sense that more attention and care shall be paid where little or none was paid before; and this is not to the *special* advantage of women or blacks, for example, but for the equalization of their opportunity, in the face of prior disadvantage. Such preference and compensation does not discriminate against majority candidates, but puts them on an equal footing for the first time.

4. Statistical Forecasts under an Affirmative Action Plan, and the Monitoring of Equal Protection

Litigation and government inquiry are substantial risks in any case where the observable facts do not seem to support a claim of nondiscrimination. Historically, the relevance of statistics as a means of shifting the burden to come forward with evidence has most frequently been allowed by courts in respect to racial discrimination and the right to trial by jury. As the actual means which may have been used to compose a jury list are often not subject to public view, it proved virtually impossible for black defendants to establish that the persistent absence of blacks from grand juries and trial juries was, *in each particular case,* the result of willful discrimination. Where a comparison of census figures respecting the proportion of jury-eligible blacks in a given community would give rise to an expectation that over a substantial period of time approximately the same proportion of persons called for jury duty would similarly be black, but where in fact few or none were black, it became familiar that the federal courts would regard the fact of a continuing and significant disparity as yielding a *prima facie* inference that racial discrimination was a contributing element. The effect of the inference was to shift to the state the duty to come forward with evidence which would explain the result on grounds other than racial discrimination. Without doubt, this development in the law—which now has analogues in many other areas as well, including employment—was important to the effective detection and remedying of racial discrimination. We have thought it important to recall this fragment of civil rights history as a useful way of placing in perspective our several observations about "goals" and "targets," which have become misidentified as "quotas" in the litany of criticism of affirmative action plans.

In accordance with present requirements of the federal government, a "goal" and the timetable for its fulfillment are to be set by the institution itself. The means of arriving at the "goal" include exactly the kind of measures we have already discussed in the review and revision of criteria of eligibility and the review and revision of recruiting practices. In this framework, the "goal" is nothing more or less than an expectation of what an institution has reason to suppose will result under conditions of nondiscrimination, given its standards and recruiting practices, in light of the proportion of those within the field of eligibility and recruitment who are women or members of minority groups. Indeed, the word "goal" is itself something of a misnomer insofar as it suggests that the production of percentages is some kind of end in itself. Rather, what is contemplated is the specification of an expectation as to what the institution has reason to believe should appear in the ordinary course of events, given valid criteria of eligibility, proper recruiting practices, and the fair and equal consideration of equally qualified women and minority members in the actual course of selecting among candidates. Essentially, it is an arrangement which leaves open to public review the logic by which the expectation was determined, the general legality of standards which inform the criteria applied in personnel actions, the technical quality of the statistical analyses upon which conclusions are reached, and the degree of integrity with which an institution has adhered to a procedure which it has itself designed. The Committee on Discrimination believes that this part of an affirmative action plan is entirely proper and extremely important in several respects:

(a) Depending upon the unit for which the forecast is made, it will enable an institution to continue a policy of decentralized appointments recommended by the faculties of its respective departments and colleges, while simultaneously providing it with a means of insuring that racial and sexual discrimination is not in fact contributing to those staffing decisions;

(b) It provides the government agency responsible for making certain that institutions assisted by public funds are not in fact violating executive, statutory, and constitutional requirements of equal protection with a means of fulfilling that responsibility;

(c) It provides the institution with a means of rebutting allegations of racial or sexual discrimination, insofar as simplistic impressions of disproportionality might otherwise support an inference of discrimination where, in fact, no such inference is warranted.

Beyond this, conscientious efforts to project personnel needs and to forecast the extent to which affirmative action plans should tend to make a real difference in the employment opportunities of women and minority persons may serve a broader interest as well. As citizens as well as educators we all have a common interest in attempting to determine how effective our separate and combined efforts are likely to be in the abatement of discrimination and the amelioration of effects from past discrimination. The knowledge these efforts can help to provide is not without significance in assessing whether or not we have done too little in this sensitive area of civil and human rights. It may help, moreover, not only to fortify the thinking of institutions of higher learning in terms of their own role, but in considering more knowledgeably what attention needs to be given to other institutions as well—institutions not involved in higher education, but whose existence and operation nonetheless profoundly affect the equal opportunity of women and minorities.

To be effective even in the three respects we have noted, however, it is obvious that additional material and records must be made and maintained by the university—information to be periodically supplied by the various departments and colleges. An institution's willingness and ability to keep a careful and accurate record of personnel actions is of paramount importance. Among these is the requirement that educational institutions collect and analyze personnel statistics by race and sex, so to determine whether there is cause for inquiry and explanation where actual staffing practices fall short of expectations under a policy of nondiscrimination. The same need to establish reliable information on actual recruiting practices under an affirmative action plan also holds.

Finally, we think it important to note again the point, purpose, and relationships of the several parts of an affirmative action plan. It is a plan which is well designed to improve both quality and equal opportunity, but it is a plan which makes an assumption. It assumes that institutions of higher education are what they claim they are—and that all of us as teachers and professors are also what we say we are; that we mean to be fair, that our concern with excellence is not a subterfuge, that we are concerned to be just in the civil rights of *all* persons in the conduct of our profession. If the assumption is a false one, then it will quickly appear that affirmative action plans can go the way of other proposals which are intellectually sound but which so frequently fail in their assumptions about the nature of people. For without doubt, the temptation will appear to the indifferent and the cynical to distinguish between the appearance and the substance of such a plan and to opt for the appearance alone: the token production of "adequate" numbers of women and blacks to avoid the likelihood of contract suspensions or HEW inquiry, even while disparaging their presence and assigning the "blame" to the government. We do not doubt in this respect that institutions of higher learning will thus reveal more about *themselves* in the manner in which they respond to the call for affirmative action, however, than what their response may reveal about the consistency of such plans with excellence and fairness in higher education. For its own part, the Committee on Discrimination believes that plans reflected in the body of this Report are entirely sound and congenial to the standards of the AAUP, and we commend them for the opportunity they provide for the further improvement of higher education as well as for their contribution to the field of civil rights.

Marx W. Wartofsky (Philosophy)
Boston University, Chairman

Ivar E. Berg, Jr. (Industrial Relations)
Columbia University
Mary F. Berry (History)
University of Maryland
Butler A. Jones (Sociology)
Cleveland State University
Beatrice G. Konheim (Biological Sciences)
Hunter College
Margaret L. Rumbarger
Washington Office Staff
William W. Van Alstyne (Law)
Duke University

References

Aaron, B. *Judicial and Administrative Deference to Arbitration.* Reprint No. 229. Los Angeles: Institute of Industrial Relations, University of California, 1972.

"Affirmative Action in Higher Education: A Report by the Council Commission on Discrimination." *AAUP Bulletin,* Summer 1973, *59* (2), 178-183.

American Association of University Professors. *AAUP Policy Documents and Reports: 1973 Edition.* Washington, D.C., 1973.

American Council on Education. *American Universities and Colleges.* (11th ed.) Washington, D.C., 1973.

"An Industry Man Takes Over a Battered EEOC." *Business Week,* June 23, 1975, 113-115.

"Arbitration of Faculty Grievances: A Report of a Joint Subcommittee of Committees A and N." *AAUP Bulletin,* Summer 1973, *59* (2), 168-170.

Astin, H. S., and Bayer, A. E. "Sex Discrimination in Academe." *Educational Record,* Spring 1972, *53*, 101-118.

Babcock, B. A., et al. *Sex Discrimination and the Law: Causes and Remedies.* Boston: Little, Brown and Co., 1975.

Bayer, A. E. *College and University Faculty: A Statistical Description.* ACE Research Reports, vol. 5, no. 5. Washington, D.C.: American Council on Education, 1970.

Bayer, A. E. *Teaching Faculty in Academe: 1972-1973.* ACE Research Reports, vol. 8, no. 2. Washington, D.C.: American Council on Education, 1973.

Bayer, A. E., and Astin, H. S. "Sex Differentials in the Academic Reward System." *Science,* May 23, 1975, *188,* 796-801.

Bazell, R. J. "Sex Discrimination: Campuses Face Contract Loss Over HEW Demands." *Science,* Nov. 20, 1970, *170,* 834-835.

Beaird, J. R. "Racial Discrimination in Employment: Rights and Remedies." *Georgia Law Review,* 1972, *6* (3), 469-488.

Bernard, J. *Academic Women.* University Park, Pa.: Pennsylvania State University Press, 1964.

Bird, C., with Briller, S. W. *Born Female: The High Cost of Keeping Women Down.* (rev. ed.) New York: Pocket Books, 1972.

Bureau of National Affairs. *Labor-Management Decisions of Boards and Courts: BNA Labor Relations Reporter.* Washington, D.C., seriatim.

Bureau of National Affairs. *Labor Relations Reference Manual.* Washington, D.C., seriatim.

Caplow, T. and McGee, R. J. *The Academic Marketplace.* (Reprinted.) New York: Anchor Books, 1965.

Carnegie Commission on Higher Education. *A Classification of Institutions of Higher Education.* Berkeley, Calif., 1973a.

Carnegie Commission on Higher Education. *College Graduates and Jobs: Adjusting to a New Labor Market Situation.* New York: McGraw-Hill, 1973b.

Carnegie Commission on Higher Education. *Opportunities for Women in Higher Education: Their Current Participation, Prospects for the Future, and Recommendations for Action.* New York: McGraw-Hill, 1973c.

Carnegie Commission on Higher Education. *Priorities for Action: Final Report of the Carnegie Commission on Higher Education.* New York: McGraw-Hill, 1973d.

Carnegie Council on Policy Studies in Higher Education. *The Federal Role in Postsecondary Education: Unfinished Business, 1975-1980.* San Francisco: Jossey-Bass, 1975.

Carnegie Foundation for the Advancement of Teaching. *More Than Survival: Prospects for Higher Education in a Period of Uncertainty.* San Francisco: Jossey-Bass, 1975.

Cartter, A. M. *The Ph.D. and the Labor Market.* New York: McGraw-Hill, forthcoming.

Cartter, A. M. and Ruhter, W. E. *The Disappearance of Sex Discrimination in First Job Placement of Ph.D.s.* Los Angeles: Higher Education Research Institute, 1975.

Centra, J. A. *Women, Men, and the Doctorate.* Princeton, N.J.: Educational Testing Service, 1974.

Code of Federal Regulations, Title 29, Part 800 and Chapter 14.

Code of Federal Regulations, Title 41, Chapter 60.

Code of Federal Regulations, Title 45, Part 86.

"College to Fight Ruling by NLRB on Franciscans." *Higher Education and National Affairs,* June 25, 1975.

Committee on Education and Labor, U.S. House of Representatives, and Committee on Labor and Public Welfare, U.S. Senate. *Compilation of Higher Education Laws, 1972.* Washington, D.C., 1972.

Committee on Education and Labor, U.S. House of Representatives. *Federal Higher Education Programs: Institutional Eligibility.* Hearings before the Special Subcommittee on Education, 93rd Cong., 2nd Sess., Parts 2A and 2B, *Civil Rights Obligations,* Aug. 8, 9, 12, 14, 15; Sept. 17, 19, 20, 23, and 25, 1974. Washington, D.C., 1975.

Comptroller General of the United States. *The Equal Employment Opportunity Program for Federal Nonconstruction Contractors Can Be Improved.* Washington, D.C., 1975.

Education Commission of the States. *Equal Rights for Women in Education: A Digest of Federal Laws.* Denver, 1975a.

Education Commission of the States. *Equal Rights for Women in Education: A Handbook of State Laws and Policies Affecting Equal Rights for Women in Education.* Denver, 1975b.

"Faculty Salaries Shown Rising." *Higher Education Daily,* Feb. 12, 1975, p. 6.

Federal Register, Feb. 14, 1974.

Federal Register, June 4, 1975.

Fields, C. M. "Affirmative Action, 4 Years After." *Chronicle of Higher Education,* Aug. 5, 1974a.

Fields, C. M. "U. of Md. Charges Civil Rights Office Threatened It With Adverse Ruling Unless It Settled Bias Suit." *Chronicle of Higher Education,* June 10, 1974b.

Fields, C. M. "29 Universities Warned. U.S. May Withhold Contracts." *Chronicle of Higher Education,* June 23, 1975.

Fleming, R. W. "Implications for Government." In L. W. Sells (Ed.), *New Directions for Institutional Research: Toward Affirmative Action.* No. 3, Autumn 1974. San Francisco: Jossey-Bass, 1974.

"Ford Signs Title IX Regs: Will Be Published Wednesday." *Higher Education Daily,* June 2, 1975.

Freeman, R. "The Implications of the Changing Labor Market for Members of Minority Groups." In M. S. Gordon (Ed.), *Higher Education and the Labor Market.* New York: McGraw-Hill, 1974.

Garbarino, J. W. *Faculty Bargaining: Change and Conflict.* New York: McGraw-Hill, 1975.

Green, A. A. *Women on the Chemistry Faculties of Institutions Granting the Ph.D. in Chemistry.* Report of survey conducted by the Women Chemists Committee of the American Chemical Society, July 1, 1974.

Hesburgh, T. M. "Legislating Attitudes." In J. F. Hughes (Ed.), *Education and the State.* Washington, D.C.: American Council on Education, 1975.

Hochschild, A. R. "Inside the Clockwork of Male Careers." In F. Howe (Ed.), *Women and the Power to Change.* New York: McGraw-Hill, 1975.

Holmes, P. E. Statement in Committee on Education and Labor, U.S. House of Representatives. *Federal Higher Education Programs: Institutional Eligibility.* Hearings (full citation under Committee on Education and Labor), 1975, Part 2A, 72-89.

Hook, S. "On Discrimination: Part One." In L. W. Sells (Ed.), *New Directions for Institutional Research: Toward Affirmative Action.* No. 3, Autumn 1974. San Francisco: Jossey Bass, 1974.

Hornig, L. S. Statement in Committee on Education and Labor, U.S. House of Representatives. In *Federal Higher Education Programs: Institutional Eligibility.* Hearings (full citation under Committee on Education and Labor), Part 2B, 1244-1249, 1975.

Howe, F. "Women and the Power to Change." In F. Howe (Ed.), *Women and the Power to Change.* New York: McGraw-Hill, 1975.

Jacobson, R. L. "Faculty Women Earning 17 Pct. Less Than Men." *Chronicle of Higher Education,* Mar. 12, 1973.

Johnson, G. E., and Stafford, F. P. "The Earnings and Promotion of

Women Faculty." *The American Economic Review*, December 1974, *65* (6), 888-903.

Johnson, S. K. "It's Action, But Is It Affirmative." *New York Times*, Sunday Magazine Section, May 11, 1975.

Kadonaga, C. "Confusion Behind Hiring Plan Approval: HEW Power to Bargain Overstepped?" *The Daily Californian*, Feb. 20, 1975a.

Kadonaga, C. "HEW Accepts University's Hiring Plan." *The Daily Californian*, Feb. 19, 1975b.

Karst, K. L., and Horowitz, H. W. "Affirmative Action and Equal Protection." *Virginia Law Review*, 1974, *60*, 955-974.

Larson, E. R. "The Development of Section 1981 as a Remedy for Racial Discrimination in Private Employment." *Harvard Civil Rights—Civil Liberties Law Review*, January 1972, 7 (1), 56-102.

Lester, R. A. *Antibias Regulation of Universities: Faculty Problems and Their Solutions.* New York: McGraw-Hill, 1974.

Lester, R. A. "Application of the Federal Equal Pay Act to University Faculty." (forthcoming)

Magarrell, J. "Faculty Salaries Up 5.8 Pct. in Year." *Chronicle of Higher Education*, June 9, 1975.

McCarthy, J. L., and Wolfle, D. "Women and Minority Doctorates, 1969-75." To be published in *Science*.

Michigan State University. *Michigan State News*, Nov. 21, 1974.

National Academy of Sciences. *Doctoral Scientists and Engineers in the United States, 1973 Profile.* Washington, D.C., 1974.

National Board on Graduate Education. *Minority Group Participation in Graduate Education*, forthcoming.

National Education Association, Research. *Salaries Paid and Salary-Related Practices in Higher Education, 1971-72.* Washington, D.C., 1972.

National Research Council/National Academy of Sciences. *Summary Report, 1968: Doctorate Recipients from United States Universities.* Washington, D.C., 1969.

National Research Council/National Academy of Sciences. *Minority Groups: Among Doctorate Level Scientists, Engineers, and Scholars, 1973.* Washington, D.C., 1974a.

National Research Council/National Academy of Sciences. *Summary Report, 1973: Doctorate Recipients from United States Universities.* Washington, D.C. 1974b.

"New IRS Private School Guidelines Termed 'Inadequate.' " *Higher Education Daily*, Feb. 21, 1975.

Olman, R. M. *Campus 1970: Where Do Women Stand?* Washington, D.C.: American Association of University Women, 1970.

Pondrom, C. N. "Setting Priorities in Developing an Affirmative Action Program." *Journal of Medical Education*, May 1975, *50*, (5), 427-434.

Powell, J. H., Jr. Statement in Committee on Education and Labor, U.S. House of Representatives. In *Federal Higher Education Programs: Institutional Eligibility.* Hearings (full citation under Committee on Education and Labor), Part 2A, 6-69, 1975.

Princeton University. *Affirmative Action Report and Revised Affirmative Action Plan.* May 13, 1975.

Reagan, B. R. "Report of the Committee on the Status of Women in the Economics Profession." *American Economic Review*, May 1975, *65*, 490-501.

"The Rebellion of the Chancellors." *The Washington Post*. (Editorial.) June 25, 1975, p. A-14.

Sandler, B. "The Day WEAL Opened Pandora's Box." *Chronicle of Higher Education*, Jan. 22, 1973.

Sandler, B. Statement in Committee on Education and Labor, U.S. House of Representatives. In *Federal Higher Education Programs: Institutional Eligibility*. Hearings (full citation under Committee on Education and Labor) Part 2A, 275-319, 1975.

Seabury, P. "HEW and the Universities." *Commentary*, February 1972, *53*, 38-44.

"Termination of Faculty Appointments Because of Financial Exigency, Discontinuance of a Program or Department, or Medical Reasons." *AAUP Bulletin*, December 1974, *60* (4), 411-413.

"The Sixtieth Annual Meeting." *AAUP Bulletin*. June 1974, *60* (2), 139-144.

"Title IX Sex Discrimination Regulations Released." *Higher Education Daily*, June 4, 1975.

"U. of Michigan, HEW Agree on Plan to End Sex Bias." *Chronicle of Higher Education*. Jan. 11, 1971, p. 4.

U.S. Bureau of the Census. *1970 Census of Population: Educational Attainment*. Subject report PC (2)-5B. Washington, D.C., 1973.

U.S. Bureau of the Census. "Income of Families and Persons in the United States." *Current Population Reports*, ser. P-60, no. 85. Washington, D.C., 1975.

U.S. Commission on Civil Rights. *The Federal Civil Rights Enforcement Effort—1974*. Volume 3: *To Ensure Equal Educational Opportunity*. Washington, D.C., 1975a.

U.S. Commission on Civil Rights. *The Federal Civil Rights Enforcement Effort—1974*. Volume 5: *To Eliminate Employment Discrimination*. Washington, D.C., June 1975b.

U.S. Department of Health, Education, and Welfare. *Higher Education Guidelines, Executive Order 11246*. Washington, D.C., 1972.

U.S. National Center for Educational Statistics. *Projections of Educational Statistics to 1982-83: 1973 Edition*. Washington, D.C., 1974.

U.S. National Center for Educational Statistics. *Digest of Educational Statistics, 1974*. Washington, D.C., 1975.

U.S. President. *Manpower Report of the President*. Transmitted to the Congress, April 1974. Washington, D.C., 1974.

University of California, Berkeley. *Affirmative Action Program and Related Documents*. 2 vols. Feb. 18, 1975.

University of Michigan. *Affirmative Action Program*. July 1973.

University of Michigan. *The Higher the Fewer: Report and Recommendations, Committee to Study the Status of Women in Graduate Education and Later Careers*. Ann Arbor: Executive Board of the Graduate School, March 1974.

"Universities Given Revised Agreement Form for Contracts." *Higher Education Daily*, June 27, 1975.

"Universities Sign OCR Pact; Will Get Contracts." *Higher Education Daily,* July 1, 1975.

Vetter, J. *Affirmative Action in Faculty Employment Under Executive Order 11246.* Draft report prepared for the Committee on Grant and Benefit Programs, Administrative Conference of the United States, May 6, 1974.

Weitzman, L. J. "Affirmative Action Plans for Eliminating Sex Discrimination in Academe." In A. S. Rossi and A. Calderwood (Eds.), *Academic Women on the Move.* New York: Russell Sage Foundation, 1973.

"Women Sue HEW for Action on Sex Bias." *Higher Education Daily,* Nov. 27, 1974.

Index